LINKING OBJECTS AND LINKING PHENOMENA

LINKING OBJECTS AND LINKING PHENOMENA

A Study of the Forms, Symptoms, Metapsychology, and Therapy of Complicated Mourning

Vamık Volkan

KARNAC
firing the mind

Originally published in 1981 by International Universities Press, Inc.

Reissue published in 2025 by
Karnac Books Limited
62 Bucknell Road
Bicester
Oxfordshire OX26 2DS

British Library Cataloguing in Publication Data

A C.I.P. for this book is available from the British Library

ISBN: 978-1-80013-409-6 (paperback)
ISBN: 978-1-80013-410-2 (PDF)
ISBN: 978-1-80013-414-0 (e-book)

Typeset by vPrompt eServices Pvt Ltd, India

www.firingthemind.com

FSC
www.fsc.org
MIX
Paper | Supporting responsible forestry
FSC® C007915

Karnac Books is committed to a sustainable future for our business, our readers, and our planet. This book is made from Forest Stewardship Council® certified paper.

I shall rest, a loved one with him
whom I have loved, sinless in my
crime; for I owe a longer allegiance
to the dead than to the living: in
that world I shall abide forever.
—Sophocles, *Antigone*

Contents

Preface to the reissue ix

Acknowledgements xiii

About the author xv

Foreword *by Harold F. Searles, M.D.* xvii

1. Introduction: The evolution of research into complicated mourning 1

Part I
Phenomenological and theoretical findings

2. Uncomplicated mourning 21

3. Complications in the initial stage of the mourning process 41

4. Complications in the work of mourning: Reactive depression 53

5. Complications in the work of mourning: Established pathological mourning 67

6. An example of the linking object: Othello's handkerchief 103

Part II
Treatment

7. Psychoanalytic psychotherapy of established pathological mourning 127

8. The daughters of Goodbar 145

9. Re-grief therapy 163

10. Three more examples of re-grief therapy 189

11. A yellow spot in the bottom of a coffee cup 213

Part III
Living linking objects and related psychological states

12. Children's reactions to death: "Negative" outcome—the case of the stone swan 227

13. Children's reactions to death: "Positive" outcome—the case of "Immortal Atatürk" 237

14. A living linking object: The case of the *Night of the Living Dead* 255

Part IV
Coda

15. Magical inanimate objects 285

References 301

Name index 317

Subject index 321

Preface to the reissue

As human beings, we constantly face the loss of loved ones and other significant losses. Mourning is a persistent psychological condition in our lives. Throughout human history, we have also shared collective losses, particularly after wars, war-like situations, and forced displacements. Today, we are once again witnessing devastating global events, such as the Russia–Ukraine and Hamas–Israel wars. Death, destruction, and suffering continue in other regions as well, including the ongoing civil war in Sudan, which has persisted since 2023.

Many books have been written on mourning, including this one, originally published over forty years ago. It is based on fifteen years of research conducted by my colleagues at the University of Virginia and me, working with patients struggling to cope with their losses. This book introduced new findings, such as the concept of linking objects and linking phenomena in individuals experiencing complicated mourning. It also provided clinical illustrations of "re-grief therapy," offering valuable insights into the therapeutic process.

In this new preface, I want to share what led me to study the psychology of mourning after becoming a psychiatrist.

I was born in 1932 to Turkish parents on the Mediterranean island of Cyprus. During my childhood, I was exposed to a diverse mix of large-group identities, including Greeks, Turks, and, in smaller numbers, Armenians, Maronites, and those who identified as descendants of the Phoenicians. Additionally, the British were a significant presence, with all these groups living side by side. After finishing a Turkish high school on the island, I went to Turkey for my medical education.

In early 1957, I arrived in the United States of America with my medical degree and only fifteen dollars in my pocket. Fortunately, I had secured a job at a hospital in Chicago. A few years later, I became an American citizen. My move to the USA was part of the broader phenomenon known as the "brain drain," as the country faced a shortage of medical doctors and actively recruited professionals from around the world.

My arrival in the USA coincided with a turbulent time for Cypriot Greeks, who were engaged in a struggle against British rule in an effort to unite Cyprus with Greece. In the process, they began to oppress Cypriot Turks and launched attacks against both British forces and civilians.

During my final two and a half years in Turkey—first as a struggling medical student and later as a newly graduated physician—I shared a small apartment with another Cypriot Turk named Erol Mulla. Like me, he had come to Turkey for his medical education, though he was two years behind me in school. He affectionately called me "abi," meaning "big brother," and since I had only sisters, I came to think of him as the brother I never had.

Three months after my arrival in the USA, I received a letter from my father. Inside the envelope was a newspaper article with a photograph of Erol. The article described how he had traveled to Cyprus from Turkey to visit his ailing mother. While attempting to buy medicine for her at a pharmacy, he was shot seven times by Cypriot Greek terrorists. These killers targeted Erol—a bright young man with a promising future—simply to instill fear in the ethnic group to which he belonged.

When I learned of Erol's death, I felt numb. I did not cry. Alone in Chicago, in an unfamiliar country where I had no close confidants, I kept the news of his murder to myself. Even years later, during my personal psychoanalytic training, I did not deeply examine my grief over losing Erol. My mourning remained hidden, buried beneath the demands of my new life.

Looking back, I now realize that studying the mourning process in individuals and writing this book became my way of confronting not only Erol's murder, but also the sorrow of leaving behind my family and friends in Cyprus. Later in my career, I spent over three decades working in various countries, facilitating unofficial dialogues between representatives of opposing groups, engaging with political leaders, and spending time in refugee camps. Through these experiences, I developed new theories on large-group psychology and introduced the concept of "chosen trauma" to describe its impact on tribal, ethnic, and national groups.

A chosen trauma is the shared mental representation of a historical event in which a large group suffered catastrophic loss, humiliation, and helplessness at the hands of its enemies. When members of a victimized group are unable to mourn such losses and overcome their humiliation and helplessness, they pass on to their offspring the images of their injured selves and the psychological tasks that remain unresolved. This process, known as the "transgenerational transmission of trauma," ensures that each subsequent generation inherits references to the same historical event. Over time, the mental representation of this event becomes a defining element of the group's identity, linking all its members across generations.

A chosen trauma reflects the "infection" of a large group's mourning process, and its reactivation serves to unite its members. Political leaders can exploit this reactivation to fuel new large-scale societal movements, some of which may be destructive and malignant. While this book does not focus specifically on the psychology of large tribal, ethnic, or national groups, I hope that its detailed descriptions of individual mourning processes will also provide deeper insights into many world events.

Vamık Volkan

Acknowledgements

During the fifteen years of clinical study of complicated mourning that led to the writing of this book, I was joined by a number of colleagues for varying periods of time, each of whom I would like to thank for his contribution to the study. I cannot name here all those who helped me in my investigations, but I want to express special appreciation to colleagues who shared material from their clinical experience for inclusion in this book. Although their names appear at appropriate points in the text, I should like to acknowledge here those to whom I am so indebted.

Salman Akhtar, M.D., and J. Anderson Thomson, Jr., M.D., for their description of their work with two sisters whose mother had been murdered.

Anthony F. Cilluffo, Ph.D., for his analysis of psychological tests given to patients undergoing re-grief therapy.

Brian W. Hastings, M.D., for the details of the psychoanalytic psychotherapy of a young woman whose brother was killed in an accident.

Robert King, M.D., for the account of the psychoanalysis of a young woman who from childhood on kept within herself the combined image of her mother and a dead sister.

Daniel Josephthal, M.D., for his account of the re-grief therapy of a young widow whose husband had been lost in an airplane crash.

Thomas Sarvay, M.D., for his account of the re-grief therapy of a young man whose linking object was his father's ring.

Rex E. Buxton, M.D., for reporting a patient's dreams demonstrating her response to the suicide of her husband.

Burke M. Smith, Ph.D., for testing patients undergoing re-grief therapy, and for analyzing their test results with the assistance of M. B. Fletcher, Ph.D., and Nancy Phillips, M.S.

Having had the help of Mrs. Virginia Kennan for nearly ten years in the preparation of my books and papers for publication, I acknowledge once again the value of her editing and of her friendship. My secretary, Mrs. Judy Mitchell, demonstrated her customary cheerful diligence in working on this manuscript. I am also indebted to Mr. Nicholas Cariello of International Universities Press for his careful reading of the manuscript of this book and his valuable suggestions for its improvement.

About the author

Vamık Volkan, MD, DFLAPA, received his medical education at the School of Medicine, University of Ankara, Turkey. He is an emeritus professor of psychiatry at the University of Virginia, Charlottesville and an emeritus training and supervising analyst at the Washington Psychoanalytic Institute, Washington, DC. In 1987, Dr. Volkan established the Center for the Study of Mind and Human Interaction (CSMHI) at the School of Medicine, University of Virginia. CSMHI applied a growing theoretical and field-proven base of knowledge to issues such as ethnic tension, racism, large-group identity, terrorism, societal trauma, immigration, mourning, transgenerational transmissions, leader–follower relationships, and other aspects of national and international conflict. A year after his 2002 retirement, Dr. Volkan became the Senior Erik Erikson Scholar at the Erikson Institute of the Austen Riggs Center, Stockbridge, Massachusetts and he spent three to six months there each year for ten years.

In 2006, he was Fulbright/Sigmund Freud-Privatstiftung Visiting Scholar of Psychoanalysis in Vienna, Austria. Dr. Volkan holds honorary doctorate degrees from Kuopio University (now called the University of Eastern Finland), Finland; from Ankara University, Turkey; and the Eastern European Psychoanalytic Institute, Russia. He was a former president of the Turkish-American Neuropsychiatric Society, the International Society of Political Psychology, the Virginia Psychoanalytic Society, and the American College of Psychoanalysts. Among many the awards he received are the Nevitt Sanford Award, Elise M. Hayman Award, L. Bryce Boyer Award, Margaret Mahler Literature Prize, Hans H. Strupp Award, the American College of Psychoanalysts' Distinguished Officer Award for 2014, and the Mary S. Sigourney Award for 2015. He received the Sigmund Freud Award given by the city of Vienna, Austria in collaboration with the World Council of Psychotherapy. He also was honored on several occasions by being nominated for the Nobel Peace Prize with letters of support from twenty-seven countries. Dr. Volkan is the author, co-author, editor, or co-editor of more than fifty psychoanalytic and psychopolitical books, including Enemies on the Couch: A Psychopolitical Journey through War and Peace. Currently Dr. Volkan is the president emeritus of the International Dialogue Initiative (IDI), which he established in 2007. He continues to lecture nationally and internationally.

Foreword

For several years I have admired greatly the work of Vamık Volkan, and I feel, therefore, pleased as well as privileged in writing the Foreword to this, his third published book. Among his various outstanding qualities, I wish to cite, first, his scholarship. It is unfailingly impressive to me how conscientiously this abundantly talented and, in the best sense of the phrase, professionally ambitious man cites the contributions of other workers in his field and related fields. Dr. Volkan's contributions are all the stronger and deeper by reason of their grounding in the related contributions of others. He is respectful of others' contributions without being self-effacing. Whereas, in my view, his first book leaned considerably upon the admittedly brilliant contributions of Otto Kernberg, here, in this third volume, Volkan emerges as very much, and powerfully, his own man.

One of the strengths of his work derives not merely from the kind of library scholarship that is among his interests, but more than that, from the fact that so much of his work itself is done in collaboration with colleagues in academic and similar settings. Dr. Volkan writes as one whose work has been subjected, ongoingly, to searching discussion with colleagues. Work that survives such rigorous scrutiny by fellow experts tends to emerge as reliably strong and enduring in value.

His' writing is always, for me, a pleasure to read; he writes in a lively style and with enormously helpful lucidity of thought. I have learned much from his clear theoretical presentations not only of his own views, but of the writings of earlier contributors to psychoanalytic theory. The reader will find in. this volume memorably lucid discussions of—as examples—introjection and introjects, identification, projection, and externalization. Dr. Volkan helps the reader to a deeper and clearer understanding of these concepts, which, applicable to the most basic processes of human personality formation and functioning, will illuminate the therapist's work with both current and previous patients, not merely with those patients who are, or have been, involved in reactive depression or established pathological mourning.

I found the quotable, and otherwise excellent, ideas contained in this book to be so numerous that I shall mention a number of them more or less at random here, as examples of Volkan's characteristically thought-provoking, stimulating presentation. He writes of "complicated grief as a seal over other psychopathology." He observes that "Throughout our lives we are influenced not only by interaction with important living people, but also by representations of the dead that reside within us, in the form of identifications or of separate 'presences' (introjects) either in ourselves or in those with whom we interact."

He introduces the excellent concept of "living linking objects," describing how a mother may "deposit in her child's self-system the concept that he is the dead person's representative." He draws valuable diagnostic differentiations between complicated grief, neurotic depression, and unduly protracted "normal" grief reaction.

He states, with his usual vivid clarity, "If the dead person is too greatly idealized to be 'killed,' the expected process of mourning may … not be initiated." At another juncture he writes, "Besides the hallucinations of the deceased, two other phenomena—introjects and linking objects—are used by mourners to enable them to keep in touch with the images and representations of the dead and to maintain the illusion of absolute control over such images and representations. The existence of introjects and linking objects provides important clues in the diagnosis of established pathological mourning."

He presents a discussion, of the widest applicability and significance, of the role played in creativity by linking objects and other linking phenomena.

I find admirably clear his comparisons between linking objects and transitional or fetishistic objects. His discussion of how unassimilated object or self-representations located, so to speak, within the mother can be deposited within the child during early mother–child interaction, while acknowledgedly not a concept original with Volkan, is presented with rare, if not unprecedented, simplicity and clarity—a typical example of one of this book's great values for the reader.

Time and again, this book conveys, remarkably effectively, an immediate sense of the psychoanalytic process at work, as when he says, of certain patients whose treatment he has been describing, that, "Each used her character neurosis as a defense against confronting her grief. Character pathology 'contained' their grief, so that initial attempts to analyze the character neurosis failed until it was approached as a resistance to grieving."

As one who has worked much (largely in past years) with schizophrenic patients, I found especially valuable Volkan's observation that complications in the mourning process often lead mistakenly to a diagnosis of schizophrenia. He reports, for instance, that, one of his cases "provides an excellent example of the importance of postponing the diagnosis of severe conditions such as schizophrenia until it can be established that the disturbance in reality testing is based on more than denial of a loss by death. Clyde was by no means the only example encountered in our research of a patient who exhibited behavior that seemed psychotic but was in fact focalized and uniquely related to a fixation in the work of mourning."

My reading of this book proved, for me, to be of the most lively relevancy, both clinical and personal. As I read, I was reminded repeatedly of my years of work with a chronically schizophrenic woman, and with a number of borderline patients. I sensed the incompleteness of my own working through of some of the major losses of my adult life. I surmised that my work with the schizophrenic woman had been slowed, despite my best efforts at a conscious level, by her serving unconsciously for me as a linking object in my own pathologic grieving of the loss of my mother, despite my mother's having been vastly healthier than this woman has yet become. Volkan's book repeatedly enabled me to recall my own childhood in a different and clearer light. At times this was painful indeed; for example, when he wrote, of one patient, that "Her childhood fears that if she weren't good she would be sent to an orphanage poured out," I was reminded poignantly of seeing my only sibling, a sister four years older, under precisely this threat from our tyrannical father. At times, particularly when Volkan was throwing new light, for me, upon incompletely worked-through losses on my own part and on the part of my now-deceased mother, I found his book, for all its innate readability, heavy going.

On the back of one page of the manuscript I made the following note:

> *Amusingly enough, as I closed this book-manuscript today, I felt how much attached I have become to it, and I sense it has become, for me, a linking object to Volkan (I first sensed it as equivalent to a security blanket, then—all within seconds—a linking object to Vamık Volkan) whom I admire, and whom I unconsciously wish dead on a murderously competitive basis.*
>
> [A few hours later on the same day] *Am struck at finding, in sessions with both J. and N. today, how relevant V. V. 's book is—it definitely is helping me to pick up more quickly such phenomena as pathological mourning.*

Volkan's case descriptions are written with a novelist's skill. They are succinct, vivid, often memorably dramatic—as when he describes the patient who "each night became a living tombstone"—and beautifully illustrative of his theoretical concepts. But more than this, his case descriptions are examples of remarkably effective psychoanalysis and psychoanalytic therapy. I find, for instance, beautiful and moving examples of successful grief work. In addition, he gives us, from the non-clinical realm, a fascinating psycho biographical analysis of Atatürk. It is rare, indeed, to encounter so scholarly a person who is, at the same time, so masterfully effective an analyst and therapist as is Volkan.

Volkan's technical versatility, whether in conducting psychoanalysis or in doing relatively brief re-grief therapy, is admirable. He is clearly activated by deeply humanitarian concerns in his persistent, and clearly often successful, endeavor to bring the insights and techniques of psychoanalysis into the relatively brief treatment of patients who need psychoanalytic therapy but who cannot, because of their circumstances, be in treatment more than a few weeks or months.

In his research methods I find, similarly, much to admire. This volume reports his having collected hundreds of dreams from persons fixed in the chronic hope of finding the one they have lost, while at the same time fearing to encounter him or her. One of the interesting findings from this particular study is that of the "frozen" dreams typical of some of these patients, expressive of their fixation in the mourning process. Your ordinary workaday analyst, no matter how effective in his daily work and no matter how articulate a writer he may be, is unlikely to be armed with a research basis so formidable as Volkan's. I cite not only the size of the sample he has studied, but his systematic usage of psychological tests to confirm his clinical findings.

On the negative side, I find that Volkan recurrently touches base with an analytic position that is, to my taste, perfectionistically classical, and that does not sufficiently acknowledge the myriad feelings, negative ones often prominent among these, at work behind the analyst's relatively neutral external demeanor. To my mind, these feelings on the part of the analyst, far from being mere imperfections, are essential to the analyst's task; they are commonly necessary, and deeply intuitive, responses to the patient's transference reactions to the analyst. Volkan seems, much of the time, to know this well. But I cannot accept certain statements, statements reflective (supposedly) of an inner dispassionateness impossible—were it even desirable—of human attainment: "As in all other therapies whether psychoanalytic or not, the therapist must convey his non-exploitative desire to heal, and encourage his patient to express himself directly without any fear of hostile, punitive, engulfing, or abandoning responses"; and "Without either attacking or protecting that therapist [the patient's previous therapist, toward whom Volkan had reason to feel much condemnation], I stated that I seemed to have a different way of dealing with patients." Similarly, in the reports, here, of re-griefing, the therapist's countertransference reactions are relatively inaccessible to the patient or to the reader of this book. That is, in re-griefing, the therapist is functioning conspicuously as the *healthy one*—a position that must inevitably prove, on close scrutiny, highly defensive. For instance, the re-grief exercise that Showalter and Volkan term "demarcation" seems to me to involve the therapist's unconsciously demarcating himself from the patient (unconsciously endeavoring, by this demarcating, to protect himself from the patient's grief and from his own grief projected onto the grieving patient).

Similarly, when Volkan says that "I explained [to a patient] that silence on my part would mean that I was listening to her," this statement is a disavowal that an analyst's or therapist's silences may have as myriad meanings and affective tones as do the silences on the part of a patient—ranging all the way from tones of loving oneness to antagonism to basically autistic unrelatedness, and so on, from one time to another.

In keeping with the relatively classical-psychoanalytic tone of the book, the reader finds here less of autobiographical data, concerning Volkan himself, than one would wish. The few bits of autobiographical material that he provides are most welcome. He says at one point, for instance, that he was "dealing also at that time with some personal losses of my own"; but a more than merely tantalizing, that is, a relatively informative report of some of his own mourning experiences, and the difficulties that he himself encountered in accomplishing such work of mourning, would be most welcome to his readers and would not complicate—I feel confident of this—his work with current and future patients. Further, such relatively abundant autobiographical data would help to dispel an air, which appears from time to time in this book, of his dwelling in a realm somewhat above that of his patients.

But it would be grossly unfair of me to emphasize that last point too heavily. Volkan is miles ahead of most classically psychoanalytic writers in this regard—namely, in depicting his own humanness as well as that of the patient. On the one hand, it seems to me that, at this stage in his personal and professional development, he is still a bit shy or guarded, unnecessarily, in this regard. On the other hand—and here may be the proof of the pudding—it seems clear that his patients, colleagues, and students are relatively well able to identify constructively with him—and all these persons could not identify so healthily with an analyst (or therapist or teacher or colleague) who held himself, more than fleetingly, in the position of a paragon.

Volkan devotes, throughout his book, such careful and well-reasoned attention to the published contributions of his contemporaries and predecessors that the question may arise in the minds of many readers, as it did in mine, "Precisely what is to be regarded here as being an original contribution of Volkan's?" By way of reply, it seems clear that he himself regards the concept of established pathological mourning as being a relatively original contribution of his own. Further, in my own view, excellent and, so far as I know, original concepts of his are reflected in such cogent statements as this: "I maintain that the mourner is *protected* from attempting suicide when he has a stable linking object through which he can maintain external contact with the representation of the dead, and a stable introject that enables him to maintain internal contact with it."

Volkan has developed and integrated in this volume many concepts that have already been touched upon by previous contributors to the literature; but he has found new gestalts, new patterns, for some long-familiar theories and clinical phenomena. Much more importantly, his overall influence in the field of psychoanalysis and psychoanalytic therapy is—as measured by this present book, for example—authentically original in the best sense of the word. Few, if any, other contributors to this field possess his scholarship, his technical mastery as analyst and therapist, his ability to work with colleagues in investigative and clinical work, his interest in developing clinically fruitful research projects, and his ability to report his findings in absorbingly readable and lucid writing. Many colleagues possess one or another of these abilities, and a few may possess this entire range of strengths; but none in this latter connection comes to my mind. Above all, Volkan uses his formidable talents and capacities in bringing to bear upon complex theoretical issues, and enormously challenging treatment endeavors, a point of view that is uniquely his own.

Harold F. Searles, M.D.

CHAPTER 1

Introduction: The evolution of research into complicated mourning

In the mid-1960s I undertook the psychoanalytic psychotherapy of an 18-year-old woman diagnosed as having anorexia nervosa. Before beginning work with me, she had been in the hospital for many months as a psychiatric inpatient, and during her stay there her nurses had noted something curious in her behavior: whenever her weight was shown during routine weighing to be over 99 pounds she would either flatly refuse to eat or pretend to eat, while in reality taking almost nothing. This behavior naturally brought about weight reduction. When her success became evident the next time she was weighed, her eating pattern would change dramatically. She would then eat openly, and her preoccupation with the need to be thin would disappear. When she was once again over 99 pounds, she would renew this seemingly absurd cycle, resorting to self-inflicted starvation in the midst of plenty.

When she became my outpatient, I noted the nurses' report of this behavior, which reminded me of a balance scale that requires a 99-pound weight on each pan in order to stay level. There was no indication on her chart that it had excited any interest among the physicians who had been caring for her. The patient was unaware of the symbolic meaning of her need to maintain her weight at 99 pounds, and it was only after her psychoanalytic psychotherapy was well under way that I was able to grasp it myself.

Her illness had commenced three years earlier at the time of her maternal grandfather's death. Her grandfather had been her father's age, a powerful man, a leader not only of his family but of the small town in which they had lived. He had had an especially close relationship with his granddaughter. At the time he was admitted to the hospital in which he was to die within a few weeks, he weighed over 200 pounds, but he wasted away so rapidly that by the time my patient saw his body in its coffin it was shockingly reduced in size. The family had "protected" the girl, then in her mid-teens, from seeing him as he lay dying, and when she saw the body and overheard a remark that the great man now weighed no more than 99 pounds, she fainted.

Since I have written in detail elsewhere about this patient, whom I called Alice (Volkan, 1965, 1976), I will not go into the particulars of her case here, however fascinating they may be. I cite it here only as the genesis of my clinical research into the identification and treatment of persons suffering from complications of the mourning process. For it became clear to me that Alice's preoccupation with weight, and the related oddities of her eating behavior, represented at least partly an attempt to identify with the shocking fate of her grandfather.

What is particularly interesting about Alice's case is the nature of the representation of her dead grandfather with which she tried to identify. Observations of the psychological processes by which an individual identifies with some aspect of the physical appearance of the dead go back to 1897, when Freud wrote in a letter to Fliess that identification with the dead was the mechanism underlying tonic hysterical spasms he had studied in which *rigor mortis* had been imitated and sustained (Freud, 1897–1902). The work of Abraham (1911a, 1916, 1924), Freud (1917a), and, later, of a host of other psychoanalytic writers has made us familiar with the notion that after the death of a loved one we often try to preserve the representation of the deceased by internalizing it. By maintaining her weight at 99 pounds, Alice was trying to identify with the shrunken representation of her grandfather that she had already internalized. She was attempting to preserve the representation of the man with whom she had had such an intense psychological closeness.

Taking in the *shrunken* representation of her grandfather had had a special meaning as well, as I learned during the process of her psychoanalytic psychotherapy: for what she called a "stick man"—the shrunken representation—was the condensation of her own early and split-off omnipotent self-representation (a phenomenon that has become known in the psychoanalytic literature as the "little man" (Kramer, 1955; Niederland, 1956; Volkan, 1965, 1976) with the representation of her dead grandfather.

Borrowing a description from Freud, Kramer described the "little man" as a prehistoric ego structure that "remains preserved as a fossil in the body of the ego, alien to its more advanced and differentiated elements" (p. 69). The main function of the "little man" is to make available to the rest of the ego a mother equivalent from which separation would never be required. In order to hold onto her hidden omnipotent part, Alice could not let her grandfather die. She needed to identify with that representation of her grandfather which stood for the "little man" in order to keep him "alive." As her therapy progressed, Alice began to gain some understanding of her need to keep her omnipotent grandfather alive. It was no longer necessary for her to maintain her body weight at 99 pounds. Instead of trying to identify fully with the shrunken aspect of the dead man, she began to see his still-internalized representation as having an existence separate from herself. Without any suggestion from me, she embarked on a new behavior pattern that called to mind aspects of the work of mourning (Freud, 1917a). A multitude of ties to the dead man and to his internalized representation were reviewed with affect in order to loosen them. Between her hours in therapy, Alice shut herself in the attic of her home with boxes of scrapbooks and pictures from her childhood, recalling her experiences with her grandfather as she pored over photographs of him. In a sense she was doing affect-laden "exercises" in observing what her relationship with the dead man had been all about, and what he had represented to her, especially as a shrunken image. She hallucinated (externalized) his appearance and "talked" with him, at the same time as she began, in piecemeal fashion, to let him die, as it were. At this point I offered her security as she went through a process, the work of mourning, that had been postponed for years. As a young girl she had been unable to tolerate the initial phase of grief at the time of her grandfather's death; she had had a disruptive identification with his representation. Her new attempt to grieve in therapy led me to believe that she was going through "re-mourning" or "re-grief."

Other factors had contributed to her anorectic condition. Among these was the faulty body ego she had developed at the beginning of her life as a result of an abdominal hernia. There was also the simultaneous longing for and dread of symbiotic relationship that had resulted from her experience with her mother. Although we dealt with each of these difficulties in her treatment, the main obstacle we had to overcome was her "frozen" mourning process. It seemed to me that progress in the other areas of her psychopathology occurred only after she became able to mourn. The mourning process that under normal circumstances would have begun with the loss of her grandfather and continued to completion in the ensuing months, was reactivated some years later as though it pertained to an altogether contemporary event; and it was initiated by the patient herself, obviously with the stimulation of the therapy. It is of further interest that Alice mourned for the original lost person, her grandfather, and that her mourning was not displaced onto the figure of the therapist. In the usual situation of transference, the therapist would typically represent the dead man as a target of unconscious desires and defenses against them. The patient would then grieve over losing the therapist if any separation occurred between them, such as a vacation. For example, I have described elsewhere (Volkan, 1976) the analysis of another young woman who had had an abortion some years before her work with me. She spoke at the beginning of her analysis of seeing her dead fetus flushed down a toilet, but it was only after some years of work with me, when I was on the point of taking my summer holiday, that she felt sadness. I had become in her eyes her fetus; during her hours in the last weeks before my vacation, she had fantasies of my getting smaller and smaller, until, on the last day before my vacation, she perceived me to be as small as a fetus; my projected vacation was for her the separation from it. She worked through her grieving process in her transference, feeling the affects in relation to the "here and now" interaction taking place between us. The application of all this to the events of an earlier time was interpreted to her once she experienced mourning. In contrast to this patient, Alice was grieving for her original lost object.

Complicated grief as a seal over other psychopathology

At the time of Alice's psychoanalytically oriented psychotherapy with me I was a candidate at the Washington Psychoanalytic Institute. I had just begun to apply the techniques of psychoanalysis proper, which I was using with other patients under supervision. I am sure that many of the fine details and nuances of Alice's case escaped my attention, but my work with her definitely gave me the idea that when a mourning process concerned with a major loss by death is not resolved, pathological adjustments to it, basically attempting to deny the reality of the death, may seal over aspects of any other psychopathology from which the patient is suffering. Even then I sensed that unless this seal is broken, the working through of other psychopathology might be difficult or even impossible.

This surmise was borne out when the Charlottesville Study Group on Psychoanalytic Psychotherapy, which I founded five years ago, studied the reactions of two adult sisters to the brutal murder of their mother. By coincidence, the two sisters had become patients of two members of the study group, J. Anderson Thomson, Jr., and Salman Akhtar. Each saw her psychiatrist three times a week. The content of the first two years of Thomson's psychoanalytic psychotherapy with his patient was examined in the weekly meetings of the study group, and her reactions to her mother's murder were compared with those of her younger sister, Akhtar's patient. As might have been expected they had had different responses to the event, influenced by their different personality structures, their different fantasies, the different relationship each had had with the mother, and the different important inner representations each had had of her, although the responses of both were highly complicated and condensed in their general psychopathology. They were, however, alike in their attempt to identify with their mother as she was at the time of her death and in their becoming "living memorials" to her (see Chapter 8).

Thomson's patient entered treatment with denial of affects concerning her mother's death but with an awareness that she was caught up in some frantic and unusual behavior patterns. Thomson conducted her treatment by adhering to therapeutic neutrality and responding to his patient with interpretations only, as is customary in psychoanalysis proper. Before long she presented unusually open oedipal material in the therapeutic work, such as one might see in a borderline or psychotic personality organization (although this patient did not otherwise exhibit the characteristics of such organizations) or in a neurotic patient after the gradual therapeutic removal of layers of repression. Incidents of her early childhood such as specific sexual stimulation by an older brother and certain behavioral patterns of her father when drunk had greatly stimulated oedipal conflict. The therapist waited to see what would evolve without prematurely interpreting or interfering with her verbal productions. It became clear that the open oedipal material was in the service of covering up the patient's affect-laden fantasies of her mother's murder. Matters remained unchanged for many months.

The patient at last went through a stormy grief reaction. What is interesting here is that after she completed grieving, drives pertaining to oedipal material, and her defenses against them, appeared once again in the transference. The second appearance of the oedipal material, unlike the first, which the study group saw as a defensive maneuver to protect the patient from the pain of grieving, was not "open" but evolved in a more repressed manner and in more symbolic terms and with morc with immediately if the beach is to be made fit for use. Of course, antecedent pathology and pre-existing character organization usually determine to a great extent the ability or inability to grieve (unless a death initiates mourning that resembles traumatic neurosis; in such cases, the nature of the trauma is the determining element of the complicated grief, although antecedent pathology still makes itself felt). The inability to grieve seals over in turn the working through of preexisting psychopathology in the treatment situation. It is the breaking of this seal that "re-grief' therapy is designed to accomplish.

The beginnings of "re-grief" therapy

During the time I was treating Alice—and learning a great deal from her—I had an office next to that of Joseph Wolpe of behavior therapy fame. While at the University of Virginia, Wolpe was actively involved in clinical research in behavior therapy. At departmental scientific meetings, lively discussions took place between him and his followers and the faculty psychoanalysts and their followers, of whom I was one. Wolpe aggressively defended his creative propositions and methodology and provided statistical data to support them. To a new psychoanalytic candidate he was "the aggressor," and I can see now in retrospect that my research into complicated mourning had at the time elements of my "identification with the aggressor" (Anna Freud, 1936). Armed with this identification, and influenced by Alice's use of pictures and scrapbooks to promote her achievement of mourning, and dealing also at that time with some personal losses of my own, I postulated that a person with complicated mourning could be "deconditioned, " if you will, toward a disruptive introject—the representation of the dead he keeps within his bosom (Volkan, 1966). I further postulated that what Alice had initiated for herself—with the stimulation of the treatment process—could be initiated by the therapist with suitable patients in order to help them loosen their ties to the introject. Although this assumption suggests a mechanical view of the introject, I also knew that there were affective, cognitive, and dynamic processes that made the patient feel as though he had a presence (an introject) within him. I was, moreover, aware that the known loss of an object in a patient's adult life could reactivate his childhood reactions to frustration (Klein, 1940) and whatever affective experiences of loss (real or fantasied) he might have had in childhood, including the psychological losses involved in leaving one developmental level behind and going on to another. Illustrations of how adult object loss reactivates the affects pertaining to childhood experiences of loss will be found throughout this volume.

In spite of knowing that a historical object loss (the death of a loved one) in adult life cannot be seen as an isolated event, I felt that in certain selected cases brief psychotherapy, in which little or no attempt was made to deal with deeper conflicts, might serve to help patients go through their grieving; at the time, I was working in an inpatient setting in which the patient's stay was necessarily rather short. I gave the name "re-grief work" to what the patient would undergo, and I called the technique I would employ "re-grief therapy."

My first "official" re-grief therapy was conducted with the help of C. Robert Showalter, then a colleague at the University of Virginia Hospital (Volkan, 1966). Mary, our first patient, was a teenager, an average high school student who exhibited rather obsessional characteristics, and who had been brought to the hospital because of a suicide attempt. She had been able to manage her own life rather well in a household in which her parents had become increasingly quarrelsome.

However, when her mother finally killed herself with a shotgun blast to the head—after sending Mary to a neighbor's house to spare her from having to witness what she was about to do—Mary experienced a traumatic and sudden loss. She felt terrible remorse about having left the house, where she might have done something to prevent the tragedy. She was unable to go through the work of mourning and to loosen her ties to her mother's representation. She clung to this representation, to the point of identifying disruptively with it, and began to step into her mother's role in controversies with her father, and to adopt other maneuvers of her mother's. On the second anniversary of the suicide, Mary tried to blow her brains out just as her mother had done, using the same gun in her attempt. For some mechanical reason, the gun did not fire, but having pulled the trigger, Mary experienced at that moment, as we learned later, an element of conscious merger with the mother's representation as she concentrated on how her mother must have felt during the moments before her death. It was this suicide attempt that had caused her to be brought to the hospital.

During the two months that followed we applied our "re-grief therapy," seeing her almost daily. We first took a history, and then made the formulation that Mary had arrived at a level in her psychological development in which she was in possession of an integrated self-concept. Before her mother's death, her ego had been using rather sophisticated defensive-adaptive mechanisms to deal with her inner impulses and processes, as well as with the external world. Mary was not aware that she had taken over some of her mother's behavior. We helped her to place a boundary, as it were, between herself and the mother representation with which she had identified, working first on an intellectual level. Showalter and I called this exercise one in *demarcation* (Volkan & Showalter, 1968). To advance the process, we followed Alice's model and asked Mary to bring to her sessions pictures of her mother and herself, which she could review as she attempted to see where she ended and where her mother began. These intellectual exercises were supplemented by our own efforts to clarify and explain to her the unconscious aspects of her disruptive identification with aspects of her mother. She was encouraged to focus on the lost object in the supportive environment of the hospital. We observed that such a focus elicited powerful affects most of which referred to the narcissistic hurt of being abandoned by her mother. There was also anger, which was sometimes displaced onto the therapist. He absorbed it and, by means of interpretations, helped the patient confront the guilt she had felt for not having remained on hand to protect her mother from killing herself. Affects on a deeper level put a boundary between the patient and the representation of the dead woman.

At this point, the therapist, following Wolpe (1958), employed in part a continually repeated presentation of memories of Mary's relationship with her mother. Memories of this kind had been collected as the history was being taken and had also surfaced with the first application of the technique. This "desensitization" process helped Mary to be less and less anxious about her experiences with her mother, especially about her fantasied failure to prevent her death. When Mary recalled the funeral, she was sad but felt relieved. Within two months she was showing an interest in new love objects, and a check-up six months after she left treatment indicated that she was doing rather well. Although a more extensive follow-up was not possible in this case, Showalter and I felt encouraged by the outcome of the treatment and continued to use this method with a few other patients who were unable to grieve (Volkan & Showalter, 1968). I embarked on related clinical research, and the initial crude method of "re-griefing" evolved during the next few years into what Josephthal and I called in 1980 "mini-focal analysis."

Further evolution of this clinical research

I am now able to report on the clinical research of 15 years during which I have treated or otherwise seen professionally more than 150 patients from ages 16 to 58 who had come to my attention because they were "frozen"—as many such patients spontaneously described themselves—in the process of mourning. When I became an analyst, I took into psychoanalysis proper five patients whose presenting problems included symptoms related to a loss by death. To some extent, therefore, I was following the work conducted by a group at the Chicago Institute for Psychoanalysis (Fleming & Altschul, 1963; Fleming, 1972) that studied in psychoanalysis certain adults who had lost a parent to death during their childhood or adolescence. The Chicago study showed that the defense structure of the patient, built up in response to the loss of a parent, delayed the development of an analyzable transference. This was a circumstance that I had already sensed in my own therapeutic involvement with such patients. The Chicago study also showed that the therapeutic relationship activated the mourning process of these patients and, with the recall of previously repressed memories, the experiencing of grief. It is after the resolution of mourning that growth and change can begin to take place.

In comparison with the Chicago study, my sample also includes patients reacting to losses by death suffered in adult life. One patient who came into analysis after finishing his re-grief therapy (Volkan, 1971) gave me insights on a deeper level as to how re-griefing was perceived by him (see the case of Mike in Chapter 9). Another patient, one who had completed five years of analysis, asked to see me after she had lost her father; she was still having "weird" dreams about his decaying body almost two months after his death (see Chapter 2 for further notes on the case of this patient, Linda). Thus, I was able to see the reaction of an analyzed adult to the loss of a parent, a parent whose relationship to the patient had been an important subject of her psychoanalysis.

Seventeen patients were treated with re-grief therapy for three to four months, three to four times a week. Follow-up was made according to the patient's availability. Another seven patients went into psychoanalytic psychotherapy that lasted over a period of years on the basis of two or three weekly sessions. Among the others were those whose therapies were supervised by me and those seen in extended diagnostic interviews as part of this clinical research. Finally, when I was given the opportunity to study a group of people victimized by war (Volkan, 1977, 1979a), I learned about their shared reactions to the many losses, including death, that war brings with it.

Initial theoretical formulations

Normal mourning, depression, and established pathological mourning

Freud suggested the existence of a relationship between bereavement and symptom formation in the early days of the psychoanalytic movement (Breuer & Freud, 1893–1895), and later established the critical distinction between normal mourning—what I have called "uncomplicated grief'—and the reactive depression ("melancholia," to use Freud's term) that can follow the death of someone close and important to the mourner (1917a). We shall see later that the mourner in uncomplicated grief loosens his ties to the representation of the dead person by means of the work of mourning and/or identifies with selected aspects of that representation in a loving way that promotes his own growth. In contrast the depressed mourner experiences a *disruptive* identification with ambivalently related representations of the deceased that eventuates in a continuing internal struggle—a struggle between cherishing the self and wanting to do away with it.

The literature contains further accounts of the complications of grief. For example, the initial absence of a grief reaction is described by Deutsch (1937), and the chronicity of what is generally thought of as "normal" grief reactions by Wahl (1970). Nevertheless, differentiation between the varieties of complicated grief and depression over loss by death is not always made, and these diagnostic terms are commonly used interchangeably.

My research has shown me that on the descriptive level there is a clinical picture of what I call established pathological mourning that differs from the clinical pictures of either reactive (neurotic) depression or unduly protracted "normal" grief reaction. While established pathological mourning is not always an all-or-nothing phenomenon, and while one may expect to see many mixed cases, my study has shown me that the clinical picture of established pathological mourning is unique and predictable and a source of remarkable insights into the minds of the bereaved.

Application of the developmental and internalized object relations approach

From a metapsychological point of view, classical analysis, with its emphasis on drives and the ego defenses leveled against them, explains the grief process as one reflecting a conflict between the desire to maintain the old libidinal—and, I may add, the aggressive—position and the demands of reality that it be abandoned. Bibring (1953) has investigated both depression and grief from an ego psychological point of view, and

Pollock (1961), Rochlin (1965), and others have addressed themselves to the adaptive aspects of restitution following loss. Uncomplicated mourning leads to identification with the "good" aspects of the deceased and thus the enrichment of the mourner's personality structure. It also makes the mourner a solid bridge between the generations, as it were, when the one being mourned belongs to an older generation than his mourner. I believe that my studies add to these formulations the knowledge gained by recent studies on separation–individuation (Mahler, 1963, 1968) and internalized object relations (Jacobson, 1964; Kernberg, 1966, 1976; Volkan, 1976), shedding further light on the mourning process. Throughout this volume the standard tripartite structural (id–ego–superego) approach will be amplified by a developmental and an internalized object relations approach.

The theory of internalized object relations views intrapsychic conflict in terms of an individual's self- and object representations. Conflicts of object relations take place between certain units of self- and object representations under the impact of determined drive derivatives (such drive derivatives clinically appearing as affect dispositions) and other contradictory or opposite units of self- and object representations, under the impact of *their* respective affect dispositions. These conflicts can be clearly seen in patients with borderline or narcissistic personality organizations, who have not achieved a cohesive self-representation and integrated object representations. But they may also be seen in persons *with* cohesive self-representations and integrated object worlds when the death of a loved one precipitates the hypercathexis of the representation of the dead, reviving old conflicts among self- and object relationships and demanding new inner adjustments to restore the previously established, newly disturbed, balance among them.

Following the contributions of Jacobson (1964) and Mahler (1963, 1968), Kernberg (1966, 1975, 1976) stresses the building up in bipolar fashion of self- and object images that reflect the original relationship between the infant and his mother; and the subsequent development of dyadic, triadic, and multiple internal and external interpersonal relations in general. In his early interaction with the mothering person, the infant acquires his orientation to extrauterine life. The stimuli that impinge upon him may be pleasurable or unpleasurable, leaving an ever-increasing number of memory traces of the two types. (Stimuli accumulate through the instrumentality of the inborn and autonomous [Hartmann, 1939] perceptive faculty of the primitive ego.) From these memory traces the individual forms in a bipolar way what Mahler (1968) calls "memory islands," which contain "pleasurable-good" or "painful-bad" stimuli not yet allocated either to the self or the not-self. Still, his repeated experiences with need-satisfying (and need-denying) outside sources provide the infant with vague affective discriminations between "self' and "not-self." He forms self- and object *images*, at first undifferentiated, from the perceptions with which these experiences are associated. Consistent and more or less realistic endopsychic *representations* of the object world and of the self-a "more enduring schema" (Moore & Fine, 1967, p. 85) of multiple images—gradually develop out of these images. During this gradual process

> Libido and aggression are continually turned from the love object to the self and vice versa, or also from one object to the other, while self and object images as well as images of different objects undergo temporary fusions and separate and join again. Simultaneously, there is a tendency to cathect one such composite image unit with libido only, while all the aggression is directed to another one, until ambivalence can be tolerated. (Jacobson, 1964, p. 44)

Jacobson further indicates that these continually occurring cathectic shifts and changes are reflected in introjective and projective mechanisms. These mechanisms are based on the child's unconscious fantasies of incorporation and ejection of the love object and exist at least throughout the first year of life.

Kernberg (1976), who treats both self-representations and object representations as theoretical affective-cognitive structures, postulates five stages of the gradual process to which Jacobson refers. These stages reflect a process whereby undifferentiated bipolar self- and object images are first differentiated and then integrated, when "good" and "bad" image units are put together—mended. Emphasis on the bipolar development of self- and object representations and the maintenance of such bipolarity until the integration of "good" and "bad" representations becomes possible—usually in the third year of life—justifies the use of the term "splitting" to indicate the separation of opposite representations. In this connection I have consistently used the adjective "primitive" before "splitting" to differentiate this phenomenon in a primitive phase of the developmental process from other types of splitting that I will examine later (Volkan, 1975a, 1976, 1979a). Since the theory of internalized object relations takes into account the way in which "good" and "bad" self- and object constellations are invested with libidinal and aggressive drives respectively, the term "primitive splitting" also refers to the separation of representational units along affective lines according to the investment of opposing drive derivatives.

Primitive splitting reflects at the outset the primitive ego's inability to integrate. With the gradual achievement of integrative capacity, primitive splitting is used less often and is finally abandoned for all practical purposes when circumstances are normal. In some situations, however, the separation of representations may be more and more resorted to as a defensive measure, chiefly to keep internalized "good" relationships with the mother from contamination by "bad" experiences with her. Some adults, especially those who have a borderline personality organization, continue to use primitive splitting as their dominant defense mechanism (Kernberg, 1967).

Attachment behavior

Descriptions of the mourning process in the psychoanalytic literature are generally compatible in spite of some departures in terminology. There is disagreement among the writers, however, with respect to theoretical underpinnings. As I have observed, the most widely accepted psychoanalytic view of the grief process takes into consideration drive investment in the representation of the dead, and an unconscious and eventually successful struggle to loosen the ties to this representation in piecemeal fashion. Bowlby's ideas on grief, as developed in a series of papers (1960, 1961, 1969), differ drastically from this premise, and depend basically on a biological theory in which an inborn urge is assumed to tie the infants of all mammals, including man, to the mother. Behavior resulting from this tie is called attachment behavior, its function being primarily protection from predators. It remains active in adult life and is elicited when anyone, whether child or adult, is in trouble. It accounts for the extremely young age at which infants, according to Bowlby, can experience mourning. It is elicited at particularly high intensity when the attachment figure cannot be found.

> Because, in the light of this theory, attachment behaviour is regarded as a normal and healthy part of man's instinctive makeup, it is held to be most misleading to term it "regressive" or childish when seen in older child or adult. (Bowlby & Parkes, 1970, p. 202)

The core of Bowlby and Parkes's schema of the mourning process—the yearning and search for the lost figure—reflects this conceptualization of attachment behavior, a conceptualization that has been severely criticized by Anna Freud (1960), Schur (1960), Spitz (1960), and Engel (1971). I have no intention of reviewing this controversy here, but by way of epitomizing it I would refer to the remark of Anna Freud that Bowlby's emphasis on the biological urge does not deal, as classical psychoanalytic theory would, with the *representation* of these drives. Moreover, psychoanalytic theory would take into account the repercussion in the mind of happenings in the external world rather than the happenings *per se.* According to Anna Freud, "activating events" are experienced as events in the pleasure–pain series. Engel (1971), in an extensive review of Bowlby's theory of attachment behavior, criticizes him for his failure to distinguish between psychological and behavioral frames of reference.

The theory of internalized object relations that I have just described proposes a bridge between traditional psychoanalytic theory with its emphasis on dual instinctual drives, and the psychoanalytic theory of object relations. The first, to which Anna Freud would subscribe in the controversy alluded to above, views object investment as secondary to the expression of libidinal—as well as aggressive—instinctual needs. The second, to which Bowlby would subscribe, stresses the primacy of the infant's attachment to the object. Kernberg thus sees the earliest expression of instinctual drives in behavior patterns that involve interaction between the infant and others in "an average expectable environment" (Hartmann, 1939), and holds that instinctual drives are subsequently expressed in internalized object relations, which, in turn, are crucial organizers of all other psychic structures.

Internalized object relations theory thus allows us to take an additional view of cases like Alice's. Rather than ascribing her reaction to her grandfather's: death to "attachment" behavior or to libidinal and aggressive instinctual needs, we see the hypercathexis of the representation of her dead grandfather reviving old conflicts among libidinally and aggressively invested self- and object representations.

Linking objects and linking phenomena

I have found that patients with established pathological grief typically select an inanimate object—a symbolic bridge (or link) to the representation of the dead person—to use in a magical way. I have called these objects "linking objects" (Volkan, 1972) and phenomena used in a similar way "linking phenomena." Such objects mainly provide a locus for externalized contact between aspects of the mourner's self-representation and aspects of the representation of the deceased. The mourner sees them as containing elements of himself and of the one he has lost. By using his linking object, the mourner can keep alive the illusion that he has the power either to return the dead person to life or to "kill" him; that is, he has the illusion of absolute control over the psychological meeting ground that is afforded by the linking object or linking phenomena. It is on this meeting ground that the established pathological mourner seeks to restore and then finally resolve the ambivalence that characterized his relationship with the deceased in his lifetime.

In another section of this book, I will give accounts of parents who have used children as "living linking objects" to console themselves for the earlier loss of other children or persons with whom they have had a close relationship. Finally, I will compare the linking object to other inanimate objects with special psychological meaning, such as the transitional object (Winnicott, 1953) and the fetish (see Chapter 15).

Conclusion

What was originally simply a clinical search for a practical, effective, and necessarily brief therapy for hospitalized patients with complicated grief has thus evolved into a more generalized and searching clinical study of death-related issues. In this study I have used psychoanalytic theory to understand the data collected from patients in psychoanalysis proper and from those in other forms of therapy (see Chapters 7 and 9 for definitions of the several therapies). The accumulation of what has been repeatedly observed during thousands of therapy hours and hundreds of interviews over 15 years lies behind this new systematic description of complicated mourning and provides a new understanding of the psychic processes involved in it. Later in this volume I will return to the re-grief therapy that initiated my clinical research, and trace its evolution over the years into a specific treatment method, one certainly not analytic in all of its particulars but one based on an understanding of the meaning of linking objects and phenomena and on other insights that only psychoanalytic theory could have provided.

Part I

Phenomenological and theoretical findings

CHAPTER 2

Uncomplicated mourning

The literature on bereavement holds that uncomplicated mourning goes through recognizable stages. In this chapter I will first describe as an example of uncomplicated mourning the reactions to her father's death of a woman who had already undergone psychoanalysis, during which problems related to her father had been worked through. My intention in this is to show how a death temporarily revives ancient conflicts between the self-representation of the mourner and the representation of the deceased, which the mourner must resolve before he or she can fully accept the loved one's death. I then provide a brief review of the psychoanalytic literature on the stages of mourning; concluding with a discussion of the question, "Is grief a disease?" I suggest that the concept of disease is a valuable model for the phenomenological description of the mourning process.

An analyzed woman's uncomplicated mourning

Linda was a woman in her mid-twenties who had undertaken psychoanalysis after a suicide attempt following rejection by a lover. She tended to devote herself to other people, particularly when the other person was a married man. Her pattern was to become a virtual slave to her current married lover, acting as his "second wife," until this "most beautiful relationship" curdled, leaving her feeling rejected. The termination of the fifth such relationship had brought her into analysis.

The story of her family emerged slowly as we worked together. Her father, a teacher, had been very much in love with his first wife. But the death at age seven of a son born to the couple had brought them such grief that they could not hold their marriage together; the mother's infidelity finally led to divorce. The father remarried, my patient being the first child born to his second marriage. He was a withdrawn man, who had never forgotten his first wife and their dead child, and perhaps because of this, his second wife had become an alcoholic. As a result, Linda had been denied warm, loving mothering.

Her experiences with her mother while a small child, and the repeated frustrations they had brought her, had caused Linda's early self- and object representations to be contaminated with excessive aggression. The mending of such representations with her libidinally invested self- and object representations had not been fully successful, as evidenced by my clinical observation that she had kept a "savior" representation of herself apart from a representation of herself as hungering for affection. Through the activation of this savior representation, Linda wanted to "save" her mother—not for altruistic reasons, but to make her a more adequate mother. Later, however, when her father became psychologically important to her, this wish to save her mother was condensed with a wish to save him as well.

Linda's father saw in her aspects both of his first wife and of the son he had lost. He would tuck her into bed at night, as his wife lay in drunken sleep, and linger in her room on one pretext or another. As a child and as a growing girl, she had noticed that he wanted to stay with her rather than go to his wife. In her desire to please him, the girl had become a tomboy by way of giving him back his lost son. She had had intense penis envy, which she had carried into her analysis. At the same time, however, she had identified herself with her father's reportedly beautiful first wife, and her father had begun taking her around with him, introducing her as his "second wife," jokingly, but not altogether inaccurately, since, as it became evident in analysis, Linda knew that in this introduction he referred to his first wife as the one he had divorced after learning of her affair. Thus Linda, very beautiful in young womanhood, and masochistically submissive to men, sought out married men to whom she could be a "second wife," men whom she could save. At the same time, she felt intense envy of them to the extent that, as males, they represented the dead boy her father had loved, and with whom she had tried at times to identify herself. Thus, the dependent "hungry" self-representation came into conflict with the omnipotent "savior" self-representation, just as it had in childhood. Her envy of her lovers usually led to the termination of her affairs.

Other aspects of her case are not relevant here. During her analysis, which took five years, she came to understand the deeper meaning of her repeated behavior as a "second wife." She was able to examine clearly her early representations of herself and her parental figures. She felt rage at first against both her parents, then came to feel sympathetic with her father's unresolved grief and better able to see his "human nature." Her own grief over her early mother enabled her to ignore the urge to drop everything in her own life to make yet another attempt to save her mother, who was still going from one crisis to another at the time of her analysis. The "fragments" of which Linda was composed—savior of her parents, child still in need of attention; tomboy/envious, castrated girl, submissive woman, and seductress—came together (mended), and she was able to mend the representation of the grieving and needy withdrawn father with the representation of the father who was slyly human.

What interests us here is Linda's coming to terms with her conflicting representations of her father. The literature holds that an uncomplicated response to death can be expected when the bereaved person has little or no "unfinished psychological business" with the departed and when he is capable of a rather realistic appreciation of what the deceased person represents for him. Linda and I spent years together; in her transference displacements and externalizations I became the different aspects of her father, and in the course of our work together, I observed with her the completion of her unfinished business. Let me cite one example to illustrate how Linda had come to terms with her conflicting representations of her father.

Her father was a Jew who had come to America as a child and later changed his Jewish name in an effort to avoid prejudice. This had alienated his relatives, all of whom had continued to use the original name.

Neither of the women he married w.as Jewish, and Linda, brought up as a Christian, denied strongly and defensively having any Jewish characteristics as an adult. Moreover, she denied that her father might still retain a Jewish identity of his own, however hidden.

On the day after the Israeli athletes were murdered at the Olympic Games in Munich she spoke to me about the murder without feeling. She told me how surprised she had been the day before to hear the guests at a party express rage over it. I was moved by her need for denial and realized I was sensing in myself—through projective identification—a part of Linda that was full of sorrow. In conveying to her my observation of her denial, I suspect that my voice betrayed the feelings I had had about the tragedy. Our interchange caused in her a deep sadness, and she wept for the athletes for days as she lay on the couch, arriving at some understanding of what her father had had to endure to survive as a Jew. New memories of him now showed her that he had felt a secret pride in his background, and she came to realize that his need to deny his Jewishness had been to a considerable extent practical. Her deepened appreciation of her father's heritage allowed her to integrate her conflicting perceptions of him, leading, in turn, to a further integration of her own identity. Although she remained a Christian, it was no longer difficult for Linda to admit that she had Jewish blood and to declare that she was proud of having Jewish blood. Her analysis terminated soon after this.

Two years later Linda's father died. Although she called me two months after her father's death, the "weird fantasies and dreams" that had occasioned her call were of very recent appearance. She explained over the telephone that they had not made her especially anxious, but that she had found them puzzling. She wondered if these fantasies and dreams might indicate the return of a pathological state, and she proposed our getting together for a check-up to see whether her reaction to her loss was "abnormal" or not. I agreed to see her, and we met for four hours over a period of two months, having two hours together soon after she called and another two hours two months later.

In our first meeting, she reported that her father had visited the home she lived in with her husband—for she was now married—two days before he died. He was aging and known to have some kind of cardiac problem, but he gave no signs of imminent death. She felt close to him. Both seemed to enjoy their brief time together. At the end of his visit, the father returned to his own home at some distance in the country. Two days later, Linda was called to the telephone to learn of his death. On hearing the news she felt numb, and her mouth was dry. As she hung up the telephone she continued to feel that her father was still alive, although she realized that the caller had spoken the truth. The belief that he still lived alternated with the reality of his. death. At times she was able to entertain both views simultaneously. She did not know what to do. Her husband was away from home and out of reach, but even had he been available, she felt too aimless to get word to him. But as soon as the observing ego that she had developed in analysis gave the signal, she became keenly aware of her psychological processes.

By the time her husband came home, she was able to talk to him feelingly about her father's death. She saw the solicitous friends who called as shadowy, and she had a sense of her own remoteness from the environment, a feeling that alternated with her being fully able to do whatever was necessary; she began calling her relatives and making arrangements for the funeral. She watched herself become a "savior," just as she had tried to be for both her parents as a child. She was taking things over, saving her mother and other relatives from the responsibility of arranging for the burial rites. She was able to perceive this familiar maneuver—the adoption of the role of savior—at the same time as she recognized that in reality she was the best person to take care of things. She felt no internal conflict about her actions.

She went to the place where the death had occurred. She wept throughout the first night there and wept again often during the first week, feeling great pain. The sight of an aunt at the funeral—one of the relatives who had kept the family's Jewish name—enraged her. She wanted to cry out, "Why didn't you pay attention to my father's dilemma? His having to survive as a Jew in this hostile place?" She wanted to scream, "Where were you before?" She was able to maintain outward control, but was bothered by the wave of rage she felt, was reminded of the rage she had once felt toward the dead man himself, and pondered whether she might be projecting onto her aunt her own self-condemnation. As she observed the waves of anger, she had an intimation that she was also angry at her father for dying. Things had been going well for the first time in her life, and his death had now activated some extremely distressing feelings in her.

She was able to get through the Christian funeral rites. Her anger against her father over his concealment of his Jewish origin alternated with an appreciation of what he had faced during his lifetime. She participated fully in the service and returned later for a visit to the grave.

During the ensuing months, her crying spells diminished. She realized that because of her father's chronic illness and advanced age she had on one level of awareness been prepared for his death. She continued, however, to be preoccupied with images of him and with the different memories of her life that pertained to their experiences together. Feelings of guilt, centering mostly on her having taken him for a walk shortly before his death, intruded on her preoccupation with him. The place where they had taken their walk was windy. Although she wondered if this might not have hastened his death, she was not intensely or unbearably guilty about this possibility.

A few days before getting in touch with me she fantasied the body of her father lying in the earth. She found it bizarre that she could imagine it decaying bit by bit. Such fantasies came into her mind before she fell asleep and continued in her dreams. She reported the process of her grieving during the two hours we had together at this point and spontaneously expressed her opinion that her fantasies and dreams might represent her letting her father die. In fact, after calling for her appointment with me, she had come to this conclusion with relief, but had wanted, in spite of this, to keep the appointment she had made. She felt that her "learned" ability to observe her inner processes made possible the interpretation she had arrived at. She was, in other words, psychologically "killing" her father in order to adjust internally to an external loss.

Two months later, during the two hours we used for a subsequent check-up, she described her perception of what she called "a new energy" that had become available to her as her preoccupation with her father's image had lessened. She had felt an increased interest in life and had thought about acquiring a pet. Even before she had spoken of the wish for a pet, however, her husband had apparently sensed it, and given her a puppy. She observed how this puppy fascinated her and how much she loved it.

Some years earlier, before her marriage and after her last intense relationship with a married man, she had purchased a puppy. That love affair, which had taken place during her analysis, had been colored by an externalized transference neurosis. Her partner had been, like myself, a university professor. It was when she brought the externalized transference phenomenon into the analytic setting that this last affair stormily ended, with an understanding on her part of her desire to be my "second wife." During the working through of this phase, the puppy replaced her lost lover, who, because of his habit of complaining to her about his wife, was identified by Linda with aspects of her own needy father. She named her male puppy "Baba." She knew that I am Turkish, but denied when asked about this name any realization that it is the Turkish name for father, although the similarity of the name to "papa" did not escape her. When, later, Baba sired pups, Linda was given one of the males. She insisted during her analysis that I accept him as a gift until I interpreted her perception of me as the grieving father, for whom the new puppy was perhaps a representative of the boy so long ago dead. Through this proposed gift, she sought to save me from fantasied sadness and to free herself magically from the need to be my savior.

I felt that the puppy she had acquired after the death had again represented her lost father. During our brief consultation, she had made no attempt to connect the new puppy with the old one, on which she had spent so many hours during her analysis; nor was any attempt made on my part to induce curiosity about it. I felt she knew that her intense interest in her new pet reflected the withdrawal of interest from the inner representation of her father and the investment of that interest in a symbolic and living representation of him. I surmised that the puppy served as a bridge for her to pass over in order to find other human love objects to which her "new energy" might be directed. Although her observing ego suggested to her that the new pet might be a substitute for the dead father, this thought did not interfere with her continuing delight in simply having it.

Many years later I saw Linda professionally again. By then her intense involvement with the puppy was a thing of the past. She now had children in whom she was, appropriately, intensely interested. She consulted me at this time because she had uncovered one of the reasons why she had married the man she did. She now realized from her continued self-analysis that aspects of her husband represented aspects of her own previous needy self as well as the needy self of her father. In spite of her husband's many achievements, he had had a difficult relationship of dependency with his parents, and unacknowledged hostility toward them. Linda realized that she had married him partly to save him—as a representative of her own needy-hostile self. She was certainly not his slave, as she had been the slave of her several lovers, but she could still observe remnants of her old behavior. Once she understood this, her relationship with her husband underwent change. He responded to this change with hostile feelings, and Linda wanted to discuss this with me. Before long she persuaded him to go into psychoanalysis himself.

During these last professional interviews with Linda, years after her father's death, I was able to learn what kind of a representation of her father she had retained. In the sense that it reflected her collected and integrated perceptions of him, it was realistic. When memories of him surfaced, they were not accompanied by pain, sadness, or anxiety. During the routine conduct of her daily life she had no need to hypercathect, as it were, the representation of her father. Still, unrepressed memories of him were available to her. She had no exaggerated anniversary reactions.

Generational continuity

As Linda said during her last visit with me, we never really "kill" anyone, especially anyone with whom we have had a meaningful pleasurable or painful relationship. With this I agreed, as Freud (1908) would have done. Freud held that we never actually surrender anything but simply exchange one thing for another. In discussing psychic reality, it makes better sense to speak of the various fates of the "immortal object" (Schafer's term, 1968) than to speak of object loss pure and simple. The representations of the dead live on in our memories and feeling states until we ourselves die, but, in the course of time, we come to a point at which we no longer have a pathological need to activate the representation of the dead person so as to complete any "unfinished" psychological relatedness, unfinished psychological relatedness that we may have had with him in reality but that fantasy has subsequently embellished.

It is, of course, "normal" and expectable for the representation of the dead person to be activated on occasion, as on the anniversary of the death. Engel (1975), Mintz (1971), and Pollock (1970, 1971, 1975a) have written at length about anniversary reactions, which may or may not generate chronic psychological trouble, depending on the nature of the mourning. Pollock (1971) states:

> For the vulnerable individual a specific time of day, a specific day of the week, a specific season of the year, or specific holiday can serve as a trigger or activator for the appearance of a symptom related to anniversary reactions. (p. 123)

He holds, moreover, that in the cases he reports "internal unconscious determinants were the significant factors" (p. 130), and the external temporal referent served only "as a trigger for the release of the repressed conflict" (p. 130). Thus, he states, anniversary reactions derive from complicated mourning and disappear—"leaving only a memory as a memorial"—when analysis effects resolution of intrapsychic conflict.

Linda noted the anniversaries of her father's death but had no particular affective experience or preoccupation with his image on these occasions. She did, however, give me an example of another sort of typical reactivation of the representations of the one mourned.

I had already observed in my work that when one comes to a milestone in life such as marriage, promotion, or a move from one place of residence to another, one typically activates the images of dead others who have been realistically or symbolically significant in one's life. Engel (1975) writes of finding himself thinking about his father as he received recognition for his accomplishments four decades after his father's death. I have observed that a son, leaving behind him the city in which he had lived with a mother now dead, is likely to experience some modified work of mourning, as though he were making his farewell to the dead mother's representation in the environment that they had both known. The converse may also be true. The return after many years to their common homeplace may evoke an aspect of what Novey (1968) calls "a second look": the son remembers his dead mother by reactivating her representation. Again, whether we call such reactivation "normal" or pathological depends on its degree and on the course that it takes. In Chapter 5 I tell of a young woman's selecting as her wedding day the anniversary of her father's death, without being aware, until the day before the scheduled date, that she had condensed an anniversary and life milestone; she then had a severe reaction and attempted suicide. I demonstrate that this was, among other things, chiefly an attempt to join her father so as to get his blessing on her marriage.

Linda bore two children during the five years after her father's death. The birth of the second child, a son, reactivated a special image of her father—the grieving father—that she related to internally. At first she felt remorse and sadness over his not being able to see her beautiful boy child. As the activation persisted, however, she felt discomfort with it—until she realized that she herself had tried as a tomboy to replace the son that her father had lost. In other words, she saw that the child's birth had reactivated a version of the old conflict-ridden psychological story: now that she had a son, the new baby could replace her father's lost child. She could please her father in this, save him from his depression, and, in turn, be free of obligation herself. Her unusual ability in self-examination allowed her to work through this situation once she recognized it, and the reactivation of her father's representation ended.

I used the term "generational continuity" for the first time to describe a phenomenon I observed in myself while watching a parade with my little son during the first anniversary of the 1974 war on the island of Cyprus (Volkan, 1979a). It had to do with my feeling that I was a link between the representation of my dead father, who had died during the time of turmoil in Cyprus, and my son, the grandson he never saw. Linda also provided an example of generational continuity. The representative of the first generation, the father, responds with complications to the death of his son, and to the loss of his wife to another man. His daughter in the second generation has a mission to make him for get his grief, and tries to replace the dead boy as well as the lost wife. Her little son in the third generation is perceived by his mother, for a time at least, as representing the first dead boy and as a solace to the representation—kept alive within his mother—of the dead grandfather he never saw. If Linda had not undergone psychoanalysis, and if her "psychological business" with her father had remained unfinished, it is possible that her son might have assimilated into his self-concept his early mother's distorted perception of him, becoming an instrument, as it were, for healing the wounds of the long dead person of the first generation. Throughout our lives we are influenced not only by interaction with important living people but also by the representations of the dead that reside within us, in the form of identifications or of separate "presences" (introjects) either in ourselves or in those with whom we interact. Influences of the latter type may cause psychological problems in some people, while in others they may direct creative urges according to their psychological "obligations."

The phases of uncomplicated mourning

Different investigators studying the self-limited sequential patterns of behavior experienced after the death of an important other have systematized them into schemata of their own, which, in spite of some theoretical and semantic differences among them, I find similar from the phenomenological point of view. Some investigators see an initial acute stage that is followed by phases in which the relaxation of ties to the lost one are worked through in order to achieve a new inner adaptation, in terms of which the loss can be accepted. Others do not separate the acute stage from what follows, seeing the phases together, in a continuum.

No one case, however typical it may be, will exhibit all the expectable manifestations of uncomplicated mourning. But Linda's case, particularly because analysis had made her an unusually alert observer of her own psychological processes, is quite instructive. Let me briefly review the phases of Linda's reactions to her father's death.

On receiving word of her father's death Linda observed a numbing of feelings and a division of her ego functions. She knew that the death had taken place, but she felt as though her father were still alive. She thus experienced a split in her ego functions pertaining to her perception of the death as a reality. Such splitting generally follows by a full attempt to deny the occurrence of the death, but while Linda could clearly see the split over the news of her father's death, she did not report an initial full denial of it. There were other symptoms: her mouth felt dry, others seemed shadowy, she felt distanced from them. She also noted the revival of an old symptom—her zeal to become a "savior" of others.

Numbness was followed by pain and weeping, then by anger. The anger was directed toward her aunt, although Linda eventually realized that her father was its true target.

Her crying spells diminished in less than a month, during which time she was conscious of her preoccupation with the dead man, especially in connection with experiences she had shared with him. Her good feelings about these memories were then challenged by her guilt over the possibility that she had contributed to her father's death, guilt that never became overwhelming, however. Two months after the death her fantasies and her dreams referred to her father's decaying body. She concluded that these were reflections of her acceptance of his death, and represented her "killing" him in the service of that acceptance.

Four months after the death Linda's preoccupation with the different images of her father had almost disappeared. She observed a new surge of energy within herself, and felt the need for a new love object. In a repetition of an earlier pattern of dealing with loss, she acquired a puppy. The use of a puppy as a substitute object had been examined in connection with her earlier experience, and I now considered the second puppy to be a bridge, similar in function to the first puppy, whereby she could transfer the investment of emotion in her father to other living and important human beings. Her preoccupation with the dead had disappeared, and for all practical purposes the mourning process was at an end.

Similar reports from equally self-observant people are, of course, available. Poets and novelists have often reported, at least symbolically, the initial and continuing inner processes of the grief experience. Psychoanalysts in mourning have written in psychoanalytic terms of their self-observation. Four examples come to mind: Pollock's (1961) essay includes observation of the processes at work in a mourning adaptation of his own and of other family members after the death of his mother; Engel (1975) describes his reaction to the death of a twin brother; Smith (1973) movingly tells of his mourning for a brother, Clint, also a psychoanalyst; I have examined my postponed mourning for a roommate in medical school who was murdered in the interethnic conflict on Cyprus (Volkan, 1979a).

A review of the literature on the phases of uncomplicated mourning

What Linda's case shows, and what the psychoanalytic literature verifies, is that the behavioral sequence of the mourning process is predictable—it goes through stages—and that it has an identifiable beginning and end, although when we take into account the diversity of antecedent experience (and other factors that I will note), some diversity of response can be anticipated within the prototype. Even those who have had no previous experience with death have experienced psychological loss of various kinds from infancy on; in an absolute sense, a form of mourning is involved with the psychological separation from the mother, although I believe that a certain maturity of psychological structure is required if one is to mourn in the sense being considered here. On this account, the following review of the work of a few selected investigators deals only with adult mourning.

Lindemann's classic work (1944) describes the symptoms of "acute grief" among 101 patients, some of whom were bereaved in the Coconut Grove disaster, others of whom were the relatives of military casualties, and others simply psychoneurotic patients undergoing treatment at the time they lost someone by death. The reactions to death were remarkably uniform throughout this rather diverse group. All reported having waves of somatic distress lasting from 20 minutes to an hour at a time; a feeling of tightness in the throat; shortness of breath; the need to sigh; an empty feeling in the abdomen; a lack of muscular strength; and exhaustion. They had no appetite. Food tasted like sand to them. Their sensorium was clearly altered, and they felt a slight sense of unreality and of increased emotional distance from other people, sometimes seeing others as shadowy and small, as had Linda. Lindemann also notes their sense of guilt and hostility and their urgency in speaking, especially when talking about the deceased.

Lindemann also observes another characteristic, "the appearance of traits of the deceased in the behavior of the bereaved, especially symptoms shown during the last illness, or behavior which may have shown at the time of the tragedy" (p. 142). For example, a mourner may find himself walking with his father's stride, or someone else may notice that he is doing so. Lindemann views this particular feature of acute grief as manifested by those who "border on pathological reactions" (p. 142).

Pollock's "acute stage"

Pollock (1961) differentiates between the acute and chronic stages of reaction to the death of an important other. He holds that the bereaved person in the acute stage goes through three sequential phases: shock, acute grief (affect) reaction, and separation reaction. I examine these phases here with reference to the work of Pollock and others, as well as to what I have observed myself in working with grief-stricken patients.

Shock reaction. Pollock sees this as resulting from the mourner's inability to integrate the excessive stimulation occasioned by initial awareness of the loss. Intensity of such reaction is closely related to how suddenly and without warning the loss came about. Usually of short duration, shock reaction may become evident in panic response, with shrieking, wailing, and moaning, or in an opposite state, complete collapse and motor retardation.

Most other writers on the subject (Engel, 1961; Lipson, 1963; Schuster, 1969) speak of disbelief or denial as accompanying shock. Schuster emphasizes that shocked disbelief is not just an attempt to deny the loss or obtund the pain accompanying it, but that it provides a chance to deny or undo the hostile intent one feels for the dead. "The death stirs our infantile hatred for past rejections and our magic belief that thinking ill of someone will result in harm" (p. 88). Freud (1915), Moellenhoff (1939), Sterba (1948), and Wahl (1958), among many others, point out that denial of the reality of death is an attitude general in Western culture. Lipson (1963) notes the effort to make the dead person look alive by use of cosmetics, the custom of speaking in whispers around a dead body lest it be disturbed, and the consideration given the selection of a comfortable and seemly coffin. Any culture reflects the unconscious processes shared by its adherents. Denial is in the service of the pleasure principle, which governs all mental activity. It is when the traumatized and shocked ego can no longer deny the reality principle that the loss of the object is finally acknowledged. Denial is usually accompanied by splitting of the ego (Freud, 1927, 1940). The mourner may then behave as though the death has not occurred, even though intellectually he is aware of its reality. When the course of grieving is uncomplicated, the reality principle prevails, and the integrative capacity of the ego triumphs.

Acute grief (affective) reaction. Pollock (1961) includes in this phase the anorexia and feelings of fatigue and exhaustion that Lindemann describes. This is also the phase of intense psychic pain in which spasmodic weeping occurs, slowly changing to tearful lamentations and verbal communications broken by sobs. The crying that accompanies psychic pain in this phase is compared by Pollock with the very earliest communications of life: it is an alarm signal as well as an expression of unpleasant feelings and emotions. Pollock also includes in this phase fantasizing and daydreaming about the deceased. The mourner may even have inner dialogues with an unassimilated introject in which the object may continue to exist.

What is most interesting about this phase is the nature of the psychic pain experienced by the mourner. Freud stated (1912, 1914b) that as libidinal interest and investment are drawn away from a love object to the ego, libido in the ego is dammed up, at least in some cases of pathology. Pain is experienced with this increase in tension. Referring to this formulation, Pollock notes that this conceptualization of Freud would permit a view of the acute stage of the mourning process "analogous to the model of actual neuroses": when libido is withdrawn from the person who has died, pain increases; "when libido is discharged, the pain diminishes" (p. 347). Pollock hypothesizes that the pain characteristic of the acute stage of mourning represents a "regression to an ego state where the pleasure–pain principle is the chief axis of mental functioning … . This pain may result from the heightened non-discharged 'energic cathexis' due to the absence of the object" (p. 347). "This early intense pain," he continues, "is seemingly … tied to the reaction to frustration over the object's absence," in contrast to the pain of the chronic stage, in which the pain seems to be caused by the realization that there is no longer any hope that the lost object will meet the mourner's needs (p. 347). That is, the reality principle has gradually prevailed. (It should be noted that Freud himself regarded this matter of the psycho-economics of pain in the mourning process with some perplexity throughout his career. See Freud, 1916, pp. 306–307; 1926, p. 169.)

There are other explanations of pain in the mourning process. Melanie Klein, for example, emphasizes the presence of a sense of guilt and fear of retaliation (1940). Bowlby (1961) associates the pain with a yearning to recover the lost object, a view shared by Parkes (Bowlby & Parkes, 1970; Parkes, 1972). I will examine this view more closely in a subsequent section.

Separation reaction. Pollock's third phase of the acute stage of the mourning process is separation reaction, reflecting the start of decathexis of the internal representation of the deceased. Anxiety comes with reaction to the separation, along with anger, as the perception of the loss in time and space is integrated. The appearance of anger is important because

> … it is indicative that the separation is recognized and acknowledged. In this sense anger is restitutive, as cathexis can be discharged through the affective experience of anger. Thus the anger is in the service of mastery of the shock, panic, and grief. As to the reasons for the anger, we must recognize that the rage is narcissistic rage. (p. 351)

The rage Pollock identifies is like the lament of a child who asks why tragedy has afflicted him when those responsible for him could have prevented it. When rage is discharged diffusely, frustration over being abandoned and feelings of helplessness are avoided. The target of this rage is usually displaced from the deceased to others. Linda's anger with her aunt substituted for narcissistic anger at her father for abandoning her and causing her pain.

Schuster (1969) also emphasizes the role of anger in reaction to death, holding that the mourner's rage confirms for him the actual event of the death. He continues:

> The loss, in that it depletes one's object libido, leaves one less nourished, more empty, has an obvious depressive effect. But no one losing anything can help but feel abandoned—to one degree or another, and feeling abandoned leads to anger for the rejection and a desire for retaliation. Life, being what it is, consists of a ceaseless series of losses and abandonments and consequently leads to an entrenchment of one's ambivalent attitudes toward both the living and the dead. (p. 89)

Pollock's "chronic stage"

Pollock's "acute stage" is followed by a "chronic stage" characterized by "various manifestations of adaptive mechanisms attempting to integrate the experience of the loss with reality so that life activities can go on" (p. 352). He equates his chronic stage with Freud's "work of mourning." In the case of Linda, the work of mourning took a relatively short time not only because she had previously undergone analysis, but also because she had not been unprepared for the death of her father, an elderly man in poor health. In general, however, analytic writers usually suggest that the work of mourning may take about a year, although Freud spoke of a year or two. Greene (1965) states that one cannot make a judgment about the degree of resolution of grief until the end of the second year, after the first vacation, first birthday, or other milestone is experienced in the absence of the one who has died.

Bowlby and Parkes's classification

The classification of the mourning process offered by Bowlby and Parkes differs in that it makes no clear-cut distinction between an acute and a chronic stage. Bowlby (1961) identified three phases of the total mourning process, although he and Parkes (1970) later worked out a schema with four, basing it on data from the work of Lindemann (1944) and Marris (1958), as well as on Parkes's own research (1964a, 1964b, 1972).

Descriptively, the first phase is numbness that usually lasts from a few hours to a week. This phase is interrupted by outbursts of extremely intense distress and/or anger. Bowlby and Parkes obviously refer to the "shock" reaction and denial noted by others when they write that most of their patients "felt stunned" on hearing of the death and that some reported having failed altogether to grasp what they were being told (1970). Bowlby and Parkes then see the second phase as one of yearning for the lost figure, and indicate that this phase may last for months or years, during which the mourner may also be aware of an urge to search for the dead person. A widow may, for example, misperceive someone passing in the street as her dead husband. The third phase is one of disorganization, followed by a fourth phase, one of reorganization to a greater or less degree.

Classification of the mourning process in this volume

While I think it correct to divide the responses to death into two general stages, as does Pollock, I will not use Pollock's terms, "acute" and "chronic," to refer to them. The terms "acute" and "chronic," with their reference to time, are best used here to refer to the persistence of any sign or symptom. To avoid semantic difficulties, I will speak here of the *initial stage* and of the *work of mourning*, which is, in effect, a longer second stage.

The initial stage includes the period of initial numbness and shock; denial of the death, followed by the splitting of ego functions with respect to the perception of the death; the activation of certain images of the death and of inner relatedness to them; painful emotions accompanied by weeping; and the appearance of an anger indicating the ego's attempt to accept the loss and its psychological implications. This anger, a narcissistic response to separation, initiates the integration of the previously split ego functions in the service of the reality principle. If no complications supervene, one can expect the manifestations of initial grief to disappear within two to six months after the death, depending, of course, on the circumstances of its occurrence. During this period, signs of the initial stage not only follow one another but may suddenly disappear and reappear again, until the mourner, after acknowledging his anger, settles into the next stage, the prolonged work of mourning with its piecemeal advances. The work of mourning includes a slow-motion review of the relationship to the dead person; the struggle to keep or to reject a close tie with his representation; and an initially regressive disorganization that is followed by a new inner organization, able to test reality more fully for confirmation that the death, with all its psychological implications, has indeed taken place.

I leave for later chapters (see Chapters 4 and 5) discussion from a metapsychological point of view of the inner reorganization that takes place at the end of the work of mourning. I will briefly state here, however, that both projective and introjective mechanisms are activated in the mourning process, and that, if this process is completed without complication, an identification with positive aspects of the dead person may occur, enriching the mourner's ego. Certainly Linda, as a result of her analysis, was able to identify with her father's secret pride in his Jewishness, as well as with his practical protection of himself in a hostile environment. During his funeral, which had taken place in a Christian church, Linda had briefly clung to an old image of the weak father, but as her mourning progressed, his many different object images competed for her attention. With further progress in mourning, her preoccupation with these images lessened, to be replaced by a more nearly integrated representation of her father. She then identified with that aspect of her integrated representation of her father that honored his Jewish heritage, and in her daily life, could herself be comfortable with being a Christian of Jewish extraction.

"Is grief a disease?"

Since, from a practical point of view, the mourning process has a recognizable beginning and end, the behavioral scientist who scrutinizes it is like the scientist who examines an organic process with predictable sequential patterns—perhaps a wound or a burn. He is justified in saying that, just as a wound or burn can be infected in ways that make for different possibilities of outcome, so can mourning become infected, as it were, and be what we call "complicated." And just as a wound may be closed by the formation of a keloid, so can the mourning process "heal" in a way that leaves scars in the form of peculiar kinds of psychological adjustment.

In a paper that Engel (1961) describes as having "more the qualities of a philosophic than a scientific discourse," he asks, "Is grief a disease?" Although grief is a natural reaction to a life experience that we all have sooner or later, it does, like disease, have an etiological factor—object loss, whether real, fantasied, or simply threatened—and meets all the other criteria for a discrete syndrome, having relatively predictable symptoms and course. Indeed, a grieving person may be so manifestly distressed and disabled that others see him as being seriously injured. Engel holds that inasmuch as the psychological stress—the actual or fantasied loss of an object—disturbs the organism's total adjustment, it is in fact an etiological factor of such general importance as to justify its classification with other noxa of first importance, e.g., physical agents, microorganisms, etc. He states:

> The concept of grief as a disease requires that we keep in view and in perspective aspects of the external environment other than what we have been accustomed to heretofore—namely, the environment made up of the significant psychic objects. This becomes one reason why the persons, job, home, goals, etc., in the life of our patients cannot be disregarded in our consideration of illness,

> at least not until it has been proven that the vicissitudes of object relations, including grief, the disorder consequent to object loss, plays no role in the pathogenesis of disease. (pp. 21–22)

He goes on to say that if object loss is a potential stress, then the maintenance or replacement of objects must be considered important variables in sustaining health and adjustment.

Engel is not alone in thinking of grief as an illness in a general sense. Klein (1940) states that the mourner is, in fact, ill. Lindemann (1944) gives the impression that he is writing about illness in the usual sense when he writes of acute grief. Bowlby (1961) also agrees that the consideration of grief as an illness is "a useful way of approaching the problem" (p. 332). I would elaborate on this thesis: when I speak of grief that takes a predictable course, like the healing of an uninfected wound, I will refer to it as Engel does, as "uncomplicated" grief; when I speak of grief for which the analogy of an infected wound is apt, I will refer to it as "complicated" grief. As is true of some infections, certain complications may be fulminant and yet short-lived, disappearing to let the healing process take its expected course. Other complications may become chronic, however. A chronic complicated reaction in the work of mourning will be referred to here as *established pathological mourning*, which I will later compare with *reactive depression*, another chronic complicated reaction. I believe that in the long run most chronically complicated grief reactions culminate in one of these two states, which may be either patent or hidden behind other symptoms.

Grief seen as a disease has one quality, however, that distinguishes it from most other diseases: when it is "healed," the healing may include creative restitution and adaptation that actually enrich the mourner in general ways. In an analogy to this, Bowlby points out that sometimes a healed bone may be stronger than it had been before having been broken. When there is benefit from the "healing" of grief, the process of adaptation may have far-reaching implications. I once wrote that uncomplicated grief is nature's exercise in loss and restitution (Volkan, 1970). Pollock (1961, 1977) and Rochlin (1965) have made useful studies of the adaptive process following grief, and I will enlarge on this later, examining it particularly from the point of view of linking objects and linking phenomena.

CHAPTER 3

Complications in the initial stage of the mourning process

This chapter deals with temporary or chronic fixations in the initial stage of the mourning process. I will describe factors that contribute to such fixations and give clinical examples of ways in which these fixations are manifested. The mourner arrested in one phase of the initial stage and unable to move into the next may manifest in exaggerated ways the characteristics usual to that phase of the mourning process; or he may exhibit none of them at all.

A severely disturbed clinical picture in the initial stage does not necessarily indicate that the patient will be unable to resolve the disturbance and move into the usual progression of mourning. The lancing of an abscess often gives dramatic relief; similarly, the resolution of severe initial reactions to loss by death may cause a dramatic change in the patient's state and enable him to pursue the uncomplicated course of mourning.

Factors on which initial responses to death depend

The occurrence of complication in the initial stage of grief depends on the ego's maturity and on the circumstances of the death—chiefly, whether or not it induced in the mourner a condition like traumatic neurosis (Volkan, 1972). Trauma occurs when a stimulus, usually a sudden and disruptive one arising from an external situation (some writers include the possibility of its arising from massive inner sexual and aggressive excitement), overwhelms the ego's capacity to mediate various demanding forces, creating a state of helplessness. It is, as Freud (1926), Fenichel (1945), Anna Freud (1965), Furst (1967), and others have stated, a relative concept that cannot be assessed in terms of external events alone. Factors of mental economy dependent on the constitution as well as on past experience, the phase of development attained, the nature of fixations and internalized object relations, the actual conditions before and during the trauma, etc., determine how greatly the excitation will overtax the individual's capacity to tolerate it.

Traumatic neurosis itself is characterized by a block or decrease in various ego functions; by spells of painful affects, usually anxiety or rage related to the traumatic experience; and by sleep disturbances. Until mastery of the trauma is achieved (usually not without some persistent psychoneurotic symptoms), it is relived in dreams, and its mental representations appear in the waking state. The repetition of the trauma in dreams and memory seemed at first to contradict the pleasure principle, a concern addressed by *Freud in Beyond the Pleasure Principle.* Freud stated that the mental apparatus is "flooded" when the pleasure principle is "put out of action" by the trauma (1920, p. 29). Regression, in which primitive modes of functioning are resorted to so as to bind and master the stimulus, occurs. Freud considered unpleasurable dreams that refer to the trauma to be manifestations of this function among patients suffering from traumatic neurosis. Although the appearance of such dreams "does not contradict the pleasure principle," it "is nevertheless independent of it and seems to be more primitive than the purpose of gaining pleasure and avoiding unpleasure" (p. 32).

The initial response to death will also depend on the nature of the mourner's psychic structure and on the kind of rapport he had with the one who has died; thus, the more mature the rapport, the greater the likelihood the mourner will experience deep sadness—sadness being a feeling without guilt, a personal and intimate feeling like love, something more difficult to convey than depression (Smith, 1971). When the relationship has been highly ambivalent and stormy, however, the mourner's reactions are apt to be complicated by a variety of component feelings.

Another determinant is whether or not the death has been expected. Lindemann (1944) coins the term "anticipatory grief" to describe an individual's accommodation to the loss of a significant other whose life is clearly coming to an end, and to the mourner's passage through some or all of the phases of grief, including some of the work of mourning, before the death actually takes place. Lindemann states:

> While the reaction may well form a safeguard against the impact of a sudden death notice, it can turn out to be of a disadvantage at the occasion of reunion. Several instances of this sort came to our attention when a soldier just returned from the battlefront complained that his wife did not love him anymore and demanded immediate divorce. In such situations apparently the grief work had been done so effectively that the patient has emancipated herself and the readjustment must now be directed towards new interaction. It is important to know this because many family disasters of this sort may be avoided through prophylactic measures. (p. 148)

I had as a patient once a young woman in similar circumstances. Her husband had been sent to Vietnam soon after their marriage, and she had been sure that he would die there. I discovered genetic reasons for her expecting this: as a young girl she had suffered the sudden loss, of a significant person. When her husband returned from Vietnam without a scratch, she perceived him as a stranger, a virtual "ghost" to whom she did not want to be married and who should not touch her. She retained in her mind an idealized image of her husband that did not correspond to the real man returned from the war zone. In her brief treatment with me, she described what was clearly an instance of "anticipatory grief."

Anticipatory grief that is not exaggerated can prepare the mourner for the shock of death when it actually comes. A family is seldom deeply shocked when an aged chronic invalid dies; a sudden death is obviously a more crushing event.

Another factor in determining the nature of the initial response to death is whether the death occurred from what could be considered natural causes, or whether it involved violence: suicide, homicide, or mutilating accident. I have found that violent death, because of unconscious connection with the mourner's aggressive drive derivatives, fosters guilt that precludes the expression of "natural" angry and aggressive reactions following the death. The case of Fred, to be referred to shortly, will provide an example. If the dead person is too greatly idealized to be "killed," the expected process of mourning may again not be initiated. This situation may occur when an idealized leader dies suddenly, or when the mental representations of those fallen in battle are perceived as saviors and memorialized in the minds of those left behind. Such memorialization is discussed in my work on Cyprus in reference to the aftermath of the 1974 war there (Volkan, 1977, 1979a).

Yet another factor is whether or not death has brought about drastic changes in the real world for the bereaved, such as the loss of one's home or a sudden severe reduction of income. My patient Mike, for example (see Chapter 9), had to face, among other difficulties, real changes in respect to the wealth of his family. At the time of his death, his father had just completed building a house in a location of considerable prestige, and had obtained membership in an exclusive club. When he died, his family was forced for financial reasons to return to its former comparatively very modest home. In cases of altered circumstances, it is important to know how the mourner internally perceives the meaning of the external changes he is obliged to undergo.

I have also noted (Volkan, 1970) that the type of funeral, the nature of the mourner's participation in it, even the type of coffin chosen, are factors that influence the initial stage of mourning. As psychoanalytic studies (e.g., Fenichel, 1945) have revealed, funeral rites and religious rituals are attempts to deal with the common psychological components of the initial stage of grief—the emergence of aggressive feelings, for one. Consequently, the mourner should be allowed to indulge fully in mourning rituals (Volkan, 1966). It often happens, however, that the persons who may be most vulnerable to complicated responses to death are not allowed to participate in the funeral rites. I know of many cases in which teenage boys who have lost their fathers are "used," because they are the only male in the family, or the oldest male child, to take care of some business on behalf of the family, perhaps some legal requirements of the funeral. Thus, they are treated like adults but also calculatedly "protected" from the pain of having to take part in the actual funeral rites. Mike was again an example of this. During Mike's later re-grief work, a national leader was killed, and when Mike saw the ceremonies for him on the television and saw one of the dead leader's children acting as pallbearer, he burst out angrily, "During *my* father's funeral I was made to be an errand boy!" (Volkan, 1970).

My patient Solomon, described in detail elsewhere as a living statue (Volkan, 1979a), had to interrupt his Jewish religious rites for his dead father when his mother decided that the 13-year-old boy should be sent to the country for fresh air. While in the country he caught a snake and put it in a glass bottle with some sort of acid fluid. Having thus been interrupted in his religious ceremonies, he created his own ceremony for "killing" his father. With the dead snake representing the dead man, the son made a daily ritual out of checking its progressive deterioration in the bottle. His unfinished psychological business with his father was so complicated, however, that he could not successfully reactivate the mourning process. While the snake's skin rotted away Solomon himself fell victim to severe dermatitis. His skin became infected and gave him considerable pain and discomfort. Although one cannot presume to know all the etiological factors involved in his dermatitis, it is safe to say that it also reflected identification with the decaying father.

Although I speak here of relatively apparent factors that seem to influence the initial responses to death, it is obvious that only a penetrating psychological study of the mourner, whenever the opportunity presents itself, can reveal the highly personalized perception of a given ego to a given death, and the condensation within it of representations of psychic events vital to it, such as those initiating separation and castration anxiety. Idiosyncratic responses of a given mourner can, moreover, be understood only by identifying their symbolic meaning for the individual in question.

Examples of complicated responses to death during the initial stage of grief

I will now offer a number of vignettes to illustrate the manifestations to be expected from complications in the initial stage of mourning. My clinical research indicates that the severity of an initially complicated response to death does not necessarily forecast chronic complications. In fact, patients may work through their exaggerated initial responses, usually in a dramatic fashion, as one may work through a typical traumatic neurosis. Even if they are not worked through, however, the patient can be expected in due time to embark to some extent on a somewhat more advanced stage, carrying the burdens of the first along with him to be condensed in those more characteristic of the next.

I have indicated that the shock and denial phase of the initial stage is usually brief. If the patient is using denial extensively (whether in the form of outright denial or its usual replacement, splitting of ego functions), others around him are sure to see his state as pathological and see to it that he goes promptly to a professional such as a minister, priest, rabbi, or psychiatrist for help. Among the 150 patients I saw, only two had severe fixation at the denial phase. One of these, Fred, responded not only to the suddenness of the accident that took the life of his younger brother but also to the mutilation involved.

In his early thirties, Fred was his brother's senior by two years. Although the relationship between the two men was friendly and loving, some feeling that the younger brother had replaced him in the eyes of their parents lingered on in Fred. When his brother was killed, Fred's childhood anger at him was reactivated, and he found it necessary to deny the death so as not to feel guilty about his anger.

As a child Fred had pushed his younger brother in a somewhat unfriendly argument, causing him to fall on a broken glass and to cut his leg so badly that it bled profusely. It was a month after the fatal automobile accident—in which the victim's legs were badly cut—that Fred was seen by our psychiatric team.

He had been at the service station he managed when he noticed an ambulance speeding by. There soon followed a telephone call from the hospital asking him to come to identify his brother's mutilated body. Fred felt numb. He denied the possibility that his brother was actually gone. He saw the body with its cut legs at the hospital and identified it as his brother's but soon returned to work, insisting that the episode was actually only something he had dreamed about. He clung to his dream theory for a month in spite of his brother's disappearance, and did not attend the funeral.

At this point he was brought to the hospital for treatment. One of my assistants began his inpatient treatment with a review of his relationship with his brother and gentle confrontations of his denial. After a month, Fred went into abreaction over the viewing of his brother's body, recalling his guilt over hostile wishes he had entertained toward the dead man and his remorse over having wounded his leg. It was only then that he entered the initial stage of grief. On his own, he paid a visit to his minister and prepared a delayed funeral rite with him, taking flowers to the grave.

This type of death-denial is somewhat different from the "rejection of emotion" described by Deutsch (1937) in a well-known essay on the absence of grief. While in Deutsch's cases, the expected initial grief (affect) reactions did not appear, there was no actual denial of the knowledge that death had taken place. She suggested that when there are no reactions at first they must appear at some later time, as in the case of Will below.

Will was in his late teens when his father died. He was sitting with his mother and young sister in their family room one evening when someone came to the door with word that the father of the family had died. Death had come suddenly. The father was a miner and the roof of the mine he was working had collapsed. The news sent Will's mother and small sister into "hysterics" and forced him to become at once "the man of the house." His history indicated that in the initial stage of grief there had been none of the pain and weeping to be expected, and, later, none of the usual rage. His inability to experience and resolve the phases of initial grief had caused him to be chronically fixated at this stage; it was only ten years later, and then only with professional help, that he was able to express his feelings of grief.

He was in his late twenties when he was admitted to the neurological ward of the hospital (he was later transferred to psychiatry). He had been admitted because his knees gave way, leaving him unable to stand. He had been having attacks of this disability for a year, and had seen one neurologist after another. The first attack, as I discovered later, had come on the ninth anniversary of his father's death: all of his attacks, including the first, came in the early evening, the time of day when the news of his father's death had arrived.

Will had a repeating dream in which he saw his father buried under a collapsing ceiling. He would try to pull away the stones from his father's body, but always awakened in anxiety before accomplishing the rescue. This repeating dream had come during the first year after his father's death. It had faded away to a considerable extent, but returned at the time he began to have his attacks of being unable to stand. Throughout all these years, Will felt no emotion about his father's death.

I uncovered one important cause of his symptom's appearance nine years after the death. An insurance policy providing for the family was to terminate when the youngest child—Will's sister—became 18, which she did nine years after her father's death. Will had by then made a place for himself as a professional man, but he now felt obliged to take over most of his mother's and sister's expenses. Being "the man of the house" was a heavy burden for him, not only in real responsibility but also in psychological terms, since he now felt that he was replacing his father. He felt very much the loss of the original family provider, and his symptoms were in the service of further trying to deny his father's death, by identification with his collapsed representation. Moreover, they yielded secondary gains, since any illness clearly made it impossible for him to have to support his mother and sister. In his case, brief inpatient psychotherapy was effective and led to the disappearance of his symptoms. They were abandoned to the accompaniment of clinical manifestations of painful emotions, weeping and anger, that are characteristic of the initial phases of grief.

I have no follow-up information on Will's case, and I do not know how well he faced the working-through stage of mourning, given the fact that he had experienced the initial stage of grief fully ten years after his father's death. I simply cite his case here as an example of the complications of affective experience at the initial stage of grief, and as an example of the way in which the initial stage can be postponed for years, requiring resolution long after a death. Will's complications manifested themselves not as exaggerations of expectable affective experiences, but as a defensive denial of them. This stands in contrast to patients who are arrested in the weeping phase of initial grief, who, for years after the death, will weep easily whenever their attention is turned to any reminder of it.

Carl's case dramatically illustrates not only fixation in the anger phase of initial grief, but also that the exaggeration of the initial grief response does not necessarily result in chronic difficulty; such a patient returns to the usual track of mourning under the influence of a triggering external event or professional help. Carl was in his early thirties when he came to our attention.

Carl had been deserted by his parents in childhood. His father had been sent to prison and had later disappeared altogether from his life. His mother had then left him in the care of her parents, although she had occasionally visited and looked after him. To all intents and purposes he had been brought up by his grandparents, and he had looked to his grandfather for escape from the psychological pain of his early childhood.

Carl had been an adult at the time of his grandmother's death, but had experienced no exaggerated mourning for her. He had long been his grandfather's shadow and had continued living with him in their rural home until he married, at which time he built a house for himself and his wife next to the old man's. In the psychoanalytic sense he had continued to use his grandfather as an external ego–superego.

His first reaction to his grandfather's death included denial. He experienced splitting at the funeral in that he knew that the body being lowered into the ground was his grandfather's but was nevertheless certain that he saw the old man moving about his house, which was visible from the gravesite. For a month after the funeral, he engaged nightly in a bizarre ritual, going to the grave and sitting on it until sunrise. He was a living tombstone, reflecting the psychoanalytic notion that the placement of a stone on the grave is a response to the shared unconscious wish for certainty that the dead will not rise. This notion is consistent with a finding of mine that those prone to complicated grief are preoccupied with the kind of coffin chosen and usually select heavy coffins or concrete vaults to prevent the dreaded return of the dead (Volkan, 1970). In Carl's case, the other side of his ambivalent feelings about his grandfather was also evident: while each night he became a living tombstone, he also kept a shovel in the trunk of his car, fantasizing that if the old man wanted to rise out of his grave he would help him.

A new behavior pattern emerged after a month went by.

Carl still worked by day, although his nightly vigils permitted only dozing at night and left him exhausted. In the late afternoon, anger would overtake him—anger diffused and directed toward the world at large. (The exaggerated quality of his anger becomes readily apparent when we compare it with Linda's controlled rage at the aunt she saw at her father's funeral.) Carl found a bucket of paint and a paintbrush and wrote on walls and rocks the legend "Kill L.B.J.! Kill L.B.J.!" He began sitting on a hillside armed with a rifle, and talked about shooting the people who drove by on the road below. This alarming development led his family to call the police. Because of what seemed to be threats against the President, the F.B.I. was also called in, and Carl, in a state of angry excitement, was rushed to a psychiatric hospital. There it was discovered that the initials L.B.J. were his grandfather's as well as the President's. Carl had no conscious awareness of his having condensed his grandfather's image with that of another father figure, Lyndon Baines Johnson.

Because the first appearance of Carl's symptoms could be traced to the time of his grandfather's death, hospital personnel called in the re-grief team, which had been treating other inpatients on the same unit. In view of the exaggerated quality of Carl's symptoms, we suggested the need for an initial treatment designed to calm him down.

A few days after his arrival in the hospital a fell ow patient committed suicide by hanging and Carl was the first to find the dangling body. He tried furiously to restore life, giving mouth-to-mouth resuscitation and pounding on the dead man's chest. The emergency team arrived within minutes and pronounced the man dead. Someone noticed that Carl was touching the fingers and saying, "They are blue! They are blue! There is such a thing as death!" Carl then shut himself in a room and began sobbing and crying, continuing this throughout the afternoon and night, according to the nurses' reports. Exhausted, he fell into a sleep from which he awakened a dramatically different person, one engaged in uncomplicated mourning which he shortly thereafter completed. I regret not having complete information about Carl's genetic background, his ego functions, and so on, but I think his case sufficiently fascinating on the descriptive level to report here. Did his encounter with the dead body of the suicide quell his powerful anger and attempts at denial? Did it cause him to deny his excessive anger for fear that he would actually kill someone? Did his efforts to bring the dead man back to life assuage his feelings of guilt? Did his encounter with the suicide help him to test reality? Carl himself claimed that the last was true. I have a five-year follow-up on Carl since he moved away from the farm and came to the city where I live. (One wonders if this was not another act of avoidance.) None of his bizarre symptoms returned during these five years, and he and his wife, who now have a child, claim to be living a normal life.

Complications in the initial stage of grief may leave the patient extremely preoccupied with the image of the dead, either in dreams or in waking consciousness. Wahl (1970) has written about "normal" grief manifestations of this type that later became chronic. Since chronic preoccupation with such images can also be a manifestation of the state I call the work of mourning, it is at times difficult to determine whether such a picture truly reflects a complication of the initial stage or the condensation of complications of both stages. One must know if this preoccupation began in the first weeks or months after the death, and did not lessen thereafter.

One patient, Gregory, reported that since the death of his father four years earlier, his father had been daily in his thoughts, and in his dreams several times a week. In the dreams he lay in his coffin, buried but still with the appearance of life. It will be remembered that Linda, who grieved in an uncomplicated manner, had similar dreams, but in hers the body evidenced decay within two months of the death, indicating the beneficial "killing" of the one lost. Unlike Linda, this patient spent at least four years in preoccupation with the image of the dead.

Rex Buxton gave me a personal account in 1971 of a case in which such initial excessive preoccupation with the images of the dead came to an abrupt end with the help of psychoanalysis. His patient was a middle-aged woman, already in analysis, whose chronically depressed husband had often threatened suicide. At last she found her husband's dead body hanging from the kitchen ceiling as she entered their home. She cut the rope with a kitchen knife and gave mouth-to-mouth resuscitation until she could no longer tolerate her revulsion at having his stomach fluids enter her mouth. After the death, the woman continued to see her analyst, and for a little more than a month, she reported dreaming the same dream each night: a realistic reenactment of her return home, her discovery of her husband's dead body, her cutting it down, and her efforts at mouth-to-mouth resuscitation. The dream ended before the stomach juices entered her mouth, at which point she would awaken. A month and a half after the death, she reported having the same dream once again, but now with a different conclusion, one that protected her from awakening. In the new version, instead of trying to resuscitate her husband, she seized the knife again and stabbed him through the heart, thus, in a psychological sense, "killing him." After this, the repeating dream ceased and her preoccupation with her husband's image in her waking hours diminished.

Thus far I have given examples of complications of the initial stage of grief. At times, such psychological responses can be mixed with psychosomatic responses, as in the case of Solomon; or they may give way to recognizable psychiatric conditions such as hysterical neurosis, as in the case of Will. The following two chapters will examine complications of the work of mourning.

CHAPTER 4

Complications in the work of mourning: Reactive depression

This chapter describes the factors that can complicate the work of mourning. It is suggested that such complications may in the long run result in either reactive depression or established pathological mourning. All other recognizable disturbances to which a mourner is subject are likely to spring from one or the other of these conditions and/or can be reduced to them.

Since the metapsychology of both conditions can be explained by terms such as introjection, introject, identification, projection, etc., I will clarify my use of them at the outset.

A case of depression following the loss of a loved/hated object illustrates the phenomenology of depression and permits an examination of its metapsychology. In reactive depression, there occurs an "in toto" disruptive identification with the ambivalently related representation of the dead person. Suicide in this condition reflects the way in which the depressed mourner has become a battleground for the tensions formerly existing between the mourner and the deceased. These tensions are carried over into the relationship of the mourner with the representation of the dead person he now maintains.

The work of mourning

After passing through the initial stage of mourning, the mourner settles into the piecemeal work of mourning. He yearns and searches for the dead (Bowlby & Parkes, 1970) and painfully tests the reality of his loss. During this time, he cathects and decathects hundreds of memories of his experiences with the one who has died. He examines the dead person's images and his own corresponding self-images, and uses these in a process of introjection–projection. Within a year or two, psychic ties to the representation of the deceased are loosened, and the work of mourning comes to a practical end when the mourner no longer has a compulsive need to cling to the representation of the dead person. Meanwhile, however paradoxically, the mourner identifies with certain aspects of the dead and comes to resemble him in these particulars. Thus, when such mourning is concluded, the ego will often have been enriched.

Regression in the work of mourning, invoking early introjective–projective mechanisms, is obligatory, and is in the service of the new organization that will appear when mourning has ended. This new organization will include some identifications with certain aspects of the dead and adaptive mechanisms for dealing with an external world in which he is no longer sought. Such regression is not unlike the regression in the service of development that Blos (1979) ascribes to the second individuation phase of adolescence. Blos contends that adolescent regression in the service of development results in "the disengagement of libidinal and aggressive cathexes from the internalized infantile love and hate objects" (p. 179) and "brings the more advanced ego of adolescence into contact with infantile drive positions, with old conflictual constellations and their solutions, with early object relations and narcissistic formations" (p. 180). It is no wonder that Wolfenstein (1966, 1969) developed the hypothesis, with which I agree, that passage through adolescence is a necessary pre-condition for the ability to mourn, as mourning is described here.

Complications in the work of mourning generally take two forms: reactive depression or established pathological mourning. There is, of course, no lack of evidence in the literature of psychiatry, psychoanalysis, and psychosomatic disorders that neuroses other than depression can be precipitated by a death. It is also suggested that when the course of mourning is not successfully completed, somatization, the use of primitive defenses that lead to a break with reality, and other solutions are resorted to (Cobb, Bauer, & Whiting, 1939; McDermott and Cobb, 1939; Peck, 1939; Lidz, 1949; Lehrman, 1956; Greene & Miller, 1958; Schmale, 1958; Parkes, 1964a, 1964b; Volkan, 1965; Brown & Epps, 1966; Evans & Liggett, 1971; Crisp & Priest, 1972; Hill, 1972; Parkes & Brown, 1972). Nevertheless, I will focus here only on established pathological mourning and reactive depression as sequelae of loss by death.

Although both states involve the use of internalization, they can be differentiated on both a descriptive and metapsychological level. The distinction between them depends basically on what the mourner does with the representation of the one he has lost; whether, as in depression, he keeps it within himself or, as in established pathological mourning, he also externalizes it onto the outside world; whether, as in depression, he identifies totally and disruptively with the ambivalently related representation or, as in established pathological mourning, he struggles between "killing" the representation or "not killing" it. In established pathological mourning, the failure to resolve this struggle permits the maintenance of a continuing relationship with the representation of the dead. The mourner remains in limbo, so to speak, clinging to the representation of the dead at the same time as he tries to loosen its hold on him, so that we can fairly say that established pathological mourning *directly* reflects fixation in the work of mourning.

Since the same psychoanalytic terms—introjection, introject, identification, projection, externalization, along with a few others—are used in discussing phenomena associated with the representation of the dead in either case, and since there seems little definite agreement among different investigators as to the precise meaning of each of these terms, I will clarify here how they apply in this context.

Clarification of terms

During the years when psychoanalysis was being accepted as a new theory for understanding the mind, Freud used the terms introjection and identification, as well as related concepts of incorporation and imitation, interchangeably. As interest in these concepts grew, attempts were made to clarify them (Fuchs, 1937; Hartmann, 1939; Knight, 1940;

Greenson, 1954; Koff, 1961; Hartmann & Loewenstein, 1962; Miller, Pollock, Bernstein, & Robbins, 1968).

It was Schafer (1968), however, who made the most telling attempt to distinguish them.

Schafer uses *internalization* to refer to *all* "those processes by which the subject transforms real or imagined regulating interactions with the environment, and real or imagined characteristics of his environment, into inner regulations and characteristics" (p. 9). He sees *introjection* and *identification* as two distinct types of internalization, and I will follow his example here. He uses *incorporation* to refer to a specific wishful primary process ideation about taking the object in through the mouth or other body orifice. (It should be noted that he later [1972] argues that internalization is an unworkable metaphor, referring to a fantasy rather than a process, and that it should be avoided in psychoanalysis altogether.)

Introjection, as I use it here, "signifies an activity"—the taking into the self-representation of an object representation—that may in turn lead to *identification,* which is something more static—"a state of affairs" (Fuchs, 1937, pp. 276–277). In identification, the self-representation resembles the object representation. While both can be seen as efforts to maintain a close tie to an object or its representation (Freud [1921, p. 105] spoke of identification as "the earliest expression of an emotional tie with another person"), they may at the same time be seen as opening a way for relative independence from an object or its representation when identification finally occurs. When self and model are perceived as one, relative independence from the original model is achieved.

When the act of introjection does not eventuate in the kind of melding of object representation into self-representation that characterizes identification, the object representation is felt as existing within the patient himself, and is perceived by some patients as an ongoing and persistent phenomenon. It is usual for psychotic patients and children (Schafer, 1968), as well as those suffering from established pathological mourning (Volkan, 1976), to describe such a representation as an inner presence. (It may also be spoken of as a "frozen" entity [Giovacchini, 1967].) These inner presences are referred to as *introjects.*

Should we call all object representations introjects? Schafer (1968) states that objects become introjects in a crisis—when, for example, they are "urgently needed" but unavailable, or when the individual is caught up in extreme ambivalence toward the object. He indicates that "both the coming into being of an introject and its continued existence represent attempts to modify distressing situations with the external objects" (1968, p. 73). Giovacchini (1972) refers to introjects as "experiences and objects that have become part of the ego but have a structure of their own that distinguishes them from the rest of the ego" (p. 157).

Elsewhere, I have indicated that introjects are a specific kind of object representation that the individual strives to assimilate in his self-representation (thereby achieving identification) but that he fails to assimilate in some respects (Volkan, 1976). Introjects are functional in the sense that they exert great influence on the self-representation. They do not, however, lead to structural changes in the self-representation (and therefore in the ego organization) as do identifications.

It is interesting that most introjects are perceived by the patient in bodily terms. He talks about feeling or sensing the head of another person within his chest, for example. It is only when the introject is depersonified—when the self-representation can perform the functions originally performed by the object representation (in other words, when the introject has been assimilated into the self-representation)—that we can speak of identification as having occurred. What I describe here is similar to, or identical with, Kohut's (1971) "transmuting internalization."

The "little man" phenomenon (see Chapter 1) reminds us that not all inner presences are unassimilated object representations (introjects). The "little man" is an unassimilated *self*-representation that the patient perceives as a "foreign body" buried in his chest. Moreover, it seems to me that in practice most introjects are to some extent contaminated with corresponding self-representations. For example, when a schizophrenic patient perceives and describes a demoniacal presence in his head, it is revealed in treatment to be his early perception of the early "bad" part object condensed with aspects of the early "bad" part self.

Another concept—that of *projection*—is related to that of identification. It was originated by Freud in 1895, and he later used five interrelated but differentiated applications under the general heading of projection (Novick & Kelly, 1970). Rapaport (1952) describes different conceptualizations of projection. He envisions a continuum "extending from the externalization of a specific type of tension in paranoid projection, to that of a whole system of attitudes and tensions in transference phenomena, to where it imperceptibly shades into the externalization in the form of a 'private world' defined by the organizing principles of one's personality" (p. 463). What I will refer to here as *projection proper* may be defined as a putting out into the external world of a painful impulse or idea.

Novick and Kelly (1970) use the term *externalization* to refer to a specific type of projection in a conceptualization that I will follow in this book. It is striking that externalization, as Novick and Kelly describe its application in the psychoanalytic literature, is not directly opposed to what would appear to be its contrary—internalization. They use the term externalization as it pertains to the projection of aspects of the self, differentiating it from projection proper, which is motivated by the sequence of fantasied dangers that arise from drive expression. Projection proper may, however, be condensed in externalizations. Novick and Kelly state that "with the emergence of the self from the state of 'primal confusion,' the child faces the extremely difficult task of integrating the various dissonant components of the developing self. ... The earliest conflicts confronting the child" relate to his attempts to integrate "seemingly incompatible aspects of the self" (p. 83). Some aspects are valued because they are associated with pleasure—or, more importantly, they meet with favorable responses from parents. Others become dystonic and are externalized. The origin of Novick and Kelly's understanding of externalization—and its place in object relations—can be traced back to Melanie Klein's (1946) term *projective identification*, which she describes as referring to "a combination of splitting off parts of the self and projecting them on to another person" (p. 108). In 1955 she adds to this "the feeling of identification with other people because one has attributed qualities or attributes of one's own to them" (p. 58). The concept of externalization can be enlarged if we include whole or part objects, ego ideals, or parts of the superego as elements to be externalized (Zinner & Shapiro, 1972).

Jaffe (1968) describes how the mechanism of projection is used, on the one hand, to effect the other's annihilation by distancing the object from the self, and on the other, to preserve a tie with it (the object is not sufficiently distanced to be lost, and can still be identified with). We shall see later the relevance of this concept to linking objects and linking phenomena.

Having briefly reviewed the related concepts pertaining to the maintenance of a tie with the representation of the other, and/or the establishment in one way or another of a resemblance to the other's representation, I will now return to the consideration of reactive depression and established pathological mourning.

A case of depression following a death

When Tina was 14 her parents were divorced, and her father moved out of the family home to live in an apartment nearby. Tina's mother had been acknowledged to be a heavy drinker, and Tina, the only daughter and the eldest of the siblings, assumed much of the mothering responsibility for her siblings whenever her mother was on a drinking spree. She also felt responsible for her father, and often visited him in his apartment, enjoying his companionship and his flattering remarks about her. At first he took her out occasionally, and they acted together like "a happy couple." Within a year, however, Tina began to notice women's clothing in his apartment and was obliged to conclude that he had a woman friend. This was not a subject they discussed together, however. Soon she realized that her "honeymoon" with her father was at an end. He seemed cool toward her, and she responded accordingly. At first she hated him for his defection but she kept seeing him, trying to regain his undivided attention. When she felt her efforts were successful she was filled with affection for him. This soon turned to hatred, however, when the feminine clothing reappeared in his bedroom. Ambivalence dominated her relationship with him.

At home, when her mother talked scornfully of the gossip linking her ex-husband with a new woman friend, Tina learned the woman's identity, although she never encountered her in her father's apartment. Her father seemed to be making a point of preventing any such meeting. At 17 Tina learned from her mother that her father and his friend had parted, news that was borne out by his all too evident distress, which filled her with relief and guilty joy, encouraging her to believe that she and her father could resume their former relationship. But with irritation she observed that this was no longer the father of her earlier years—he no longer seemed dashing to her, and he seemed to have little interest in life. She wanted to shake him up and bring him to his senses. Although she thought of talking openly to him about his collapsed affair, she never did.

Now, whenever she visited him, she found him occupied with shining his shoes and dusting his books, cast down and withdrawn. Thus, when he shot himself in the head, she was shocked but not altogether unprepared. She attended his funeral with her mother and her siblings, and wept for weeks, feeling nevertheless that she experienced not genuine sadness but anger instead; she also continued to feel numb. Rumor had it that her father's lover had been in the back of the chapel at the funeral, and for months Tina, who had not seen her there, reviewed the scene of the funeral to see if she could pick her out, sometimes imagining a confrontation. Her anger was directed to the image of this woman.

Tina recognized that she was feeling extreme guilt, and thought that if only she had been smart enough she might have talked with her father about his lover and about the depression that had been so evident to her, and thereby saved his life. She had difficulties with her schoolwork, but her teacher sensed what she was going through and was lenient with her, although Tina could not bring herself to appreciate this. She would find herself imagining her father's representation, sulky and detached, endlessly cleaning his shoes; it acquired a life of its own inside her head, where Tina would relate to it. Sometimes 'she felt that she had succeeded in stopping him in his dreary work, but sometimes she could not do so. When her inner interaction with the father's representation (introject) was not successful, she would find herself telling him inwardly, "Go to hell!"

Within six to ten months this phenomenon, so bothersome for her, disappeared. By that time people were telling her that she had changed in character, becoming more solemn, slower, and more concerned with order and cleanliness. She knew that she had also become rather callous, incapable of a genuine love for others. Once, as she dried dishes, she found herself rubbing the towel a second time over a dish that she had already dried. This reminded her of her father's endlessly cleaning his shoes in his depression.

By the time she went to college the memories of her father's introject and related memories were mostly gone. She had little social life in college and was aware of fearing to be hurt by a relationship with a young man. Her excessive attention to cleanliness persisted. Her hard study led to her being called "a brain." Although her father had shot himself in the head, she made no conscious connection between this circumstance and the name given her by fell ow students. Once, while visiting the Smithsonian Institution, she "accidentally" saw a display purporting to be the shattered gray matter of a suicide shot through the head. It was this event, in her last year of college, that triggered a strong feeling of worthlessness in her. In spite of the intellectual ability that she had shown and the jealous regard of her fell ow students, she continued to feel worthless to an exaggerated degree. She began to think that life was not worth living, and contemplated suicide with no conscious acknowledgment that her father's self-destruction might be influencing her. Once, with serious thought of shooting herself, she was obliged to remember that she had no gun and that in any case this kind of termination was "messy." One day she decided to kill herself with sleeping pills, after carefully cleaning her dormitory room, dusting all of her books, and replacing them on the shelves. But a friend happened to call and sensed that something was amiss. When the friend persisted in her questions, Tina told her of her suicidal intent, and wound up taking her advice to consult the college psychiatrist, who sent her to me for treatment.

She was still depressed when she came in. Her initial reaction to me was ambivalent, but as therapy progressed she gained authentic awareness that there was a connection between her suicide plan and her father's suicide and that her worthlessness and preoccupation with cleanliness were connected with his depression. She came to realize that after keeping the introject of her depressed father within herself for about a year she had finally identified with it. This realization was prompted by the manifest content of a dream in which she reported, "I was with my father. He took off his shoes and I wore them. I was in my father's shoes!" Her association to this dream revealed her identification with the dead man, whose obsessive shoe-shining had been such a crucial image of his depression. The dream also produced other associations that revealed the sexual meaning she had attached to her father's shoes.

It is beyond the scope of this discussion to give further particulars of this patient's psychopathology and treatment. I have introduced her here simply as an example of depression following a death. I do want to note, however, that after her identification with the representation of her depressed father was loosened, she went through the process of mourning. During this time I learned, of course, about many other aspects of her life, but it was only after her mourning for her father was substantially resolved that I could deal more effectively with problems of her psychosexual development, which included the sexual meaning attached to her father's shoes, her defensive character traits stemming from early interaction with a rather narcissistic mother, and so on.

Disruptive identification with the representation of the dead

Similarities and dissimilarities of uncomplicated mourning with depression following a loss by death can be seen in a comparison of Linda's case (Chapter 2) with Tina's. Unlike Linda, Tina experienced complication in the initial stage of mourning; her numbness persisted. Although Tina could cry as Linda did, she was unable to experience sadness. But what basically differentiates the two cases was the different degree of guilt each woman felt.

Although Linda recalled many images of her father, she was able to loosen her ties to them eventually. By means of the puppy, she became able to invest her attention in other objects. Although she felt some guilt about her father's death, it was not so overwhelming that she had to recreate his image internally and identify with it. She had already resolved her ambivalence toward her father in analysis.

Tina's creation of an introject of her father during the first six to ten months after his death was dramatic. Her interaction with it suggests an attempt to work through her mourning and overcome her guilt as she tried to rescue her father from depression, but her negotiation with it did not come to resolution—it simply disappeared. Identification with this ambivalently related introject—the father's depressed representation—was marked by the change in Tina's character that made her behave like the depressed father. There was also evidence of an effort to repair the father by becoming "a brain." As in her initial introjection of her father's representation, her identification had its source in Tina's powerful feelings of guilt. It was, in one sense, the Smithsonian visit that impressed her, at least unconsciously, with the futility of her attempt to repair her father. The loss of this "hope" caused her reactive depression to surface fully, reflecting identification with the representation of the depressed father. Unlike Linda's loving identification, this was disruptive. Five years had gone by since her father's death and Tina's mourning had still not been resolved.

Freud (1917a) showed how the general conditions prevailing in both "mourning" and "melancholia" justify their being seen in relation to one another. Mourning is seen as a typical and expectable reaction to the loss of someone loved, whereas melancholia may be a more selectively determined response to a similar kind of event. As Freud described it, the phenomenology of the latter state involves "profoundly painful dejection," a loss of interest in the world outside the self, a loss of the ability to love, and the inhibition of any activity not connected with thoughts of what is lost. These occur also in mourning, but what distinguishes mourning from reactive depression on the descriptive level is the "disturbance of self-regard" that appears in the latter condition. From the depressed patient one hears statements full of "self-reproaches" and "self-revilings," "culminating in a delusional expectation of punishment" to come (Freud, 1917a, p. 244). Note how the phenomenological characteristics mentioned by Freud coincide with Tina's feelings of worthlessness and dejection and her sense that she was unable to love. In order to understand Tina's disturbance in self-esteem, we must understand more about the depressed patient's disruptive identification with the representation of the person he or she had lost to death.

I have indicated that when the mourning process is uncomplicated, identification with the representation of the dead is in the service of healing and growth. (For more on such identifications, see Hartmann, Kris, & Loewenstein, 1946; Loewald, 1962, 1973; Stierlin, 1973; Volkan, 1976.) The patient's self-system is enriched as he selectively identifies with unambivalently perceived representations of the dead.

In reactive depression, however, internalization results in an "in toto" type of identification, to borrow a term from Ritvo and Solnit (1958); such a designation refers here to the process rather than to the representation of the person taken in. Smith (1975) writes about the difference between the "in toto" identification in depression, which he calls defensive, and the identification entered into for the purpose of healing and growth.

> Identifications for purposes of growth are not imperative, emergency, "in toto" internalizations. The various aspects of the objects can be experienced and specific ones can be relinquished or coordinated

> as enduring aspects of the self. The difference is between relatively enforced and relatively optional identifications. The latter tend to be with the loved and admired traits of the object. (p. 20)

Jacobson (1971) also writes about identifications in the uncomplicated grieving process. She notes that when libido is liberated, as the ties to the representation of the dead are loosened, it cannot immediately be invested in new object relations in compensation for those lost. "Instead, it is absorbed by the identifications and used for investments in new sublimations and ego functions" (p. 100). As proof of this, Jacobson refers to the well-known clinical observation that when the stages of mourning are passed through without complications, mourners "begin to double their efforts in work or start new, absorbing activities founded on identifications with the lost object" (p. 100).

In contrast to the normal mourner, the mourner in depression preserves through disruptive identification the ambivalent relationship he had with the person who has died. In Tina's case, the preservation of the ambivalent relationship is evident in her identification with just that aspect of her father—the depressed and dejected father—that in his lifetime she had so strongly rejected. Unable *because* of her unresolved ambivalence toward the historical images of her father to identify selectively with the aspects of him that she had cherished, she experienced the "in toto" identification of reactive depression. The representation of her father used for identification was invested not only with libido but with aggression as well. Aggression in the self resulting from identification makes for guilt and self-reproach.

As Freud (1917a) indicates, "If the love for the object—a love which cannot be given up ... takes refuge in narcissistic identification, then the hate that is also felt for the dead person comes into operation on his substitutive object, abusing it, debasing it, making it suffer and deriving sadistic satisfaction for its suffering" (p. 251). Fenichel (1945) summarizes this state in terms of structural theory and shows how it reflects a struggle between the superego and the ego. After identification with the representation of the dead person takes place (Fenichel uses the term "introjection" to describe what I and most other psychoanalytic writers refer to as identification), "sadism enlists on the side of the superego and attacks the ego that has been altered by the introjection" (p. 397). "The superego treats the ego in the same way that the patient unconsciously had wished to treat the object that was lost" (p. 398). Fenichel describes here how the identification is assimilated in the ego, and how the ego combined with the assimilated introject is set up against the superego. He also describes how in certain situations the identification is mainly associated with the superego, causing it to change and oppose the ego.

Fenichel's ideas on depression also yield important answers as to why every mourner does not become depressed. He writes that the individual prone to depression is one who is "fixated on the state where his self-esteem is regulated by external supplies or a person whose guilt feelings motivate him to regress to this state" (p. 387). Such a person is an orally dependent individual, and when the representation of the dead symbolically represents "narcissistic supplies" for him, the death brings about a lowering of self-esteem.

Fenichel's summary of the classical psychoanalytic understanding of reactive depression refers to intersystemic conflicts within the mental apparatus. But Bibring (1953) states that "the oral and aggressive strivings are not universal in depression as is generally assumed" (p. 41), and studies the condition as "an ego-psychological phenomenon" (p. 21). Thus Bibring's emphasis is on the intrasystemic conflicts within the ego. I agree with Jacobson (1971) that certain depressions, especially psychotic depressions, in which "the conflict is between the wishful self image and the image of the failing self" (p. 177) are the kind that mainly reflect a tension within the ego. However, as Jacobson and Mahler (1968) would both agree, Bibring leaves out the role of object relations, aggression, and hostility conflicts in the type of neurotic (reactive) depression that I describe here. These issues should also be considered in order to more fully understand the suicide that may occur in reactive depression.

Suicide in reactive depression

When Tina seriously contemplated suicide she was not consciously aware of her disruptive identification with the father who had himself committed suicide. She had no observable inner relatedness to a differentiated image of her dead father, nor was she preoccupied with such an image. Her suicide attempt will be compared in the next chapter to that of a patient in established pathological mourning.

Fenichel (1945) notes that "the thesis that nobody kills himself who had not intended to kill somebody else is proved by the depressive suicide" (p. 400). Love for the representation of the dead makes the mourner keep it within himself, but hate for the same makes him want to destroy it. Since there is an "in toto" identification with this ambivalently related object representation, the mourner becomes a battleground; when the object representation is destroyed, its host—the mourner's self—is also destroyed. In structural terms, suicide in reactive depression is evidence of the unbearable tension brought to bear on the ego by the superego. In some persons it represents passive abandonment of the struggle, but in others the suicidal impulse is more active. Fenichel states that some suicidal acts

> ... assert themselves as desperate attempts to enforce, at any cost, the cessation of the pressure of the superego. They are the most extreme acts of ingratiatory submission to punishment and to the superego's cruelty; simultaneously they are also the most extreme acts of rebellion, that is, murder—murder of the original objects whose incorporation created the superego. (p. 400)

Jacobson (1971) states that suicide or other self-destructive behavior is no indication that "the aggressive drives are beyond the pleasure principle." Although "in neurotic suffering the pleasure principle has lost most of its power ... its efforts to reassert itself must not be underrated." Jacobson holds that the self-destructive act of suicide "aims at the total elimination of tension " (p. 37).

> The explanation would be that, first, the pleasure principle is sacrificed in the effort to restitute the psychic equilibrium; in trying to enforce a lowering of the high tension level at any cost, the constancy principle eventually also fails in the function of self-preservation and can accomplish a total elimination only by self-destruction. (p. 37)

Having described the phenomenology and metapsychology of depression following the death of a loved/hated other and the suicide that sometimes occurs in this condition, I will now turn my attention to a related clinical condition—established pathological mourning—which has, more than depression, been the focus of my clinical research.

CHAPTER 5

Complications in the work of mourning: Established pathological mourning

This chapter examines the clinical entity I call established pathological mourning from the phenomenological as well as the metapsychological point of view. The patient in established pathological mourning, like the depressed mourner, has experienced complications in the work of mourning. His state more directly reflects his fixation in the work of mourning, however, in that he is conflicted about "killing" or "not killing" the one he has lost. The ambivalence that had characterized his relationship with the deceased persists, leading him simultaneously to yearn for and dread the dead's return from the grave.

Unlike the depressed mourner, the established pathological mourner does not develop a disruptive identification with the representation of the dead, but maintains such a representation as an unassimilated intro ject. He also invests certain inanimate objects of his own selection with magical qualities.

Such "linking objects" furnish an external locus at which the self-representation can meet with the representation of the lost object. The person in established pathological mourning can thus keep alive an illusion of continuing communication with the dead, communication over which he feels himself to have absolute control; he accomplishes this internally by means of an introject, and externally by means of a linking object (or linking phenomenon).

I include a discussion of dreams and hallucinations in established pathological mourning, and illustrate how suicide in this condition differs from suicide in depression. Case histories are given.

Two fatal events

The case of Phyllis illustrates on a descriptive level how established pathological mourning differs from reactive depression. Phyllis was in her early twenties when a mentally deficient sister five years her junior died. The sister had lived in the family circle until puberty when, fearing that she might become pregnant, her parents had sent her to an institution. She had returned home on weekend visits, however, and on one such visit, she fell on a stairway and broke her neck, dying instantly.

At the time of the accident Phyllis was out with "an exciting new date." She had had the usual shock reaction when she learned of the accident, but later recalled that for a few days she had had "unwelcome thoughts" of how the event had interrupted the fun she had been having. She had exhibited irritability that those around her had attributed to grief but which she recognized as due to rage over her sister's death spoiling her pleasure. This "selfishness" made her feel very guilty. She had episodes of weeping, but at the time of the funeral and thereafter, she could not help but wonder how soon it would be seemly for her to go dancing again with her new boyfriend, who had made a call of condolence.

During the next few weeks, Phyllis was flooded with memories of how her dead sister had so often spoiled her fun, and with recollections of her own childhood fantasies of curing her. She felt renewed guilt over having supported her parents in their decision to send her sister to an institution. But within three months she felt fairly well adjusted to the tragedy. After all, the dead girl had been out of the family home long enough for Phyllis to have become used to her absence.

It was about this time that she was driving in the country with a woman friend when their car hit a horse that had strayed onto the road. It was thrown into the air by the impact, and the fall to the ground broke its neck. Horrified, the two women got out of the car. While her friend went to a nearby house to call the authorities, Phyllis watched the animal thrash about in its death throes. She was helplessly convinced that fate was playing a trick on her and as she noticed some rocks by the roadside, she told herself that she "would have to be as hard as these rocks" to bear so savage a reprise of her sister's death. As the horse gave its last gasp she picked up one of the stones, a flat one, kept it in her hand for a while, and dropped it into her pocket. When she got home she put it in a box in her bedroom closet.

She still had the stone when she became my patient five years later, although by then she had moved into an apartment she shared with another girl. She recognized the fact that it held some kind of magic for her, and felt compelled to keep it. She disliked looking at it but she had to know where it was. She connected it with her sister's death as well as with the accident that had killed the horse. It was a relic of the horse's final moment, and she was intellectually aware that its flatness reminded her of her sister's flat chest, and that its hardness had something to do with the hardness she needed to endure the tragedy of violent death. Moreover, she recalled with both affection and guilt how her family had defensively joked about her handicapped sister and how one brother had said she "had rocks in her head."

Phyllis realized that in her mind the two deaths were interchangeable. For a year after the accident, she was preoccupied with a slow motion picture of the horse hurtling through the air and plunging to the ground, which would then switch to the picture of her sister huddled at the bottom of the stairs, the latter drawn from the scene as described by family members present at the time. She was in fact so preoccupied with these images that she was obliged to give up her work as a secretary and take a vacation of some months before resuming work elsewhere.

By then the image of her sister on the stairs seemed to be buried within her chest. She would reactivate it from time to time at work. It had its own autonomy, to which she would relate. In her mind's eye she would kick the dead girl to bring her back to life, although sometimes the violence of this fantasied act made her feel guilty, so that she would then try more gently to arouse her sister. Her sister's image appeared to her spontaneously at times, and at other times it was triggered by idiosyncratic associations. For example, the sexually charged term "necking" would be associated with the sister's and the horse's broken necks, and would reactivate the introject enough to bring it into her full waking awareness; "frozen" images of her sister persisted in her dreams.

At home, she still looked for her sister whenever she was reminded of her. But she dreaded the possibility that she might find her there on a weekend visit as in the past. Once, while she was in her apartment, she heard a noise outside as though something had fallen from a nearby tree. She felt compelled to look to see if it were her sister, even though, intellectually, she knew that this was impossible.

She felt "normal" except for her preoccupation with death and her sister's image. She continued to use the present tense when speaking of her sister, and during the year before coming to see me joined a "religious" group that emphasized achieving contact with the dead. She did not experience lowered self-esteem or self-reproach but felt that if her sister had not died her own life would have taken a different and more productive course.

Established pathological mourning described

Phyllis was engaged in a continuing search for her dead sister at the same time as she was seized by a dread of finding her. Her need to know where the rock was at all times and yet her dislike of looking at it, her disorganizing and painful preoccupation with the image of her sister's dead body, her need to violently arouse the introjected representation of her sister buried within her chest, her dread seeking for her sister at home, all testify to the conflict she felt between seeking and dreading to find the dead girl. In terms of the work of mourning, Phyllis was conflicted about "killing" or "not killing" her. She had not completed the loosening of her ties to the dead girl, nor had she identified with her sister's representation "in toto." Instead, like other patients in a similar state, she clung to an introject and to a symbolized inanimate object (her flat rock). I will later describe linking objects in detail, and interpret their meaning and their connection with the introject.

It is, of course, normal for anyone bereaved to long wistfully for the return of the one he has lost, often for a year or even two years after the death (Parkes, 1972). But in established pathological mourning the mourner also dreads the return of the dead. The conflict within the mourner reflects the ambivalence that had marked the relationship before death intervened. (As already indicated, of course, ambivalence also plays an important role in the depressed mourner, but in a different way.)

Bowlby and Parkes account for the mourner's yearning and searching as an aspect of attachment behavior (described briefly in Chapter 1) but put little emphasis on the accompanying dread. Parkes (1972) writes:

> The study of bereaved psychiatric patients provides some evidence to suggest that ambivalence does indeed contribute to pathological reactions, but the evidence is not as clear-cut as one would wish. (p. 134)

My experience with patients whose mourning work becomes complicated impresses me greatly with the importance of ambivalence as a determining factor to a degree that Parkes does not acknowledge. I suggest that not only is ambivalence characteristic of the person in established pathological mourning but that its very relevance is an indication that the yearning for the lost object cannot be understood on the basis of attachment behavior alone: the dread of bringing the lost one back to life reflects the negative aspects of investment in the representation of the dead. And while the aspect of dread may escape attention at first because of the intensity of "the persistent seeking of reunion" (Bowlby, 1961), I see this "persistent seeking" itself as

> ... unconsciously intensified, and ... habitual and specific enough to be called a mechanism of defense—defense mainly against the tension of ambivalence and the eruption of derivatives of those aggressive and libidinal drives originally directed toward the deceased. (Volkan, 1972, p. 216)

Thus a diagnosis of established pathological mourning should not be made on the grounds of longing alone. However, since the mourner does cling to a chronic hope that the lost one may return, and since, psychologically speaking, he has not given up all hope of resolving the ambivalence that characterized his historical relationship with the deceased, he has no need to identify wholly with the representation of the dead and his ego state is such that he does not exhibit the self-hatred and self-reproach that one sees in depression.

Evidence of wanting but fearing to bring the dead to life often appears in the interest in reincarnation typical in established pathological mourning, or in the mourner's preoccupation with the continued existence of the dead person after death. I have noted Phyllis's affiliation with a group that emphasized the possibility of achieving contact with the dead. While wanting and fearing the return of the dead is usually accompanied by anxiety in the average person in established pathological mourning, the more sophisticated may deal with it by sublimation in some scientific hypothesis or tangentially related interest. Of course, since some cultures and religions cherish a belief in life after death, the mourner's concern with this matter cannot be considered symptomatic unless it is exaggerated. Similarly, his preoccupation with reincarnation may be congruent with a commonly accepted belief system. Some cultures, even though anticipating the return of the dead in a general way, are not free from anxiety concerning this possibility. The widely known work of Boyer and Boyer (1972, 1977) at the Mescalero Indian Reservation shows that Apache Indians traditionally believe that only the spirits of those who have died after a "full life" and have gone away to some nebulous "happy hunting ground" are regarded without much fear. The Boyers believe that these were "a happy few," since the same tribe felt quite differently about the spirits of those who had met some violent death before their time, or who had had a reputation for meanness or witchery. These, the Apaches felt, hovered about in the darkness, taking vengeance, driving the living to insanity or suicide. They also saw the possibility that the loneliness of a spirit might cause it to effect the death of someone living in order to have companionship in the beyond.

Some persons with established pathological mourning are compulsive about reading obituary notices. This compulsion betrays not only anxiety over their own dying but an attempt to continue to deny the death of the one they mourn, i.e., by finding no current mention of it. Conversely, the memory of the death notice as it appeared at the time of the death makes the death final—"kills" the lost one. Some people with established pathological mourning fancy that they recognize their lost one in someone alive whom they encounter or see at a distance. One such patient, ten years after his father's death, heard about another man who bore his name. This news was enough to make him travel for hours to spy on this stranger in order to make sure that it was not his father, although he knew very well that his father was not alive. My patient Solomon was for years vulnerable to the conviction that his father might possibly be alive when anyone with a resemblance to him passed by. He would rush forward to look over and over again to see if this were his lost parent. I have seen identical behavior in other patients. It represents not only an effort to return the dead to life but, once the illusion is recognized, the wish to "kill" the deceased as well.

The mourner in established pathological mourning uses the present tense when speaking of the one he has lost, making such confident statements as, "My father likes to go to the movies," or, "He has curly hair." One joked nervously during his first interview with me, saying, "You can't talk against dead people because if you knock them down they come back to get you!" I have noted that Phyllis used the present tense in referring to her dead sister.

In established pathological mourning, the mourner may make daily reference to death, tombs, or graveyards in a ritual way. The listener gets the impression that the speaker's daily life includes some actual relationship with the deceased and that the mourner continues to watch over him. Bernard was a man in his thirties who had lost the invalid wife to whom he had remained faithful throughout her final tragic ten years. He had assumed all responsibility for a young daughter during that time. On his wife's death, he had had her buried in an appropriate cemetery away from his country home. Within a year, however, thinking that a move would make her "happier," he had had her body buried in a grave "under my bedroom window." Before another year went by, he had decided that she still was not pleased with this arrangement and had her coffin returned to the cemetery. He was contemplating a third move when he was brought to our attention.

In established pathological mourning, visits to the grave are made with ritual beyond anything demanded by religious or social tradition—or, more usually, the very existence of the grave is denied.

A 20-year-old college student who had lost a grandfather she called "the most important person in my life" was surprised, a year and a half after his death, to be asked if she had ever visited his grave. She was quick to find an excuse for never having done so; she doubted that she could find it in a cemetery as "big" as the one in the small town where he was buried. Her preoccupation with her grandfather was evident in her frequent daydreams about him and in her search for him in a conflict-ridden affair with a married man 30 years her senior. Another patient in established pathological mourning, a man in his mid-twenties, had to walk along a country road each day to catch the bus that took him to work; it passed the cemetery in which his mother had been buried for four years, and although her tombstone was visible from it, he invariably averted his eyes, morning and night, in an attempt to deny its existence.

Typical dreams in established pathological mourning

Ambivalence often declares itself most clearly in the dreams of established pathological mourners. I have collected hundreds of these dreams from people fixated in the chronic hope of finding the one they have lost while at the same time fearing to encounter him. My collection indicates that such people have typical dreams, the manifest content of which falls into three categories: "frozen" dreams, dreams of a life-and-death struggle, and the dream of death as an illusion. The existence of such dreams in cases in which established pathological mourning is suspected should be an important diagnostic clue. Reflecting the fixation that has stalled the mourning process, they tend to be repeating dreams.

Pollock (1961) suggests that normal mourners have "sequential dreams," the manifest content of which corresponds to the sequential phases the mourner passes through as he moves toward the completion of the mourning process.

> Changes occurring in the perception of the lost object in the dream reveal the gradual withdrawal of cathexis from the object and its associations. Thus in one instance, initial dreams of the departed object immediately after the death still kept the object alive, functioning and communicating. Gradually the object disappeared from the dreams *per se*, and in late phases of the chronic mourning process, a dream was reported wherein an individual spoke of a funeral and burial that had occurred several months previously. Associations to the dream dealt with "finally accepting" that the figure was dead, buried although still remembered. (p. 352)

Pollock shows that when acceptance of the reality of the loss is achieved, secondary process behavior, utilizing memory and oriented to the reality principle, becomes evident. One of Pollock's patients stated that his dreams began to lose color as he accepted the reality of his father's death. They actually became gray until, in one, a "sprig of green" appeared. Pollock writes:

> His associations dealt with "something coming to life again." It was as though the freed energy heralded "the arrival of spring, when things begin to grow again after a long cold grey winter." (p. 352)

Parkes (1970) also collected dreams, from 22 widows under 65, interviewing each of these at least five times in the 13 months after their loss, and asking at each interview if the subject had dreamed about her husband since the preceding talk with the investigator. Eleven recalled such dreams, the most striking feature of most of them being their vivid and realistic quality. Parkes suggests that they illustrate the effects of the urge to recover the lost object. It is not altogether clear, however, whether the mourning of all the widows interviewed followed an uncomplicated course; Parkes notes that two had violent dreams in which there was a killing. In any event, dreams collected in repeated but widely spaced interviews, although providing valuable information, might fail to show as much of significance as would a closely monitored sequence, like that available to the therapist in the treatment situation.

It would appear that both those mourning with and without complications have the same kind of sequential dreams, but those of the dreamer whose mourning is arrested will not "march" until his treatment reactivates the mourning process and brings about responses long postponed. The repeating dreams of established pathological mourners can be classified in three categories:

"Frozen" dreams. Many of my patients used the term "frozen" to describe their fixation in the work of mourning and to describe their dreams as well; dreams that are in effect composed of one tableau after another, in none of which there is any action. One patient likened his dreaming to seeing a slide series being projected, and another used the analogy of watching slices of bread fall out of a package. The term "frozen" refers also to lifelessness. It is interesting that Pollock's patient

with "grey" dreams associated this neutral color with a long, cold winter; when what is "frozen" thaws, life (spring) can commence again. Schuster (1969) uses the term "frozen grief' to describe a state "where no affect is felt or expressed and where there is no restitution nor working through of the grief' (p. 87). Although he does not explain why he uses the word "frozen," I suspect that, like myself and other workers in this field, he was made familiar with the use of it in this connection by his patients. Giovacchini (1967) also makes use of the term in describing the "maternal introjects" of two patients following the death of a mother. These introjects were "frozen" defensively; they were neither dead nor alive. Giovacchini describes a dream of one of these patients in which he saw frozen bodies in the rooms of an old castle.

As they associate to the pictures that compose each slide of the dream, patients usually talk about death-related stories and the inability to mourn.

Dreams of a life-and-death struggle. In this type of dream, the dreamer sees the deceased still living but engaged in a life-and-death struggle. He may be lying on a hospital bed or caught in a burning vehicle. The dreamer then tries either to save him or finish him off. The outcome remains undetermined because the dreamer invariably wakes before it can be resolved.

It is interesting that in the dreams typical of established pathological mourning, with their evidence of fixation and ambivalence toward the dead person's representation, both the dreamer and the one he mourns usually appear undisguised. One explanation may be that the ego concentrates on the struggle to "save" or to "kill," so that symbolization of the characters involved is secondary. Another explanation might be that the ego's censoring capacity is overtaxed by the strength of the conflict arising from the mourner's past relationship to the one he mourns and its reactivation by the death.

Anna Freud (1967) writes about a similar phenomenon. She had noticed that in some persons in analysis "the later stages of mourning are characterized by a series of typical dreams [in which] the dead person appears, either manifestly or slightly disguised, and makes every effort to bring himself to the notice of the survivor" (p. 17). The dead person may complain about loneliness and desertion and plead with the survivor to join him.

> The dreamer feels in the grip of conflicting emotions and alternates between pure joy about the reunion and remorse and guilt for having stayed away from the dead, neglected him, etc. He wakes up, usually, with anxiety and finds it difficult to realize that the whole experience has "only been a dream." (p. 17)

She states that it is fairly easy to understand the latent content of such dreams; they reflect an ambivalence—"the simultaneous urges to remain loyal to the dead and to turn toward new ties with the living" (p. 17).

She also notes that her patients dreamed such dreams at the point in their mourning process at which they were "becoming disloyal to the dead." In established pathological mourning, the repetition of such dreams without moving on to dreams indicative of the resolution of the mourning process gives evidence that the patient is caught in this conflict between remaining loyal to the dead or turning away from him.

The dream of death as an illusion. In this type of dream, the patient dreams of observing something about the dead body that denies the reality of death. The body lying in a coffin may be sweating visibly, for example, or a long-buried body may be intact, with no sign of decay. Such dreams are not unusual immediately after a death among those whose mourning is uncomplicated. In such cases, however, the dreams eventually cease, or change toward greater correspondence with the reality of death. The person with established pathological mourning will dream of an intact body many years after the death.

Hallucinations in established pathological mourning

Chronic hallucinations of the deceased occur less often in established pathological mourning than do dreams about the deceased. All mourners are likely to hallucinate the lost person in the period immediately following a death. Parkes (1970) speaks of the hallucinations mourners in an uncomplicated process of mourning often have in their first year of bereavement. When hallucination does continue in established pathological mourning, it constitutes a specific isolated "eccentricity" and does not indicate the break with reality that speaks of psychosis.

Matchett's (1972) study of the Hopi Indians of Arizona reveals the unique and interesting ways in which death is dealt with in a culture isolated for centuries. He cites the cases of three women between 58 and 69 years of age. One had experienced the death of a close cousin only a few months earlier, and the other two were hallucinating the appearance of persons long dead. Their hallucinations were reminiscent of the dreams of persons in established pathological mourning in Western culture. But while Matchett acknowledges their dreamlike quality, he notes that "the apparition is real enough to the beholder to be conversed with, to be described in great visual detail, and even at times to be struggled with physically" (p. 185).

The two Indian women who hallucinated the dead many years after their deaths had occurred exemplify the ambivalence seen in the dreams of persons in established pathological mourning. Such visitations of the dead were in a sense welcomed, but they were also feared: the women "killed" their visitants. One of the women nailed cloth over the window in which she had "seen" her dead person, so as to prevent his appearing there again. Subsequent appearances came only in darkness, and she would terminate these by rising and turning on the light. The second woman, whose husband had died two years earlier in an automobile accident, regularly saw him standing before her in the evening dusk. He would caress her hair and then softly touch her cheek, but one night these gentle movements gave way to an attempt to strangle her. She sprang to her feet in terror, turned on the light, and suddenly he was gone. She was able to tell the interviewer that by then his appearance showed signs of decay. What had taken Linda (Chapter 2) less than two months to experience—in the dream of her father's body decomposing—had taken this Indian woman two years to experience, after which her husband appeared before her once again with the face of a skeleton and told her, "Don't bring me back any more."

What Matchett describes recalls aspects of the work of the Boyers, to which I have referred. They write of the Apache's "ghost sickness":

> In traditional Apachean thinking, to remember a dead person, to speak or even think his name, will call his ghost. The shade, either because it is lonely or wishes to avenge itself for past factual or fancied wrongs, is apt to make a living individual extremely ill or to drive him insane, causing him either to commit suicide or behave foolishly so that he gets killed. (Boyer & Boyer, 1977, p. 33)

Introjects in established pathological mourning

Besides the hallucination of the deceased, two other phenomena—introjects and linking objects—are used by mourners to enable them to keep in touch with the images and representations of the dead, and to maintain the illusion of absolute control over such images and representations. The existence of introjects and linking objects provides important clues in the diagnosis of established pathological mourning.

The individual in established pathological mourning speaks of his introject as another person (the person who has died), or as part of that person, such as his head, or as a symbolic or spiritual representation of him that dwells like an invasive foreign object in his breast or mind. My patient Phyllis gave a good illustration of the way in which such patients let us know about their perceptions of the introject. Yet, although the patient describes his introject as a concrete entity, the analyst or therapist should not so perceive it. (It is perhaps for this reason that some—Jacobson [1971] and Kernberg [1975, 1976], for example—prefer the term "introjection" to that of "introject"—because of its more abstract reference.) What the patient feels to be an inner presence is an affective, cognitive phenomenon, an inner link to the representation of the dead.

I have noted that introjects appear in crises to modify distressing situations with the object (Schafer, 1968). In established pathological mourning, such distressing situations arise from the loss of the external object and become chronic. The patient is able to describe the existence inside himself of a part of the deceased that retains its own definite boundaries and that remains separate from the mourner's own physical and mental self-representation. Clyde, the patient described in Chapter 11, not only continued to have an introject of his dead half-brother lodged in his breast but conducted "inner conversations" with it. When he allowed himself to grieve in the course of his treatment he shouted, "Get out! Get out!" to the man, part of whom he still felt to be present within himself (Volkan, Cilluffo, & Sarvay, 1975). Mike (Chapter 9) railed against the introject of his dead father in the same way.

In established pathological mourning, the relationship between the patient and the introject of the deceased reproduces the original ambivalent relationship that obtained before the death. The patient perceives his relationship with the representation of the deceased as being to all intents and purposes a relationship between two persons. It is not some value-laden, primitively split-off, "all good" or "all bad" aspect of the deceased that is represented, but the whole person as he was historically and ambivalently experienced by the mourner before death. When, as is usual, a part of the deceased (face, head, voice, etc.) is introjected, the part represents the whole, ambivalently perceived person, not merely some aspect of him. In contrast, some psychotics may evidence an introject that reflects a pre-ambivalent condition, either an absolutely need-satisfying "all good" or a devilish "all bad" image; the introject of the psychotic may appear to have an existence unconnected with other images of the person maintained by him; and the location of the introject in the psychotic is not fixed—it can be quickly externalized, re-internalized, and re-externalized. In neurotics—and I adhere to the classification of established pathological mourning as a neurosis—the part of the dead person that constitutes an introject is congruent with other images of him, and the neurotic's introject is in a considerably more stable location than the psychotic's, being felt within, without quick shifts of internalization and externalization.

Consistent with the retention of the ambivalently regarded representation, the introject described in established pathological mourning is usually a personified image of the deceased (as indeed it is in psychosis, but with the differences noted above). Depersonification—a shift from the total human context of the object's personality to certain of its specific functions so necessary for effective (transmuting) identification (Kohut, 1971)—does not occur. Its occurrence contraindicates the diagnosis of established pathological mourning.

Linking objects and linking phenomena in established pathological mourning

While the person in established pathological mourning keeps inner contact with the representation of the deceased by means of an introject, and thereby maintains the illusion of absolute control over it, he also maintains the illusion of external contact with it by means of a linking object. A linking object is something actually present in the environment that is psychologically contaminated with various aspects of the dead and the self.

Of course, any mourner may at the time of a death invest considerable affect in an item closely connected with the one who has died. But it is typical of the patient in established pathological mourning that the significance of this object does not fade as it does in uncomplicated mourning. Rather, it increasingly commands his attention with its aura of mystery, fascination, and terror. Phyllis's flat rock, for example, which included elements of the flat-chested sister with "rocks in her head," and the hardness of which symbolized her defensively established self-image, hard and resistant in the face of tragedy, persisted in just this way.

Barbara Jones's (1967) chapter on "relics and mementoes" speaks of the interest almost every mourner feels in some external object that recalls the one lost to death. Pollock (1961) writes:

> Variations of this denial of separation may be manifested by displacement of cathexis from the object onto auxiliaries which are reminders of the departed. Thus old letters, keepsakes, portraits, eyeglasses, bits of hair, clothing, and other intimate possessions are treated as if they have to be constant reminders of the existence of the object. (p. 352)

He states further that, in some instances, clinging to such objects reflects the inability to let the dead die and be buried and to pick up one's own life and go forward.

Early in my work I noticed how patients with complicated grief reactions "symbolize certain objects which belonged to the dead one," and how "through this process, they are able to control a tie with him" (Volkan, 1970, p. 242). In one of the examples I offered, a patient had symbolized a photograph of his dead father. Ritually, he would isolate himself in a room with this picture and look at it closely until he began to feel that his father was coming back into life toward him through the frame. Another patient, Joe, continued for eight years to symbolize the clothing of his brother, who had been shot in a holdup. Joe was obsessed with the idea that he would grow to a point where these garments would fit him. I later coined the term "linking objects" to describe these objects and closely examined them both descriptively and metapsychologically (Volkan, 1972). As I began to understand their significance, I saw that they were a variation of the reactivated transitional object

(Winnicott, 1953) and grasped the role they played, along with other linking phenomena, in creativity and in certain adjustments mourners were able to make.

Anna Freud (1967) observes the obsession of adolescents with holding onto what is valuable to them after a loss, such as the termination of a romance. She speaks of their listing their friends, etc., after having received such a blow, and I believe that death may be included as a cause for such a jealous inventorying of what remains. Tessman (1978) describes the revival of transitional objects and transitional phenomena by children faced with object loss. Tessman seems unaware, however, of my contribution in this field and of the difference established between the transitional object (or phenomenon) proper and the linking object (or phenomenon), which is a special reactivated version of the former (Volkan, 1972, 1976; see also Chapter 15).

Just as not every object image or representation of the deceased is an introject, so not every object kept by a mourner as a keepsake or memento is a linking object, invested with symbolism and magic. It is sometimes only during treatment that its possession and use are openly acknowledged; until then the patient may not have been fully aware of the power it had over him. The person likely to go into established pathological mourning usually selects his linking object soon after the death. Then, rather than putting it to its appropriate use—wearing the watch or taking pictures with the camera, for example—he will put it in a safe place, often out of sight. He may make a rite of occasionally getting it out and allowing himself to come under its spell. He must be confident of its whereabouts, although he may avoid contact with it for a considerable period of time. One of my patients kept his linking object in his car. When he had an accident, he went to extravagant lengths to retrieve it from the wreckage; it was the only item he salvaged.

A great variety of things may serve as linking objects, and unlike transitional objects and fetishes, for example, they are chosen without regard to characteristic color, odor, or texture; nor do they have qualities in common from one patient to another. I have seen the following used as linking objects: (1) a personal possession of the deceased, often something he used routinely or wore on his person, like a watch; (2) a gift to the mourner from the deceased before his death, such as something a husband gave his wife before perishing in an accident; (3) something the deceased used to extend his senses or bodily functions, such as a camera (an extension of seeing); (4) a realistic representation of the deceased, the simplest example being a photograph—or a symbolic representation such as an identification bracelet; (5) something at hand when the mourner first learned of the death or saw the dead body—what could be considered a "last minute object."

Phyllis's flat rock was a variation of the "last minute object," since it became magical at the moment of the horse's death. (The horse's death, of course, represented for Phyllis the death of her sister.) Clyde (Chapter 11) had a more typical "last minute object." He had been about to play a stack of his favorite records when the phone rang with the news that his half-brother had drowned. The records became Clyde's "last minute objects." My patient Helen had an unusual last minute object, her psychiatrist's appointment card. In her mid-thirties, Helen had been seeing a psychiatrist twice weekly for two years. Her treatment had reached a stalemate insofar as the psychiatrist had gratified many of her dependency needs, leading to severe countertransference problems. She had lost her father when she was three, when he divorced her mother and disappeared from their life. A careful review of her treatment indicated that she had transferred to her physician many of her expectations as to being gratified by a father. When at one session Helen noticed that her psychiatrist seemed depressed, he denied it. Just as she was about to go to his office for a subsequent session, however, word came that he had hanged himself. Her appointment card for that day then became a linking object, and during the next week she bought an urn in which to keep it on her living room mantel, where it stayed for three years. She never removed or looked at the card, although she was always conscious of its presence in the urn. By keeping it at a physical distance (representing psychological distance), she kept it under her absolute control. She continued to be preoccupied with the image of the dead physician, and dreamed typical dreams of having to choose between saving or killing him. She would often keep her appointment with the dead man by parking her car in his office parking lot near the place formerly assigned to him. After three years she noticed that the railroad tie marking off the dead man's parking place was beginning to rot, and this observation made her anxious, seeming to be an indication that her link to him was slipping out of her control. She was in any case disturbed because her husband, wearying of her preoccupation with the dead physician, left her. It was at this point that she sought out a new psychiatrist.

I cite this instance of a last minute object at some length because a comparison of this phenomenon to the fetish serves as a useful introduction to the theory of the linking object. Freud (1927) used an idea like that of the last minute object in connection with the fetish. The choice of an object to use as a fetish seems to be determined by the last impression made on the child before he had the traumatic experience of observing the anatomical differences between men and women—the absence of a penis in the woman. Both disavowal and affirmation of castration can be discerned in the construction of the fetish itself, which is a substitute for the penis the little boy supposed a woman (his mother) to have. Freud stated that the fetish is thus "a token of triumph over the threat of castration and a protection against it" (p. 154). In the same way, the last minute linking object (like other types of linking objects) is a token of triumph over separation (more generalized than castration, which is itself a highly specialized form of separation) that also protects the individual from the anxiety of wanting to keep and to "kill" the deceased. I will discuss the psychodynamic understanding of linking objects further at a later point, and compare them with fetishes in greater detail, examining their relationship to childhood transitional objects.

I have also observed in my patients what I call linking phenomena—fantasies, sensations, and behavior patterns that perpetuate the possibility of contact between the mourner and the one he mourns without reference to any tangible object. Religious belief in the hereafter, already mentioned, may be an example of this (though, of course, in a culture that fosters this belief, only an exaggerated concept of it will be considered unusual and suggestive). Something with sensory impact, like a song, would qualify as a linking phenomenon as well, satisfying the psychodynamic requirement of the linking object by providing an opportunity for the mourner's representation to meet externally the representation of the one he mourns and to keep the circumstances of this meeting under his absolute control.

The psychodynamics of established pathological mourning

Psychoanalytic studies have shown that the surface clinical picture presented by an individual may be a symbolic expression of conflicts and/or content from different levels of his development; and, further, that any one symptom may appear in a number of different disorders. For example, Rangell (1959) and, later, Dorpat (1976) argue convincingly that conversion symptoms are not necessarily the symbolic expression of conflicts at the phallic and oedipal levels but may express conflicts and/or content of several different developmental levels. Moreover, a conversion symptom is not inevitably linked with one psychoneurotic disorder—hysteria—but may appear in other disorders, even schizophrenia (Noble, 1951), and should be regarded as only the visible tip of an iceberg, the unknown character and dimensions of which must be explored further. The diagnosis should thus be approached with caution.

In the same way, not all bereaved persons whose clinical picture features the search to recover the dead and the concomitant dread of finding him have similar psychic structures. Without knowledge of the patient's psychological organization, any formulation will be little more than descriptive and any treatment a shot in the dark. I identify the form of neurosis that I call established pathological mourning when the sufferer has achieved object constancy, has an integrated self-concept, and an internalized object world in which the elements are appropriately differentiated—in other words, has a high-level character structure. To be sure, a clinical picture such as this kind of mourner exhibits may also be presented by persons with borderline personality organization or even by schizophrenics; thus it is essential, particularly in planning treatment, that established pathological mourning be differentiated from conditions in which a similar clinical picture is supported by a character structure of a lower level.

The tripartite (id–ego–superego) model of the mind is conceptually adequate for dealing with neurotic difficulties at the oedipal level, but we hear more and more in contemporary psychoanalytic literature of the need to supplement—or even replace—this classical model whenever we are faced with a patient who is operating on the preoedipal level, or with those whose disturbances originate largely from an infirm cohesion of the self and an accompanying impairment of object relations. Although investigators differ slightly—or even drastically—in respect to the theoretical reference they use, a number of them (Boyer & Giovacchini, 1967; Kohut, 1971, 1977; Gedo & Goldberg, 1973; Kernberg, 1975, 1976; Dorpat, 1976; Modell, 1976; Volkan, 1976; Greenspan, 1977; Volkan & Akhtar, 1979) have addressed themselves to this issue, and have inquired into the development of the self-system and/or internalized object relations when examining psychopathology, applying the structural theory when faced with the neurotic patient or the patient with high-level character structure, and a theory of the self (Kohut) and/or object relations theory when dealing with those who are fixated on the preoedipal level.

Kernberg (1978) justifies our search for a specialized psychoanalytic approach by stating that the use of the tripartite structural model with patients who have severe psychopathology, i.e., those with borderline personality organization, has led to puzzling and contradictory findings. First, such patients present a constellation of defense mechanisms centering around the dissociation of contradictory ego states (primitive splitting) rather than around repression. Second, they develop a form of transference that differs from the usual transference developments in better-functioning patients, evidencing contradictory ego states that "incorporate contradictory, primitive internalized object relations within an overall matrix that does not present a clear differentiation of ego, superego, and id" (Kernberg, 1978, p. 80). (Elsewhere, I examine the differences between these two types of transference in some detail [Volkan, 1981a]). Third, and perhaps this is the most important consideration, patients with severe psychopathology exhibit their impulses in a fashion that is unrepressed but which still reflects mutual dissociation in consciousness.

Although I apply the term established pathological mourning to a condition on the neurotic level, I believe that when examining it one must amplify structural theory by reference to issues of development and internalized object relations. The individual frozen in the work of mourning is regressed, and the basic issue of dealing with the representation of the dead activates aspects of object relations conflicts. It is not enough to analyze instinctual urges and the defenses against them; the nature of the representation of the dead and the corresponding self-representation of the patient, along with their respective affect dispositions, must be understood, and the conflicts pertaining to the relationship between them must be explored. But unlike the person with psychopathology at a lower than neurotic level, i.e., a borderline patient, object relations conflicts in the established pathological mourner are not generalized. What saves him from sinking into a borderline condition or psychotic state is his use of the mechanism of splitting on a high (neurotic) level. It is unfortunate that in psychoanalysis the same term is sometimes applied to different phenomena; thus I find it necessary here to differentiate this kind of splitting from other manifestations sometimes so designated.

High-level splitting

Lichtenberg and Slap (1973) review the various psychoanalytic applications of the term "splitting," including Freud's many different ways of using it. The term has recently come into widespread use, largely because of Kernberg's (1966, 1967, 1975, 1976) work and his findings concerning the borderline personality organization and narcissism. Persons exhibiting borderline personality organizations keep their contradictory or opposing self—and object units—with their respective affect dispositions—apart. The characteristic absence of any integrative ability of their primitive egos changes in function, becoming their basic defense mechanism. The term "splitting" as used in this context describes the maintenance of a separation between contradictory ego states, and thus a separation of "all good" self- and object representations, invested with libidinal drive derivatives, from "all bad" units, invested with aggressive drive derivatives. To distinguish this kind of lower-level splitting from the high-level splitting characteristic of established pathological mourning I denote it as "primitive splitting" (Volkan, 1975a, 1976, 1981a). High-level splitting in this context refers to divided *ego functions* rather than divided *ego states*: contradictory *ego responses* are kept apart, responses that are related to a compromise accommodation to impulse-defense constellations.

In 1927 Freud briefly described the case of two young men who, at the ages of two and ten, respectively, had lost their fathers. Although as adults they both knew that their fathers were dead, they behaved otherwise (although neither became psychotic). Freud referred to these two patients in trying to explain fetishism: the child knows that his mother has no penis but behaves as though she did have one. The ability to do so—the child's reply to a conflict with two contradictory reactions—Freud (1940) explained as an ego defense mechanism called "splitting." This type of splitting divides ego functions in the interest of protecting the ego from a global break with reality.

In the same way, the ego splitting of the person in established pathological mourning is selective, concerned only with the issue of the death that has taken place. The mourner maintains his contact with reality in the sense that he *knows* that the death has taken place but at the same time harbors a contradictory perception that allows him to behave as though the dead person were not lost, High-level splitting is thus *not* concerned with keeping apart contradictory ego states: splitting the representation of the dead along contradictory affective lines or doing the same with corresponding self-representations. The mourner on the neurotic level is capable of maintaining an integrated representation of the lost one. He may internalize and externalize only a part-object representation of the deceased, but this part is always congruent with the total representation. If, however, the mourner is functioning on a lower than neurotic level, using elements of primitive splitting as he mourns, the part-object representations of the deceased and the corresponding part self-representations become autonomous, so to speak, and cannot easily be fitted into representations of the total object or self. The situation is not always this simple, of course, since in some cases higher-level splitting is condensed with repressed lower-level splitting, and as further regression occurs, the lower-level splitting emerges from the shadows. Although the initial reaction to death usually includes higher-level splitting, the need to maintain splitting wears away when the initial stage of the mourning process is uncomplicated; that is, when in the work of mourning, the ego rather totally accepts the reality of the loss. If the work of mourning is complicated, however, if it is weighted, for example, with separation/castration anxiety, splitting is maintained.

Some patients can actually identify the point at which this splitting of ego functions begins. The mourner may have gazed at the corpse in full knowledge that it was a dead body but convinced himself that he saw perspiration on its brow as though life were still going on. Even when the ego perception that does not accord with the reality is not fully conscious, its existence may be inferred. I have noted the reflection of this situation in some of the repeating dreams reported by persons in established pathological mourning.

The defensive–adaptive processes of internalization and externalization foster the illusion of continuing contact with the deceased, thereby supporting the split-off functions of the ego in maintaining the belief that death has not occurred. The result is that splitting, internalization, and externalization contribute to the patient's continued existence in a limbo of uncertainty, although the dominant split-off ego functions that still test reality—those that protect the patient from going into a generalized psychosis—can, aided by repression, cover over aspects of this uncertainty so that it may be betrayed only by symptom formation or symbolic expression. The object relations approach, as an adjunct to the structural approach, becomes particularly useful when we examine the internalization and externalization processes.

Internalization

As noted, following Schafer (1968), I use the term internalization to encompass the act of introjection, the formation of an introject, and identification. The nature of the patient's internalization is crucial in determining his clinical picture. It is upon the issues of introjection, the introject, and the type of identification adopted that the distinctions between uncomplicated mourning, reactive depression, and established pathological mourning are based.

Uncomplicated mourning. In uncomplicated mourning a successful resolution of the grief process depends on a depersonified, healing identification with valued aspects of the deceased person. The uncomplicated mourner is able to discriminate realistically among the traits of the deceased and identify those he values positively in an assessment process that is unconscious. These traits are thus ego-syntonic, and identification with them is functional, leading to the enrichment of the mourner's self-concept and his ego functions.

Reactive depression. Depression in the mourning process results from an indiscriminate, total identification with an ambivalently regarded representation of the deceased. This representation of the deceased is completely assimilated in the mourner's self-concept. The patient has no gross identity change resulting from identification, unlike the psychotic individual, but his self-concept is nevertheless strongly affected. In that ego-alien traits of the dead person are necessarily identified with, the total and indiscriminate identification of depression is disruptive. The depressed mourner at once loves and hates the representation of the deceased that he has identified with, an ambivalence reflected in the simultaneous struggle between cherishing the self and wishing to destroy it.

Established pathological mourning. In established pathological mourning the mourner unconsciously *strives toward* healthy identification with the deceased by means of the introject. Identification has not yet occurred in the mourner, neither the total, disruptive identification with the deceased of full-blown depression, nor the enriching identification of the healthy mourner. The person in established pathological mourning thus maintains his introject of the deceased in a middle ground between healthy identification and neurotic depression. In that the introject exists as a stage prior to normal mourning or depression, it has the potential to eventuate in either of those conditions. It cannot eventuate in "normal" mourning until the introject is no longer ambivalently perceived. In the sense that the established pathological mourner chronically maintains the introject in the hope of resolving the ambivalence, he can be said to "strive toward" healthy identification. Unlike the depressed mourner, the established pathological mourner has not surrendered all hope of resolving the ambivalence. This is the real significance of the introject in established pathological mourning, and this is what distinguishes it from all other object representations. "The adult caught up in established pathological mourning is in a continuing but tenuous position between the processes of depression and those of uncomplicated mourning as he maintains his introjects" (Volkan, 1976, pp. 75–76).

The self-concept of the person with established pathological mourning is unchanged and/or is less influenced than it would be in depression, but the inner relatedness to the introject continues to absorb the ego's energy. Unlike the introject in psychosis, the internalized representation is consistent with other images of the deceased.

Where identification and introject overlap

Thus far in describing the two major chronic complications of the work of mourning, and showing how one leads to depression and the other to established pathological mourning, I emphasize total identification in the first state and the introject in the second. In practice, however, one must bear in mind that some patients who disruptively identify with a representation of the dead may at the same time maintain an introject. These are, metapsychologically speaking, mixed clinical cases. Moreover, there are cases in which—especially after treatment has begun—what has been metapsychologically and descriptively considered depression turns into established pathological mourning.

I have stated that the introject in established pathological mourning strives toward depersonification and healthy identification but, typically, falls short of it. There is empirical evidence that persons prone to established pathological mourning and to depression are orally dependent, but that the former have less severe superego characteristics; more study will be necessary to show fully why one category of patient develops established pathological mourning while the other goes into depression. In any case, in the treatment of some initially depressed mourners, identification sometimes becomes personified and reverts to an introject. The following clinical vignette will shed further light on this metapsychological understanding.

Martin was a physician in his early thirties, the pride and joy of the medical firm of which he had been for several years a member. He had been known as a family man devoted to his three children until his behavior suddenly changed: after an affair with his wife's best friend, he entered into liaisons with two of the firm's secretaries. When his wife heard about this she left him. As his medical associates watched him lose his serious devotion to his work and waste much time flirting, they urged him to seek psychotherapy.

In his first therapy hours Martin said that he was confused, that he truly loved his wife and wanted their marriage to continue, but that he could not help himself and felt driven to have affairs, about which he felt strongly conflicted. He broke down and wept as he spoke of his guilt and low self-esteem. I learned that the alteration in his behavior began after the accidental death of his youngest brother a year and a half earlier. When he first came to see me, he had had no conscious awareness of any connection between the death and his uncharacteristic behavior, nor did he attribute his present affective state to the loss. He was not referred to me as a man exhibiting complicated responses to the death of a loved one.

I learned that the brother had died in a motorcycle accident, and that Martin had been sent for. Because he was the oldest brother and a physician, the family had depended on him to take care of the necessary arrangements, including the funeral. The dead man had been a Don Juan, and his parents had taken delighted pride in his sexual exploits—so much so that they had found it appropriate to put a Playboy Club key in his hand as he lay in his coffin, to be buried with him. Martin's last remembrance of his brother was the sight of the key placed in the dead hands crossed on his chest. Further therapy revealed that Martin identified with his ambivalently regarded brother, identified, that is, with what he considered the "bad" aspect of him as well as the "good," and thus felt obliged to carry on his lifestyle of hedonistic sexual activity. I would call his state one of depression.

As Martin came to understand the mechanism involved in his behavior pattern, disruptive identification with his brother came to an end. He then experienced an inner presence—an introject of his brother, whose face he felt to be buried within his chest. He sensed a differentiation between himself and the part representation of his brother, and whenever during this time he felt the urge to have some new encounter with a woman ripen into a full-blown affair, he felt anger. He told me that he now recognized that it was his dead brother in him that impelled him toward each new affair. As his anger grew he pointed an accusing finger at his chest and screamed at the representation of the dead man, "Why don't you leave me alone?"

The role of merging in internalization

My major interest in this chapter has been to describe identification that follows upon the formation of an introject. Schafer (1968), however, has reminded us that all identifications are not necessarily the end result of an introject's conversion into identification. Some are the end results of the merging of self-representation with object representation. We see this often among psychotics, but I have also seen it in persons in established pathological mourning (Volkan, 1972). In such cases, the merging is either transient or traceable to some event such as a death anniversary, which has caused the patient's longing for reunion to dominate his dread of it.

Schafer states that in merging it is

> ... as if self and object freely substitute for each other, as if interest in individuation has been pretty much suspended, and as if, ultimately, it is undifferentiated unity that is experienced or sought rather than the relation of one person to another.
>
> One patient, for example, reported that it was as if she were her mother when she yelled at her own children. She made it clear that she was not making an intellectual comparison and was not speaking of resemblance; nor did she mean that her mother was speaking through her as an alien presence (an introject). She meant that at that moment she was her mother and that, accordingly, she felt disoriented as to her subjective self. (p. 152)

In 1972, focusing only on merging such as one sees in the mourner whose work of mourning has become complicated, I wrote:

> The clinical difference between relating to an introject and actually merging with the deceased is clear. The introject is regarded as if it has existence of its own. In merging, however, the mourner loses awareness of his differentiation from the one he mourns, in a total but temporary identification with him. This transient experience is usually abrupt, and many patients have spontaneously used the word "merging" in speaking of it. An example can be seen in the patient who, throughout a therapy hour, feels that the tone of his voice and the gestures of his hands are not only his but those of the one he mourns. It is usual for such an experience to be "shaken off," only to reappear suddenly on occasion. (p. 216)

The merging type of identification in established pathological mourning will be the focus of my consideration when I examine the occurrence of suicide in this condition.

Externalization and projection

Not unlike Zinner and Shapiro (1972) and Berg (1977), I have used the term externalization to encompass not only the projection of aspects of the self but also the projection of internalized object representations, and, indeed, ego ideal and superego elements as well, expanding the concept to a degree perhaps beyond the intention of Novick and Kelly (1970) (Volkan, 1979a, 1981a). An important aspect of the psychodynamics of the person in established pathological mourning can be best understood, I believe, by applying this broadest sense of the concept of externalization and the view of such externalizations as being aided by and condensed with projections. The high degree of utilization of externalization and projection in established pathological mourning differentiates it from its sister condition, reactive depression following a loss by death.

The linking object is evidence of this kind of externalization. It stands symbolically for aspects of both self- and object representations as well as elements of the ego ideal and superego. It functions as an external meeting ground for these representations, permitting the illusion of reunion to be kept alive. At the same time, of course, the phenomenon of the linking object allows the person in established pathological mourning to maintain the possibility of psychologically "killing" the object, the representation of which, kept at a distance from himself, he has not yet identified with. The patient distances his linking object as though those of his ego functions that still test reality need to avoid contamination by split-off self-representations in conflicted relatedness with ambivalently regarded object representations.

Since the person in established pathological mourning exhibits higher-level splitting, keeping ambivalent contact with the representation of the dead internally through the introject and externally through the linking object, it is necessary in each case to understand in what kind of relation wish and conflict exist; this will reveal much about the patient's level of character pathology. Some patients on the neurotic level do not "kill" the representation of the dead because they still want oedipal gratification from it. Nevertheless, they suffer from superego guilt concerning the *wish* to "kill" it.

Suicide in established pathological mourning

Loewenstein (1957) states that, while suicide more frequently "gratifies aggressive tendencies toward a hated object or fulfills the demands of the superego," it may sometimes result from "a wish to return to the mother" and to achieve "complete reunion" with her. Loewenstein cites as an example of the latter situation the longing for death on the part of an older person in whom "regression to earlier, pregenital stages of libidinal development" occurs with "the gradual disappearance of genital gratification." Such regression "may bring with it a wish for complete reunion with the mother, for eternal sleep." Loewenstein notes that both of these purposes are served by certain suicides (p. 212).

Suicide may occur in many different diagnostic categories as well as in a diversity of personality organizations, and may have different meanings for different victims (Pollock, 1975a). Nevertheless, it is possible that all of its forms—except the one described by Kubie (1964) as organically determined—can be traced back to, or will at least be contaminated by, one of the two main psychological types—the melancholic (superego–ego struggle) or the reunion (merging) type. In the psychotic, for example, the magical merging of fragments of self- and object representations may be contaminated with fantasies of afterlife reunion that may make suicide seem inviting; on the other hand, in obsessional neurosis one may see suicides that reflect the superego–ego struggle as manifested in the melancholic type.

The empirical evidence from my clinical research indicates that the likelihood of suicide is not as great in established pathological mourning as it is in reactive depression. Furthermore, I maintain that the mourner is *protected* from attempting suicide when he has a stable linking object through which he can maintain external contact with the representation of the dead, and a stable introject that enables him to maintain internal contact with it. Thus, should the person in established pathological mourning attempt in spite of this to kill himself, it will be in the search for a "magical reunion," with a goal quite other than that of the "melancholic suicide" of depressed individuals described in the previous chapter. In comparing the two main types of suicide, one should keep in mind the distinction I have drawn between the end results of internalization—and externalization—in established pathological mourning and reactive depression. The act of suicide in reactive depression is an effort to solve a defensive, disruptive conflict of identification. The aggression directed toward the representation of the dead person results in aggression directed toward the self—which now includes the object representation.

In established pathological mourning, the situation contrasts with that of reactive depression inasmuch as the process of internalization is fixated at the level at which an introject is formed: the object representation of the deceased falls short of being assimilated in the self-concept of the bereaved and thus is not brought into play in the ego–superego system as much as it would have been in depression. Such an introject creates much less havoc than an "in toto" identification. It permits the relationship between the mourner and the one he mourns to continue, as it were, internally. The sadism that might have been involved in an intersystemic struggle has been absorbed by and contained within the introject. Moreover, the fostering of an unassimilated introject of the deceased, with its boundaries maintained, is like keeping the dead person alive. Thus, guilt feelings that would have arisen from "killing" the dead individual are reduced.

The introject's protective function in staving off suicide of the depressive type is reinforced by the linking object (and/or linking phenomenon), with its external reference. Through the utilization of the linking object or phenomenon, the bereaved person has the illusion of contact with the representation of the deceased and, more important, the illusion of control over his existence: he maintains the ability to "kill" or "not to kill" the representation. This illusion absorbs aggressive drives as well as feelings of guilt. It is as though the mourner were saying, "I am in contact with the one I lost, and I can bring him back to life; I need feel no guilt, since my aggression did not destroy him; hence, I do not need to unleash the sadism of my superego against myself." Aggressively determined contact with the dead is, as it were, locked away in a drawer, just as the linking object is usually kept locked up—or at least "distanced" from the mourner himself.

A case described by Buckman and Greyson (1977) illustrates how the development of a linking phenomenon—in this case a religious vision—protected the patient from suicidal efforts he had previously engaged in. The patient was in his early forties when his mother died. His father had died in the patient's arms many years earlier, and he had lost a sister in an automobile accident a short time before his mother's death. He had kept his mother's room unaltered after her death, as though he had been able by this maneuver to "freeze" time. It was obvious that he had complications in his mourning. Within ten months of his mother's death he had made three attempts to kill himself.

Buckman and Greyson describe his third such attempt. He had gone to the place where his parents' graves lay side by side and had sat there for hours. He had then stretched out upon the grave of his mother, positioning his head over her heart. A rifle held between his legs was aimed upward at his chin. As he pulled the trigger, he felt that the whole world was full of a rosy light and he saw Jesus Christ standing in a lush meadow with his arms outstretched toward him. Behind Jesus, he could see his dead mother, father, and sister. His mother cried, "Here comes my son!" As this vision disappeared, the patient became aware of a pool of blood beneath his head. He managed to crawl into his truck and drive some distance for help. His injuries included multiple fractures of the right mandible and maxilla. Within a few days, another vision of Jesus and his parents and sister reappeared, this time at the window of his room in the hospital.

What is interesting about this patient is that after seeing these "visions" he no longer had suicidal thoughts. The visions seemed to satisfy his need to know "where she was." I believe that, among other possible explanations for his relief, these religious occurrences put him in contact with his dead others, functioning as linking phenomena. He not only was relieved of his despair and depression, but continued to be preoccupied with religion.

Merging and suicide

I have described identifications that, unlike "in toto" identifications, result from the merging of the mourner's self-representation with the representation of the dead object. In persons with established pathological mourning, the longing for reunion with the dead, accompanied by the dread of such a possibility, is constant. Under certain circumstances, however, the dread loses its power, so to speak, and the mourner attempts suicide, which represents magical reunion. In his attempt to unite with the dead person the mourner has an impulse to claim all of his characteristics, including the fact of death. He sees that his merging will be stabilized if he is dead himself, and that the feeling of reunion will thus become permanent. Since magic is involved, and since death under these circumstances in unconsciously viewed by the mourner as a simple matter of reunion, the attempt at self-destruction seemingly does not oppose the pleasure principle, nor challenge the survival of either party. (Freud [1915] held that "in the unconscious every one of us is convinced of his own immortality" [p. 289].) The fantasy of reunion as a psychological determinant of suicide is described by Friedlander (1940), Loewenstein (1957), Wahl (1957), Pollock (1975a), and others.

My own observation is that the state of reunion identification is less stable than that of identification reached by means of the formation of an introject. Reunion identifications may suddenly appear with the stimulation of an anniversary, and as suddenly disappear. Although transient, they can have deadly consequences, as in the anniversary suicide of the person in established pathological mourning.

Millie's wish for reunion with her dead father

A 22-year-old black woman attempted suicide by taking sleeping pills in the early morning hours of October 24th, the date set for her wedding. Her recollection of what she had experienced just before and during her suicide attempt was recorded as soon as she was released from the emergency room and was able to talk to me. I will consolidate her report here with information obtained throughout her treatment.

Millie's father died when she was fourteen. Six years earlier he had taken a job in a distant city, returning home infrequently. Millie lived with her mother, her siblings, and other relatives, nourishing a secret admiration for her absent father, an admiration that she could not confess to those at home, especially her mother, lest she hurt the feelings of those already upset by her father's desertion.

When Millie was two years old, the house in which the family was living had burned. A somewhat older brother had died in the fire and the mother had been badly burned, requiring a long period of convalescence in a hospital. This event was a turning point for the family, bringing about considerable domestic disturbance. Millie felt that the severe scarring her mother had suffered had contributed to her father's withdrawal from his family. When her grieving mother returned home from the hospital to Millie and a one-year-old infant, Millie prematurely assumed an "adult" role, becoming obsessional in her daily habits and submissive to mother figures. She had a less than altruistic desire to save such figures; indeed, her desire to save them was selfish, since the goal of saving them was to enable them to give her the mothering she longed for. She secretly nourished rebellious feelings against those she tried to save.

Millie's image of her father was split. One representation was largely idealized, to be searched for. While this representation was allowed to remain conscious, it was accompanied by a devalued image of her father that Millie had to maintain if she were to get along with her mother. Consequently, after her father's death, his total representation could not be "killed"; it had to be idealized, on the one hand, in order to save Millie from the domination of mothering persons, while, at the same time, it had to be degraded, so that Millie's life with her mother would not become conflictual.

Millie was never quite certain about the exact date of her father's death because there was an acknowledged error on his death certificate; she believed it was either the 21st or 22nd of October. She was sure that burial had taken place on the 24th. She had anniversary reactions each year for eight years on the three meaningful days. Interestingly, she was always asymptomatic on the, 23rd, just before and just after a day of difficulty. Her anniversary reactions included increased preoccupation with the various images of the dead man, with whom she was only "normally" preoccupied at other times of the year. Her yearning for him would become acute at this special time, and it would awaken the memory of his whipping her as a teenager for expressing her jealousy of a woman her father had had in the city where he worked. The "bad" images would soon succumb, however, to his "idealized" images, and she would experience powerful feelings of longing for him.

At other times of the year she exhibited typical, though not exaggerated, elements of established pathological mourning. She had dreams of trying to save or "kill" her father. In one repeating dream she walked down a road to meet him, just as she had done in reality when he had come on a visit. She would see him at a distance, sometimes clearly but sometimes in a blurred way. When she approached him, she would awaken with anxiety.

She recalled having attended his funeral and knowing and not knowing that his body was in the coffin being lowered into the ground; she had maintained these opposing thoughts throughout the years. She had a typical linking object, her father's photograph, which she kept secretly in a Bible. It was a special picture that "did not belong in the family album." Although she knew exactly where it was, she refrained from looking at it. Once when she was alone, she did look at it and imagined her father coming to life, which made her feel anxious. If she spent the night with a friend, as she sometimes did, she would take the Bible with her; she never opened it, but having it with her reassured her as to the safety of her linking object. When Millie left home to get a job, she took the picture with her, hiding it again so that she could maintain a psychological distance from it.

The eighth anniversary of her father's death, the 24th of October, fell on a Saturday, just as it had done in the year of his death. Months before that date Millie had made arrangements to be married on the 24th without being conscious of the significance of the critical four-day period. There was no sign of depression, nor any sign of unusual new symptom formation. She spent the evening before the date set for the wedding with her fiancé, who returned her to her apartment late at night. Once alone, she realized that she had forgotten the anniversary of her father's death and that no one aware of the date's significance had thought to bring it to her attention. When she went to bed, she was flooded with images of her father, all idealized. She longed for his permission to marry and wanted very much to talk to him. She later described how she had then merged with him, becoming uncertain as to whether she were her father or herself. Her gestures and style of walk suggested that they were her father's. These episodes of merging came and went repeatedly, accompanied by the conviction that if she were dead she would really find him. She remembered having some pills in her bathroom and she took them in order to die and unite with her father. There was no anger in her awareness, only a wish for reunion.

After taking the pills she lay in bed and felt the approach of death. She thought that soon she would be able to talk to her father. Her landlady entered the room by a coincidence, and although Millie saw her, she could not move and remained in the "land of death" searching for her father. The landlady called an ambulance.

In Millie's case, anniversary reaction, combined with her wish to marry and find a new man in her life, served as a "releaser" for the suicide attempt. In her description of the suicide attempt, it is clear that her merging experiences, as well as her wish for reunion with her dead father, were conscious. In other patients, however, such fantasies may not be accompanied by the conscious experience of merging.

CHAPTER 6

An example of the linking object: Othello's handkerchief

My understanding of complications in the work of mourning and of the linking object was furthered by the disclosure of a young athlete that a certain handkerchief had magical properties for him. He had taken it from a drawer in his father's bedroom immediately after his father's death, and it had become the linking object in which his self-representation and the representation of his father could meet.

This chapter centers around this athlete's case report. I show how I collected data about the handkerchief during his treatment. The handkerchief, by absorbing impulses, wishes, fantasies—and the defenses against them—in the young man's interaction with his father's representation, was a serviceable linking object.

By means of the handkerchief, the young man was able to maintain the illusion of absolute control over his dead father's representation, and the illusion that he could "kill" or "not kill" that representation. In this way, he was able to stay in a kind of limbo with respect to his mourning, so as to be able to deal—however ineffectively—with conflicts centering upon his unresolved oedipal problems.

The handkerchief in the story of Othello

The young athlete whose story I will tell here let me know that a certain handkerchief held magical properties for him. I learned that it was his linking object, a connection between his own representation and his father's. I came to speak of it as "Othello's handkerchief' for reasons that will become clear with the unfolding of this patient's story.

In Shakespeare's *Othello*, the misplacing of a handkerchief "with some wonder" in it triggers a murder. It had been a gift to Desdemona from her husband, Othello, who explained that it had belonged to his mother, who got it from an Egyptian woman who made charms.

> … she told her, while she kept it,
> 'Twould make her amiable, and subdue my father
> Entirely to her love; but if she lost it,
> Or made a gift of it, my father's eye
> Should hold her loathly ....
> ... take heed on't,
> Make it a darling like your precious eye;
> To lose't or give't away, were such perdition
> As nothing else could match ....
> A sybil ...
> In her prophetic fury sew'd the work:
> The worms were hallow'd that did breed the silk;
> And it was dyed in mummy, which the skillful
> Conserved of maidens' hearts. (Act Ill, Scene IV)

Although Desdemona so prizes the handkerchief that "she reserves it evermore about her, to kiss and talk to" (Act III, Scene III), it is lost and appropriated by her maid, who gives it to Iago. Iago plants it in the chamber of Cassio, whose lover picks it up and flaunts it unwittingly before Othello, confirming his false conviction that his wife is faithless and must be destroyed.

In the case of this young athlete, I learned that his father had often recited a version of Othello's story, with sly emphasis on the role of the handkerchief as an expression of his own murderous rage against his unfaithful wife. I will show how and why his son came to use one of his father's handkerchiefs as a linking object.

Background of the case

Jerry was in his early twenties when I first saw him. He had been the star of a college basketball team before undergoing a drastic personality change following the death of his father a little less than two years before he became my patient. He had elected to drop basketball the year after his father's death, and had adopted a "hippie" lifestyle and turned to drugs. When he gave up this extreme behavior, as he did rather shortly, and returned to competitive sport in school, he found that basketball honors had gone to new players with whom he found it difficult to compete. He no longer qualified for the first team, but the coach would occasionally let him play when a first-stringer needed rest.

Jerry had formerly been an excellent student, receiving some academic honors. After his "hippie" period had ended, he was once again beginning to achieve well academically when an event took place that led to his hospitalization. The team was on the road, playing a traditional rival in a nearby state. The teams were neck and neck in the last seconds of play when, after a time out, Jerry managed to get into the game without the coach's approval. As he later explained, he was "killing the coach's authority." He took the ball all the way to the opposing court, shot, and missed. His team lost, and the coach was angry at Jerry, who was himself in such a fury by then that he went out of control and had to be taken to the hospital. After calming down there for a few days, he became my patient.

He was a handsome young man, tall and muscular, with curly blond hair. I learned from him that his good looks came mostly from his mother, who had been considered a beauty and quite a "catch" for his father, a man who lacked her advantages. He had pampered his good-looking wife, calling her a "babe." The couple had had three children, of whom Jerry was the youngest. His brother and sister were respectively five and three years older.

Jerry perceived his first years of life as having been warm and secure. The family's fortunes had slipped, however, when Jerry was four, and the subsequent changes in his environment had affected Jerry greatly. His father had lost his job because the company that employed him had not been doing well, and the father had, in any case, been no great success as a salesman. The family had then had to move to another city.

Never recovering from this blow to his self-esteem, the father had continued to go downhill, and as the family moved from place to place, both parents began to drink heavily.

Jerry was in his pubertal years when the family finally settled in a small town in which it was possible for them to seem more prosperous than their rather unassuming neighbors; they had a sizable home and a good car and clung to the illusion of superiority possible for big fish in a very small pond. This type of adaptation—the concealment of deficiency—had become Jerry's modus operandi even before puberty. The parents drank heavily off and on, but each kept a job. While drinking, the mother would sometimes tease her husband sexually in front of her son, who found it frightening as well as exciting to see her remove her slacks and ask her husband if he wanted to take her. Earlier incestuous strivings were kept alive in Jerry, who felt guilt as well as rage at his father's inability to make the mother stop behaving seductively before his son, and his failure to help the boy repress more fully his incestuous desires.

Jerry's father had an artistic, "soft" side, being a good pianist and a ready vocalist at social or church gatherings. As a child he had been called a "sissy," and his wife and son certainly perceived him as being a less than markedly virile man. Still, he had succeeded in marrying a highly desirable woman—although not without becoming her slave—and he strenuously encouraged both his sons as well as his daughters to acquire masculine strength, the epitome of which in his view was athletic prowess. Although the relationship between father and son was ambivalent at best, Jerry's athletic prowess was to compensate for his father's deficiency as a man. His mother unconsciously conveyed to Jerry that she would prefer him, as a "he-man," to his weak father.

Jerry's basketball skill began to attract attention by the time he was 13. After puberty he divided his time between studying and playing basketball, being aware even then of the solace that his success in competitive sport brought him when he felt humiliated and hurt by the alcoholism of his parents. When his father came to a game drunk, only the applause of the spectators could ease his hurt.

When Jerry was 14, he was kicked by another player during a basketball game and sustained a severe injury to a testicle, which became very painful and turned purple. Emergency surgery was necessary, and as he recovered from anesthesia, Jerry was faced by a smiling surgeon who confided that he had taken out one testicle and “dropped it into a pan, “adding that it had looked” like a scrambled egg.” Jerry was never to forget this unfortunate description or the surgeon’s expression as he offered it. In view of his family history, I suspect that even without this traumatic event Jerry would have had difficulty in handling the inevitable mourning for the abandoned parental images of childhood that leads in adolescence to the second individuation phase (Blos, 1979). In any event, the loss of the testicle kept alive in him his childhood oedipal struggle and his childhood castration fears and re-awakened anger over the notion that weak men could not “tame” seductive women. Since he was unable to disengage libidinal and aggressive cathexes of his childhood images of his parents, he kept the parents of adolescence as representative of the earlier parents of his oedipal years. In this way, he could, however unsuccessfully, struggle to resolve his re-awakened oedipal wishes.

After the loss of his testicle, Jerry’s mother, who had offered him sex education in a way calculated to stimulate him when he was eight or nine years old, lectured him about impotence, hinting that this was now likely to be his fate. Jerry handled this by strengthening the narcissistic defenses he had developed in response to castration anxiety and the humiliation caused by his parents’ drinking, deciding that he would become such an outstanding basketball player, for example, that no one would ever suspect he had but one testicle. The only substantial help he had in his distress came from a high school counselor who was also an athlete. Taking Jerry under his wing, he confided that he too had but one testicle and pointed out that in spite of this deficiency he was married and had begotten three children. His trust in this counselor relieved Jerry’s distress considerably and made him better able to tolerate the situation at home.

One night during Jerry’s last year in high school his mother announced to her husband in Jerry’s presence that she had twice recently had intercourse with a man in whom she had become interested. Her husband seemed unable to express his rage directly and undertook to do so symbolically, devoting himself to writing and revising his own brief version of the story of Othello. When he got home at night, he engaged in a ritual reading of the story, his performance culminating in his version of Othello's cry—"Fetch me that handkerchief!" He thus indirectly expressed his murderous feelings toward his wife by invoking the words of Othello at the moment before he strangled Desdemona. Handkerchiefs then took on an enormous importance in the household, the father maintaining the guise of a Shakespearean character and blowing his nose noisily in them, the mother always seeming to be washing and ironing them.

Two years after his mother's revelation about her affair, and some time after Jerry left home for college, it was found that his father had cancer. Two years later he died. While Jerry believed that his mother was responsible for his father's death, this belief only covered over his own murderous oedipal attitude toward the dead man. His oedipal wishes surfaced only symbolically, as when he tried to "kill the coach's authority" by his unwarranted entry into play in the basketball game on the night he was taken to the hospital. Interestingly enough, he had been playing against the same rival team two years earlier, just after his father's death and just before his funeral. He was unconscious of wanting to be rid of his father when he pushed into the game that night, but, as he recalled later, he *was* aware of wanting him back. It is my impression that this effort to "kill the coach's authority" was condensed with an attempt to complete his work of mourning by "killing" his dead father. But Jerry had so many unfinished developmental issues to complete that he was unable to do so. He continued to relate to his dead father's representation with great ambivalence, wanting it on the one hand to be weak, and on the other, to be strong.

I will offer here a brief formulation as to why Jerry could not "kill" his dead father's representation and as to why he continued to be preoccupied with it. The material gained from the therapy hours that led to this formulation will be reported subsequently.

Jerry had unconsciously equated the loss of his testicle at the conclusion of his pubertal years with punishment—in the form of castration—for his incestuous desires for his mother. Of course, in reality, she had helped keep such desires alive in him, and had also helped to sustain his fantasy of an oedipal triumph over a weak and effeminate oedipal father. While he liked thinking of this triumph, it also made him feel guilty so that it seemed appropriate to him that he be punished for it.

One way in which he could undo the loss of his testicle was, paradoxically, to keep alive the image of a strong oedipal father, with whom it remained possible to continue the oedipal struggle in which he had been engaged before he lost the testicle. In other words, as long as he was engaged in the oedipal struggle—as long as his victory had not taken place—castration was postponed. Moreover, the continuation of the struggle offered hope that a strong father would defeat him, allay his guilt, and offer him a reprieve from punishment—indeed, replace his lost testicle. Through "identification with the aggressor" (A. Freud, 1936), he could even identify with the representation of the strong father able to "tame" the mother. She would then no longer be a seductress to inflame his incestuous desires and expose him again to punishment.

Thus, after his father's death, Jerry maintained the conflicting representations of his father so as to replay the different aspects of the oedipal struggle that in his father's lifetime had been so imperfectly resolved. He longed for the return of the strong oedipal father (for the reasons noted above) at the same time as this longing coexisted, or alternated, with the desire to "kill" the weak father so as to taste the oedipal triumph once again. But while "killing" the father would have helped resolve his mourning, it was also far too dangerous for Jerry, since he could only expect punishment to follow, just as it had followed (seemingly) on his oedipal victory. The solution, then, was to stay in limbo, to remain capable of either "killing" or "not killing" the oedipal father to whom he was so ambivalently related. He selected a linking object to serve as a meeting ground on which he could continue his attempts to resolve the historical ambivalence, and which gave him the illusion of being safely suspended between "killing" and "not killing" his father's representation. It will be seen that other symbolic meanings were condensed in this linking object as well.

Although Jerry's case illustrates many manifestations of established pathological mourning, including preoccupation with the hope and dread of bringing the dead back to life, he did not disclose the existence of an introject during the time I treated him. One wonders if he would have done so had I had more time with him. But he invoked the magic of his linking object so often in his daily life—while at the same time observing the customary distancing from it—that I believe the expected introject was absorbed in externalized fashion with it.

He also exhibited disruptive identification with certain images of his dead father. Thus, at least in a metapsychological sense, he had elements of depression in a picture predominantly of established pathological mourning. A lowering of self-esteem was not evident on the clinical level, however. Jerry's mourning had been complicated from the first stages by his inability to feel appropriate anger toward the father who had deserted him. His early complications permeated what followed and became chronic, and when he was beset by other losses, his father's death remained his dominant concern.

Treatment

Jerry spent 118 therapeutic hours with me before circumstances forced termination. I saw him four times a week except for unavoidable interruptions caused by the cancellation of appointments. Although he was on the psychiatric ward of the hospital, he came to my office for his hours. In reviewing his treatment, I will emphasize the sequential disclosures upon which my formulation is based rather than the technical aspects of his treatment.

Jerry was polite and somewhat anxious during our first hour, in complete contrast to his bizarre and terrifying outburst at the basketball game. He stated that his problems had begun after his father's death, and told of his mother's affair, his father's lung cancer, and the attempt of each parent to commit suicide after his mother's revelation of her infidelity. Once a loud report had brought him into a room in which his mother was holding a revolver that she had just fired into the wall. Another time he had found his father trying to asphyxiate himself by running the motor of his car in a closed garage. Jerry had flung open the doors of the car and cried out, "What are you doing?" Neither attempt was ever openly referred to in the home, but they remained heavy secrets on the young man's heart.

During his first hours with me Jerry would catch himself using gestures like his father's. I believe that he was having transient episodes of identification with his father's representation, identification of the merger type that I have previously described (see Chapter 5). He also recited Shakespearean passages as his father had been in the habit of doing. He reported that after the death he had abandoned a relationship he had had with a girl, feeling that his father had disapproved of her. She had married someone else, and it was then that he had begun living in the "hippie" manner popular among young people at the time.

Soon after his treatment had begun, a new girlfriend, who lived elsewhere, came to visit Jerry and I got a glimpse of his extreme aggression. He shouted declarations of his love for her in my office and expressed a strong desire to kill her—or himself—because of that love. The girl's father had died ten months earlier, and I sensed that Jerry had identified with her in her loss and that this identification was included in his "love" for her. He had once felt great discomfort sharing a picnic with this girl, her mother, and her mother's male friend. I saw in this situation a reminder of his own mother's affair, but I did not share this observation with him.

I noticed that in several respects Jerry had accommodated to the macho model his "sissy" father had urged upon him, but that he had also assimilated his father's "soft" appreciation of art and literature. Soon he wrote a short story in which a girl who represented his girlfriend "sustained a fall" so severe that it caused her death. I pointed out how he had made his girlfriend a "fallen woman" in the tale, and it was in association to this that Jerry told me more about his mother and his feeling that she had killed his father. His rage against the fallen woman contained elements of defense against an incestuous love for her. He had taken a trip with his mother soon after his father's death, mother and son occupying the same hotel room. He had been flooded with incestuous thoughts about her, which may, of course, have been occasioned by her behavior. That night he went out and found a woman to sleep with and when he returned he found his guitar smashed. It occurred to him that his mother might have smashed it out of jealousy. The recital of this incident made him recall that he had found his mother very seductive in his childhood.

Jerry then reported his father's interest in literature and gave an account of his writing a short version of Othello. It was then that I learned about his linking object, the handkerchief that I will describe later. Since our next session came near the second anniversary of his father's death, I began hearing more about the circumstances of this tragic event. Jerry had lost his maternal grandparents during the two years before his father's death, and had attended the funeral of each.

He had seen the coffins lowered into the ground and the earth being sprinkled over them. He had not, however, witnessed his father's burial, going only to the chapel service. The day after his father's death he had driven hundreds of miles to rejoin his basketball team for a crucial game, then made a long, hurried, and frantic drive back for his father's funeral. He had then left again immediately after the service to play against an even more distant rival team, the same school against which he was playing two years later when he went berserk after "killing the coach's authority." His brother and sister were in town for the funeral but left quickly; his brother's wife was at home awaiting the birth of her baby.

The brother's wife gave birth a few weeks after the funeral, and the baby was named after its dead grandfather. The infant died at two months, and Jerry had again to make another frantic ride to attend the funeral, which involved him in some macabre responsibilities. The family had the baby's coffin placed in Jerry's car, asking him to take it to the cemetery where Jerry's father lay so that the baby could be buried next to the man whose name he bore. Jerry and his mother then embarked on a six-hour trip with the dead baby in its coffin beside them. They stopped for a meal, leaving the dead infant in the parked car. In the restaurant, the mother proposed that they have the grave of her husband opened and the tiny coffin place in the same grave. After Jerry left his mother at home, he took the coffin to the cemetery and carried out her instructions. The opening of his father's grave seemed to have symbolic importance for Jerry such that one was obliged to believe that he thought that his father would get up and walk away once the grave was opened. As he reached this point in his story, he was overcome by the thought that his father might not be dead after all. He was upset to remember that he had not in fact seen the lowering of his father's casket into the ground, and he thought that it might be well to open the grave once again so that he could see his father's skeleton and assure himself that he really was dead. He then reported that his legs felt cold and, in a transient identification with the dead man, sensed himself turning into a zombie. When he was finally able to relax he spoke of yet another death that had taken place in the family about a year before his father's death. The infant whose body he had carried about in his car was the second son of his brother to die in infancy; the first had been named after Jerry himself.

Further reports about his father's dying hours filled the next few sessions; these will be described in connection with his linking object. Jerry's accounts ended with him sobbing and lamenting that his father had left him before he could show him how to "tame women." I learned that his father had been his mother's slave and that family vacations had always been spent with her side of the family. After losing his father, Jerry had searched for a strong male figure to identify with. He had hoped for support from his basketball coach similar to that he had received from his high school counselor but had found his coach interested only in his athletic prowess, and not in him personally. Jerry felt that his present coach was using him.

At the next session he was calm and told me a dream he had had about President Kennedy, who was by then dead in reality. He had seen Kennedy engaged in a life-and-death struggle and had wanted to help him. This sort of dream is typical among people with established pathological mourning, except that the person mourned usually appears undisguised, whereas in Jerry's dream the one he mourned appeared symbolically as the assassinated President. Kennedy, of course, stood for the strong father that Jerry still searched for. In a second dream, Jerry reported having seen a tableau of frozen ground. This, too, is a dream typical of established pathological mourning, as I have pointed out (see Chapter 4). During the second month of his treatment, Jerry told me about a brief affair he had with a nationally known folk singer whom he had met a year after his father's death. He had been anxious during their first night together lest she think that, because of his lost testicle, he was less than a man. But she was too befuddled by dope and alcohol to care. I thought she represented to Jerry the drunk and seductive mother who had preferred him to other men. Since the singer enjoyed enormous popularity, Jerry felt that his association with her had brought him reflected glory in compensation for his being, at the time, out of basketball. He had remained in a castrated state, as it were, for a year after his father's death, his excellence at basketball, you will remember, being his chief means of denying the knowledge of his lost testicle to others. When the singer accepted him over other competitors for her favor, he had once again, at least for a while, an oedipal triumph. He withdrew from his hippie lifestyle and returned to basketball. She soon left him, however, and shortly thereafter died of an overdose. It seemed that those he chose to "use" for the resolution of his unfinished oedipal drama, and to allay his castration anxieties, were doomed to die, making his aggression literally murderous.

Talk about his affair reminded Jerry of his fantasy that his father could leave him one of his own testicles when he died. I will elaborate on this fantasy and its connection with his linking object later. Significantly, this reminiscence led him to feel sadness, a good prognostic sign. He then spontaneously sought out a religious leader of his own persuasion and went to an appropriate place to pray and say aloud, "May my father rest in peace!" During his hours with me he cried aloud and lamented, "He is dead! He is dead!" He reported dreaming of being helped by someone with an accent. (I speak English with an accent.) He called me a "brilliant man," but after reflection indicated doubts about my being a "terrible Turk." The ambivalence he had felt toward his father was beginning to appear in his feelings toward me.

My sense that we were making some progress was unexpectedly disappointed at this time. When I had begun work with Jerry, he had been told that his treatment as well as his hospital costs would be largely paid for by a college fund for athletes. Now it appeared that the funds from this source were less generous than had been supposed, and Jerry was under pressure to leave the hospital. This made him anxious, and he became angry at his nurses, while at the same time viewing me as a strong man able to find a solution to his dilemma. He reported a dream of being in a flower garden, where a woman picked up small buds and squeezed the juices out of them. The day residue of this dream may be found in Jerry's sense of being squeezed by women (nurses) and being left unprotected by a weak father (the sponsor) while expecting rescue from a strong father (me). His associations led to a memory of his father complaining to him, "What shall I do, fuck the flowers?" It was the first time his father had used an obscene word with him. The memory dated from the time soon after his father had learned of his illness, when Jerry felt that his father had been in a passive rage, either at having become impotent or at having been refused by his wife. Jerry then reported that his mother had sent flowers to the funeral home at the time of his father's death and had attached to them a card saying that they were from Jerry and herself. After "killing" her husband, Jerry saw her as "uniting" herself with her son. In this context, the dream's "squeezing" can be viewed as sexual stimulation, on the one hand, and a form of castration, on the other; reflecting the basic complications in the oedipal situation. Without a strong father, the representation of whom he needed to keep "alive," his mother would squeeze the juices out of him just as she had done to his father. A stimulating thought on the one hand, but how dangerous! I interpreted his need to have a strong father nearby so that he would not be at the mercy of a stimulating and powerful woman, but I made no direct reference to the sexual aspects involved. I told him further that this was one of the reasons he was unable to let his father "die."

Talk about flowers led him to reveal more about his hospital stay in a flower-filled room at the time he had lost his testicle. He then spoke of an even earlier stay in a hospital at age five, when the death of another patient in the ward, a little black girl, had exposed him to the concept of death for the first time. I will elaborate on this incident in discussing Jerry's linking object later in the chapter.

Soon I had to cancel two hours with him. In the last session before this interruption, he told me that he had broken off his relationship with his girlfriend. I saw this as a defensive move against my leaving that resulted from his fear of being engulfed and "squeezed" by her. He was repeating in the transference his expectation—and his defense against it—of being engulfed by his mother after his father's loss. He had called his mother, and had again felt that she was overpowering him. He began to tremble visibly as he sat in my office and asked how I could leave him—how could I trick him so. He wanted to hit me but restrained himself enough to ask that I remove my glasses. When he calmed down, I was able to interpret to him that he had perceived me as being like his father, who had left him—or so he felt—at the mercy of his mother and of women in general. I told him that he should be aware that his rage included the impotent rage of his father, as though he were taking aspects of his father's suffering onto his own shoulders in disruptive identification with him.

Jerry was still angry on my return. A representative of the organization that had been paying his hospital and treatment expenses had visited him during my absence. Jerry felt as though the group were getting ready to withdraw from responsibility for him now that he was no longer "a prize bull," just as, of course, he had feared that I would abandon him on my trip. He read me poems that his father had written. They were in the service of denying rejection and castration (in a general sense) and were full of hope. Jerry wept to realize how his father had tried to deny his troubles and the onset of his certain death, and how he himself was now trying to deny his own troubles.

His mother visited him, and he noticed that she was wearing on her hand what he called a "big diamond ring." He wished she would sell it to provide money for his further treatment but he kept this wish to himself. He continued to be angry and was puzzled to find himself suddenly calling one of the hospital aides, "you black bastard." When I reminded him that Othello was a black man, he felt some relief. This led to a memory of his urinating beside his father and his father's having asked him whose penis was the bigger. Discussion of these issues further clarified for him his unfinished competition with his father, his desire to have a strong father, and his dread of identification with the father who suffered. We were by then in the fourth month of his treatment, and our hours were calm. Knowing that his time in the hospital was running out, he began a feverish job hunt, leaving the hospital during the daylight hours for this purpose.

One night he dreamed of seeing his father: "He looked healthy. There were a lot of people. My father walked toward them and shook their hands. I was there too. When my father approached me he began to look like a ghoul, a zombie. He stood in front of me, but I didn't touch him." At this point he had awakened. In associating to this dream he reported that his father had been getting ready to die but that he was not yet dead. It seemed that, having survived his separation from me in the transference, and having clarified his ambivalent feelings toward his father, Jerry was now psychologically preparing to accept the reality of his father's death. As we will see, however, this was only a temporary development, for our next separation led to renewed anger toward me in the transference and a revival of ambivalence toward his father. By now he realized, with my help, that the coach had represented his father, and he went on his own to apologize to him for having "killed his authority" on the night he went berserk. In turn, the coach gave permission for Jerry to use his name as a reference in his search for work.

Jerry made a ceramic necklace in occupational therapy inscribed with the statement "I trust in me," and he wore it to show me. He wanted to work in the athletic department of the college, this time not as a star but in some behind-the-scenes role. Both the necklace and his recognition that he did not need the applause of others gave further evidence of his beginning to move unevenly toward independence and separation from his father. The coach had nothing for him this time, however, and when I had to go away on a four-day trip, Jerry hit a medical student. On my return he confronted me with a dream in which his father appeared without disguise. Someone asked the father, "How come you don't have feelings when you do things for people?" His father had replied, "But I gave to the United Givers Fund!" Associations indicated that I was now perceived as the father who, by separating from him, failed to protect him from expressing the anger and feelings of guilt that separation aroused in him. Since I had left him at a difficult time, a time of rejection by another father figure—the coach—my feelings for him were nothing but lip service; I was just finding excuses for leaving him and only pretending to care. I interpreted this understanding of the dream for him.

I learned that during my absence he had been aggressive on the ward and heard from Jerry that "women" (nurses) had "overpowered" him, arranging for the ward physician to put him down altogether with injections of tranquilizers. The nurses would now not even help him make his bed; he was "a fallen gladiator" in their eyes as well as in the view of the organization that had been sponsoring his treatment.

His mother came to visit and talked at length with the psychiatric social worker about possible solutions for the problem of continuing his treatment. She wanted to take him to their home in another state and help him find a job there. Meanwhile, I told him of my willingness to continue working with him if he could make some arrangement to stay near where I worked.

Jerry responded to all this in the last month of his hospital stay, which had lasted four months, by becoming constipated. It turned out that, on the day before his death, Jerry's father had asked his son for a bedpan and had turned purple in his struggle to defecate. There was an element of identification with the father in Jerry's constipation, since, just as the father had been on the point of separating from life, so was his son now on the point of separating from me. When Jerry used the bedpan—in the same manner as his dying father had done—the thought crossed Jerry's mind that he was unlike his father in that he would not soon die. Further associations made him recall that he had had severe constipation when he was seven, and had kept a little stick in the bathroom with which to break his feces at the rectal opening. It was embarrassing for him to recall this, but it meant to him that, since he was not going to be able to stay much longer in the hospital, it was up to him to, as he put it, "shit or get off the pot." His constipation took on further meaning when it became evident that he associated feces with corpses, and bowel movements with burial. This association was evident in a dream he had on the night he used a bedpan successfully: "I saw my father's coffin. It was in a truck. The back gate of the truck opened, and the coffin slid off."

On the following night he dreamed of "digging up the ground." Once more he became assertive but friendly. The reactions of the nurses to him altered accordingly. He was also able to be friendly with a woman he had previously fantasied as castrating. It seemed that for Jerry the entire matter of his constipation was an unconscious rehearsal of the basic conflict of his mourning: the need and the inability to separate from his father. Jerry seemed to be trying to overcome his fear of separation as he prepared to leave the hospital.

He continued to see me as an outpatient for a month. He had found some work and was earning money, but it was clear to him that the athletic organization was no longer interested. His status as a fallen star humiliated him, and he decided to return to his hometown after all, confident that he could do something there. It was summer, and I planned to go abroad for a month. Jerry said that he would return and that he hoped to be able to arrange financial support for his return to college after the next semester, at which time we agreed to pick up his treatment again. He left before I went on my vacation, and I never saw him again, although he called me twice after I returned to tell me that he had kept our plan for treatment in mind. Then one day his mother called with the news that Jerry was in a hospital. He and his brother, who had been home on a visit, had had an argument that had culminated in a fist fight, leading to Jerry's hospital admission. The physician caring for him called to tell me that Jerry had contracted an acute infection leading to septicemia, and the next day his brother called to say that Jerry had died.

A magical handkerchief

Jerry's treatment with me was relatively brief—only 118 hours—and I believe that it is only after a full analysis of a patient that one can learn the nuances of his psychopathology, identify the pathogenic fantasies that influence his symptoms or character formations, and understand the interaction of environmental and/or constitutional factors with his developmental change. But even in a situation far from ideal, Jerry's treatment revealed enough for me to understand the elements condensed in his linking object, a handkerchief.

Jerry had been alone with his father the day before his death and had seen him in an oxygen tent seemingly indifferent to everything around him. He had suddenly called out to his son for a bedpan which Jerry had gotten and had helped him slide under his buttocks. The dying man had strained and turned purple with the effort to defecate, succeeding at last in producing a small bit of fecal material that had looked like a small ball. As Jerry picked up the pan he remembered—most likely in association to his father's turning purple and the shape of his feces his stay in the hospital at the age of 14 when his scrotum had been purple and the surgeon had insisted on telling him that after he had excised one of his "balls" he had dropped it into a "pan." He had started to flush away his father's feces when the sick man called out, "Stop! Don't flush that down the toilet! Keep it!" He had apparently some notion that it should be saved for examination by his doctor. Jerry knew that, since his father was so close to death, any such examination would not be warranted, but he had felt obliged to carry out his father's instructions. Although the odor from the pan was foul and filled the room, he had kept the pan in the sickroom until a nurse removed it.

The father had died on the following day. Jerry had been by his side, repeating to him, "I am with you, Dad!" all but for one brief absence when he had left for ten minutes to find his sister. It was during this time that his father had died. Jerry regretted that he had not been with him in his last moment, and when told of the death, fell on his knees by the deathbed. He knew that others in the room had thought that he was praying, but in reality a fantasy had obliged him to kneel down to look under the bed: he felt that his father had left him something, and that he would find it there. It was only later, in treatment, that he was able to realize that what he was seeking was one of his father's testicles, so that he could have it to keep as a substitute for the one he had lost, thereby becoming a complete man.

After leaving the hospital Jerry found himself rushing home to his parent's bedroom to take out of the drawer a handkerchief that had been his father's. The one he chose was stained, though washed and ironed. Jerry folded it so that it would fit into his back trousers pocket, and put it there. The memory of all this was suppressed and recalled only in therapy. When Jerry talked about the handkerchief, he claimed to have found it "planted" among his things as Desdemona's handkerchief had been planted among Cassio's. It was this association with the Shakespearean play that Jerry talked about, feeling sometimes like Iago, sometimes like Cassio, and sometimes like Othello himself. Aspects of oedipal wishes, fears, and punishments were condensed in the handkerchief he chose to be a link between the dead man and himself. These activated oedipal elements (which included, of course, his sense of castration and the need to identify with a strong masculine figure) made him long to keep his father alive and long at the same time to "kill" him. He still clung to his magical handkerchief when I first saw him two years later. It was in the back pocket of the trousers he was wearing at our first encounter.

During his "hippie period" Jerry had bought a rectangular black box shaped like a coffin. (He was not consciously aware of the symbolism until the association was made during therapy.) Everything that belonged to him that would not fit into this "coffin" he sold, and each night before going to bed he made a ritual of placing his records, books, photographs, and other belongings away in the box, putting the handkerchief on top of them before he locked the box for the night. (His locking the box is consistent with the selection by established pathological mourners of a heavy coffin or concrete vault to prevent the dreaded return of the dead.) Only then could he go to his bed and sleep. His bed and a chair were in fact all that his room contained except for the coffin-shaped black box. When he rose in the morning he would ritualistically open the box, pick up the handkerchief, and replace it in his back pocket. He never used the handkerchief during the day, finding something else to use whenever he needed to blow his nose or wipe his face. It is typical of linking objects that they are not put to their appropriate use.

One day during his treatment, after talking about the handkerchief, Jerry took it out of his back pocket and showed it to me. It was stained and ordinary. Jerry's associations to it indicated that the stain reminded him of his father's blowing his nose during his last years, as he did very frequently, and his mother's washing and ironing handkerchiefs. His further association was to an embarrassing memory of his own ejaculation onto a handkerchief as a teenager, when the semen had dried on the linen. Now the stain on his linking object meant to him that his father had been forced to masturbate into a handkerchief because he had either been rejected by his wife or been impotent with her. The possibility of his father's impotence and his psychological castration was condensed in the linking object. It was necessary for Jerry to maintain a link with the dead man to keep alive the hope that his father would turn out to be "manly" enough to help his son repress his oedipal strivings and be someone with whom his son could identify in his struggle to overcome castration anxiety. Real images and representations of the (weak) father and (emasculated) son were, of course, in conflict with such wished-for images and representations.

Other associations to the handkerchief were revealed when Jerry began playing with it during one of his hours. He kept making a sort of bag out of the linen, and it was during the hour in which he did this that he realized why he had knelt by his father's deathbed—he had been looking to see it his father had bequeathed him one of his testicles. The bag he was making out of the cloth represented the scrotal sac awaiting his father's gift. In view of this, the use of the handkerchief as a response to castration anxiety is again clear.

It also became clear that Jerry was using the handkerchief to defend against separation anxiety. During his hospitalization for pneumonia as a child, he had experienced marked separation anxiety. He had dealt with his separation anxiety by compulsive play with a toy hammer, systematically throwing it away and retrieving it, as if to master the notion that what is separated can be retrieved. (One is reminded of Freud's famous observation of his one-and-a-half-year-old grandson's play with a spool to which a string was attached [1920]. The child's play was in the service of coping with separation from his mother: he kept throwing the spool over the curtained side of his crib until it was out of sight, then retrieving it by pulling the string.) Jerry's hospital bed had been next to that of a little black girl whose color was so strange to him that he could not bring himself to talk to her. One morning when he awoke he found that she had disappeared and that her bed linen was smeared with a greenish stain (fecal material). The little boy was told that she had died while he slept, and for years he had fantasies that his unwillingness to talk to her had had something to do with her death. Stained linen thus represented the concept of death (separation) for him, so that his later preoccupation with the stained handkerchief had a precursor. It is safe to assume that the feeling states with which Jerry responded to this childhood event colored his perceptual field, so that the stained deathbed linen had a unique symbolism that could later be transferred to like articles in his experience.

Since Jerry's linking object, in addition to linking him with his father's image, was tinged with elements of both separation and castration anxiety, it can be said to have had aspects that one would expect to find in objects of a transitional or fetishistic nature. A comparison between the linking object and transitional or fetishistic objects will be offered in Chapter 15. At any rate, given the influence of castration and separation anxiety on Jerry's psychopathology, it should not surprise us to see these same elements associated with his linking object.

Finally, I would point out how the work of mourning was externalized onto Jerry's linking object. By maintaining the handkerchief as a magical object that could not be put to its customary uses, one of which, of course, is wiping away tears, Jerry was able to avoid the tears of grief. We will see in Chapter 9 that another patient similarly externalized the work of mourning onto his linking object, a photograph of his father upon which he permitted water to drip until it looked as though it had been stained by tears.

The death of a patient

When Jerry's mother called to say that he was seriously ill in a hospital, I "frantically" tried to find out about his illness. (My spontaneous use of the word "frantically" indicates, I think, an attempt to identify with Jerry, for he had used this same word to describe his travels at the time of his father's death.) Although he had not been under my direct care for some months, I felt guilty at first on hearing of his condition. While I had undertaken intensive work with him in the belief that support for long-term treatment would continue, I was also deeply involved with his feelings. His world was so full of images and representations of dead people that every real separation of importance to him was perceived by him as a forecast of more loss. Thus, I felt some guilt that I had taken a vacation the summer before his death.

On hearing of his illness I feared that part of him would not fight against his infection; part of him, living so long with the dead, might indeed long for death. When his mother disclosed that he had failed to respond to the medications he was given, I sensed something suicidal in his physical illness. I tried to explain my concern to his mother, and spoke of wanting to have some physicians I knew in the area consult with the doctor in charge of his case. She agreed to this, but by then it was too late.

After the death Jerry's mother sent me his autopsy report and a few months later came to see me, the woman whose son had thought of her as a seductress, a killer. I have already stated my belief that a therapist should not jump to easy, quick conclusions about the "reality" of a situation until the patient's fantasies, intermingled as they are with perceptions arising not only out of reality but also out of inner drive investments, are sorted out and put into perspective. Jerry's mother sat in my office as the mother of a dead son. I felt that she had tolerated her grief chiefly by means of narcissistic defenses, much like those with which her son had defended against his anxiety or grief. She had developed an idea of "saving others," and had already begun a new job consistent with this aim. I obliged her desire to learn about Jerry's problems—his inability to grieve, for example—without going into great detail or mentioning anything that would hurt her. I emphasized that she was now the one who needed help to resolve her grief. Some months later she called again, as if to report on her adjustment after the passage of a year. She sent me a basket of fruit with a card thanking me, after which I never heard from her again.

I subsequently realized that I had made but one reference to Jerry, now so long dead, in my many writings on mourning and linking objects, and I turned an inquiring eye upon myself to account for this. Was this a denial of his death on my part? The single reference to his case among my publications appeared in a Turkish journal (Volkan, 1975b), as if my writing about him in a language foreign to his was in the service of denial. I do not want to give the impression that I had been preoccupied with his image during the years that had passed since his death, but he did come fleetingly to mind whenever I watched a basketball game. Writing about him in detail now has stimulated the work of mourning in me; as a writer and his therapist, I found myself undergoing a kind of "re-grief' work. His notes had been stored away in a "box"—there is an association here with his black box—and I got them out to go over. I even examined his autopsy report to convince myself that he had indeed died and—what was more important—that his death had been brought about by an infectious illness, and not by my departure on vacation. Now that I have written about him I can throw away my notes on his case and the autopsy report as well. But I will never "kill" Jerry altogether. I will now and then remember him—whenever I watch a basketball game, for example.

Part II

Treatment

CHAPTER 7

Psychoanalytic psychotherapy of established pathological mourning

In this chapter I examine the application of psychoanalytic psychotherapy to a young woman with complications in the work of mourning. One of my goals in doing this is to demonstrate how such complications are accessible to limited treatment—that is, treatment less extensive than psychoanalysis proper. In her case, the inability to work through her grief sealed over pre-existing psychopathology, while at the same time elements of that pathology determined the nature of her complicated response to a loss by death.

Psychoanalytic psychotherapy focuses on those of the patient's unconscious conflicts that most clearly influence the complicated response to death. It does not attempt the resolution of *all* of the patient's unconscious conflicts, as does psychoanalysis proper. My ulterior motive in developing this idea is, of course, to prepare the reader for my discussion of an even more limited, more narrowly focused form of therapy—re-grief therapy—in later chapters. I begin by briefly reviewing the distinctions between psychoanalysis proper and psychoanalytic psychotherapy.

Psychoanalysis proper and psychoanalytic psychotherapy

Bibring (1954) compares psychotherapies in general with psychoanalysis proper with respect to which of five therapeutic principles is used in the treatment. These principles are: suggestion, abreaction, manipulation, clarification, and interpretation.

Suggestion refers in this connection to the therapist's inducing various mental processes in his patient independently of—or to the exclusion of—the patient's rational or critical thinking. The therapist may, for example, induce his patient to fantasy something. Suggestion is often used therapeutically in the service of other therapeutic agents. *Abreaction*—emotional discharge—is now regarded as a part of "emotional reliving," which offers the patient evidence of his repressed impulses, etc., and convinces him of their actual existence. Originally considered a curative process, abreaction came to be employed as a technical tool in the process of acquiring insight through interpretation. Bibring states—and I agree—that in acute emotional conditions abreaction as a curative principle is to a certain degree maintained. But the value of the emotional discharge should be considered only in combination with the effects of other principles present. *Manipulation* is used technically to produce in the patient a favorable attitude toward the treatment situation or to overcome any trend toward obstruction that he may evidence. As an example, Bibring describes the patient embarking on treatment at the instance of some authoritarian influence. When his therapist convinces him that it is entirely up to him whether or not to discuss his problems in their sessions, and the patient decides affirmatively to undergo treatment, the therapist will have re-established his patient's freedom of choice. One benefit of this is that the patient then feels that he is expected to act on his own responsibility. Bibring refers to another type of manipulation that he calls "experiential," in which the therapist exposes his patient to a "new" experience with which the patient had not previously been acquainted—perhaps because of neurotic inhibitions—or had not experienced since childhood.

The use of these concepts—suggestion, emotional relief, and manipulation—do not give the patient self-understanding. The remaining two—clarification and interpretation—do. *Clarification* exposes not unconscious material but material that simply escapes the patient's attention and is more or less easily recognized by him when his attention is directed to it. According to Bibring:

> Clarification in therapy aims at those vague and obscure factors (frequently below the level of verbalization) which are relevant from the viewpoint of treatment; it refers to those techniques and therapeutic processes which assist the patient to reach a higher degree of self-awareness, clarity and differentiation of self-observation which makes adequate verbalization possible. (p. 755)

Interpretation refers exclusively to the uncovering of unconscious material; it is a prolonged process rather than a single act, and is called "mutative" in Strachey's (1934) classic description. Insight brought about by interpretation differs from that effected by clarification.

> Whereas clarification results in the detachment of the ego ... interpretation causes the ego at first to become more involved, since it leads to the reactivation of painful tendencies, memories and conflicts. (Bibring, 1954, p. 758)

Clarification, then, leads to the "strengthening" of the ego by the achievement of greater objectivity,

> ... whereas insight through interpretation initiates a process of reorientation and learning which results in more adequate solutions of the pathogenic infantile conflicts. (Bibring, 1954, p. 758)

Of course, in practice, analysts use clarification to aid interpretation.

In psychoanalysis, Bibring states, insight through interpretation is the principal agent of change, all others being subordinate, although to a varying degree all of the principles described are used, particularly at the outset of work with the patient. It should be pointed out that the interpretation used in psychoanalysis proper is made in a setting in which a transference neurosis is fully developed; psychoanalytic interpretations are thus mainly transference interpretations. Psychotherapies other than psychoanalysis employ different choices and combinations of the therapeutic agents that Bibring describes.

In a paper that accompanies Bibring's article in the same journal, Gill (1954) gives what is perhaps a more restrictive definition of psychoanalysis: a therapeutic situation in which the development of a regressive transference neurosis occurs solely because of interpretations that the analyst makes from a position of technical neutrality. Following Gill's formulation, Kernberg (1978) states that if a treatment is to be called psychoanalysis it must meet three criteria: the maintenance of a position of technical neutrality; the predominant use of interpretation as the major therapeutic agent; and the "systematic analysis" of the transference. I would add another—the frequency of treatment sessions—since I regard the close scheduling of many appointments throughout the treatment to be as necessary to psychoanalysis as is the use of the couch.

Kernberg states that all other psychotherapies—psychoanalytic or "non-dynamic"—can be described in terms of these three criteria. Thus, in psychoanalytic psychotherapy, a systematic analysis of the transference—thus of all impulse-defense configurations and the resistances they contain—does not occur. Such therapy, rather, attempts "a partial resolution of some, and a reinforcement of other resistances, with a subsequent, partial integration of previously repressed impulses into the adult ego" (Kernberg, 1978, p. 79). Technical neutrality is maintained, and clarification and interpretation are major therapeutic tools, aided by abreaction; but the therapist selects the aspects of the transference that he will interpret and offers interpretations and clarifications not only with reference to selected transference resistances but also with respect to the patient's external reality. "A systematic analysis of all transference paradigms or a systematic resolution of the transference neurosis by interpretation alone is definitely not attempted" (p. 80).

Kernberg then defines supportive psychotherapy and "non-dynamic" psychotherapies (such as counseling), and differentiates them from psychoanalysis proper and psychoanalytic psychotherapy. Although supportive therapy uses clarification and abreaction, it depends chiefly on suggestion and manipulation. Kernberg concedes that supportive psychotherapy is psychoanalytic therapy in a broad sense when the therapist is aware of and monitors the transference, and gives careful consideration to transference resistances when dealing with the patient's characterological problems and their relationship to the difficulties of his real-life situation. Counseling and other forms of "non-dynamic" psychotherapies do not include consideration of the transference process but focus exclusively on conscious, cognitive, and/or affective issues.

Here I will report the case of a patient who exhibited the clinical picture of established pathological mourning and who was treated with long-term psychoanalytic psychotherapy with the aim of resolving *some* infantile psychosexual conflicts condensed in her inability to mourn. Her treatment dealt primarily with the complication of the work of mourning but in a fashion that facilitated the resolution, full or partial, of *some* of her unconscious conflicts, especially in those areas that influenced her complicated response to death. The treatment was terminated when condensations in, and some important genetic determinants of, the obstructions to the work of mourning were resolved, and the patient became able to move through the necessary phases of grief to its resolution. I should note here that throughout this volume I use the term "analyst" only when the case in question involves psychoanalysis proper, and the term "therapist" when a form of psychotherapy is used.

A young woman whose brother died in an automobile accident

Carol was a 24-year-old unmarried elementary school teacher treated by Brian Hastings. My involvement in this case was limited to supervising it. The following account of her treatment is drawn from Hastings's extensive notes.

Carol sought treatment three years after losing one of her brothers in an automobile accident. Although she exhibited a clinical picture of established pathological mourning, it was clear from the outset that her brother's loss had activated in her fantasied losses in the psychological realm, specifically, the loss of a penis, as well as the loss involved in separation from her mother. She had already tried, without benefit, to get help from another therapist whose therapy had been educative and "supportive." It was decided that long-term, insight-oriented psychoanalytic psychotherapy, conducted by a therapist adhering to therapeutic neutrality, was indicated. It was formulated in the beginning that Carol needed to work through, in the transference, the way in which she had condensed with the experience of her brother's death her infantile fantasies and her defenses against the anxiety these fantasies had caused.

In the diagnostic interview it became clear that Carol was preoccupied with images of her dead brother. She kept a photograph of him between two candles as though on an altar. She had adopted the habit of listening to records that were copies of those her brother had owned, which she had bought immediately after his death. She sometimes felt that he might come back from the grave and hurt her, or that other cherished friends or relatives might die suddenly. She felt obliged to tell these people that she loved them, lest they die without knowledge of her love. She sought treatment because she was disturbed by feelings of jealousy toward her boyfriend, and by fear that their relationship might be "dead." She carefully avoided anything to do with murder or other violence in movies, television shows, and stories.

After her brother died she wrote a poem about his death, full of speculations as to where he had gone and what he might be able to feel or see. She later framed this poem and hung it in her living room, recalling to her therapist's mind the dreams of patients with established pathological mourning in which what appears is seen by the dreamer in frames, that is, contained and distanced.

In her initial interviews, she revealed that she had "bad thoughts," which turned out to be doubts and fears about her relations with people, and anxiety that her mutual involvement with them might "die." Her "bad thoughts" also reflected her feeling of being "damaged" or "inferior." As will become evident, her conviction of being "damaged" arose from the loss of the penis she had fantasied as a child had once belonged to her; a fantasy reactivated by her brother's death.

She was the fourth of ten siblings in a lower-middle-class family living in the suburbs of a large southern city. Her father, a hard-working factory foreman, was described as having been aloof and preoccupied, able to show affection toward his children only with great difficulty. Carol recalled his voice as loud and frightening. As a child she had been dependent on her mother, insisting until she was eleven that her mother help her with her homework assignments. However, she felt her mother to be emotionally unavailable and distant, a woman who never really understood her and with whom she never discussed anything personal. Because she had so many brothers and sisters Carol decided early that the wisest course for her would be to anticipate her parents' expectations of her, so that what little attention she did get would not be negative. As a result, she was very seldom punished.

It was revealed in treatment that Kenny, the brother whose death so troubled her, had been born when she was two, and had slept in the same room with her until she was four, so that she was often faced with the anatomical differences between them. Fascinated, she was absorbed in everything connected with his care, wondering, for example, why he stayed in diapers so long, and coming to the conclusion that because he was a boy he was treated with special affection and tolerance. Her early familiarity with the genital endowment of Kenny, who took her mother's attention from the pre-oedipal Carol (as therapy later revealed), had induced sadistic but largely repressed impulses toward the little brother.

Several early memories pointed to Carol's feeling "damaged" in some way. She thought that she had been about four when she had urinated in the bathroom in the presence of both her parents, and her father had suddenly squatted before the toilet and, watching Carol's urination, commented that the urine seemed to be coming out of the wrong hole.

Another memory dated from about age five, when a male stranger had touched her genitals at the beach. Later in the same year a retarded neighbor boy had taken her into the woods and pulled down her panties to look at her genitals. She had wondered for a long time if these episodes had in some way damaged her. Later, she became the "skinniest" girl in the family. She felt that clothes never "hung right" on her. In therapy it became evident that her "skinniness" was achieved in an attempt to provide a phallus—one now generalized to her whole body. Hastings had, in fact, been impressed with her masculine mode of dress when he first saw her, although he thought her beautiful. She was convinced that there was something wrong with her legs, thinking that they were too hairy or visibly veined. When an elementary school teacher told a story about a devil's pulling a sleeping woman's hair, Carol developed a protective ritual, which she always maintained, of bringing her long hair forward and holding onto It while she slept. She also began worrying at this time about part of her body's being chopped off if it protruded over the edge of her bed.

She described herself as having been timid and fearful, and reported feeling inferior to other siblings, especially her brothers. Longing to be touched and talked to by her parents, Carol had consoled herself with fantasies of being loved. It seemed that nobody took any interest in her when she was engaged in the typical play of a little girl with dolls or a make-believe house. Because it seemed unrewarding to be a girl, she became a tomboy, insisted on competing with boys in various sports, and wanted always to be included in their games.

Early adolescence increased the conflictual aspects of her relation with her mother; fantasies of being an attractive woman were accompanied by feelings of intense guilt. She recalled posturing before a bathroom mirror, draping herself with a towel for a dress, and then feeling bitterly ashamed.

She recalled that on one occasion her mother had called her a "sex pot"; she always felt that her mother was more strict about her dating than she was about her sisters'. When she was eleven, dissatisfied with her dependence on her mother, she decided that she would do her own homework, and refused to let her mother help her with it. Her mother slapped Carol when she spoke of wanting to dress more attractively, but when Carol stoutly objected that no other mothers slapped their daughters, her mother stopped.

When she was eleven or twelve, Carol had a period of obsessional thought about "Bonnie and Clyde," whose story she had seen several times in the movies, and about whom she had read a book. She elaborated the fantasy that she herself was Bonnie reincarnated. In this fantasy, the life of a criminal outcast and the bloody mutilation and death she suffered were the consequences of separation and sexual behavior.

She had intercourse for the first time at 16, which revived, as might have been expected, intense guilt and the fear of punishment. When the relationship with her first sex partner ended, she drew close to her brother Kenny for the first time in her life. He consoled her about her loss, and the two spent much time together, talking and listening to records in his room. It was then that she began to have what she called "masturbation dreams" from which she would awaken with an orgasm but with no memory of the dream's content. These always embarrassed her with the possibility that Kenny might have seen her as she was dreaming. It was formulated in her treatment that during this period of her closeness to her brother the affective experiences of their having been so much together in childhood were reactivated. Her envy of the boy caused a reaction formation and an upsurge of sexual feeling for him. Perhaps partly in reaction to her increasing discomfort *vis-à-vis* her brother, Carol, by then 18 or 19, embarked on a relationship with a new boyfriend and at the same time began disliking and disapproving of Kenny, allegedly because of his rebellion against parental authority. At age 20, feeling rejected by her closest girlfriend, she impulsively moved to another city to live with her boyfriend.

Very shortly after making this move she learned of Kenny's death in an automobile accident. Initially numb and angry, she had unusual perceptions during the time leading up to his burial. Kenny's motionless chest seemed enlarged, and she thought that he might get up at any moment and tell those in the room that he was really playing a joke on them, that he was not really dead. It was three years later that she became Hastings's patient after having undergone brief "supportive" psychotherapy with another therapist.

Condensation of the representation of a dead man with that of a fantasied lost penis

Her new therapist maintained therapeutic neutrality and saw Carol twice a week. At the outset of her treatment, she reviewed aspects of her personal history and emphasized the problems she had had in relating to men and significant relatives. She had had "bad thoughts" about others, which turned out to be angry thoughts. When the therapist offered neither agreement nor disagreement about the "badness" of these thoughts, she openly expressed some angry feelings about a sister. Then, afraid of going straight to hell because of her open expression of anger, she went to the grave of her brother to pray and to cry to him for help against her "bad thoughts."

Early in her treatment she told Hastings that she had had a peculiar feeling at times that she was very much like her dead brother and that she bore a striking physical resemblance to him. She was describing, in effect, a transient experience of merging with the representation of her dead brother. After being in therapy for several weeks, she made an effort to review the circumstances of Kenny's death, and recalled her poem about him with its speculations about his whereabouts. She had a vague and 'frightening dream that she was running to hide from someone in a situation that involved murder. She felt in the dream as though she were being chased by someone who wanted information from her. She was frightened about having "bad" (angry) thoughts about her therapist, and her sessions were often punctuated with long periods of silence. The therapist thought that Carol might be defending against an understanding of her own murderous thoughts about Kenny and her guilt about them. It was as though she regarded her therapist as the detective in a murder case who might point to her as the murderer. He encouraged her to feel free about talking, and declared that his purpose was not to judge her, but to respond to her curiosity about her own problems. She began saying that her angry thoughts probably came from a fear of being rejected for being dependent and inferior; but she continued to worry about the power of her angry thoughts and the possibility that one of her friends or relatives might die at any time.

After three months of therapy, she had a dream of driving down a country road while another car approached from the opposite direction. It was a convertible full of teenage boys, and as it passed, one of the boys was thrown out. Carol felt the force of the blow as he hit the ground and rolled over several times. As the boy struggled to get up, another car hit him head-on with terrible force. By then very badly injured, the boy was thrown to the edge of a cliff where he hung with his fingers until a steamroller came and crushed his hands, causing him to fall. When Carol approached the edge of the cliff, she saw that it was miles high—so high that it would take several minutes for him to hit the ground and perish at last. Her brother had been 19 when he died, riding on the passenger side of a car when another car had collided with it on that side. The force of the collision had knocked him out of the car and onto the road yards away. He had died later during emergency surgery.

Carol became increasingly uncomfortable in therapy, experiencing more and more "bad thoughts," from which she tried to protect herself by listening to the records that were duplicates of her brother's, and by sitting before his picture, flanked, as I have indicated, by two candles as though on an altar. The therapist felt that she was utilizing her linking objects more frequently so as to avoid the pain of the work of mourning. Moreover, her anger was at this point largely displaced onto others—parents, her boyfriend, and her therapist.

She explained then that she protected herself against "bad thoughts" by carefully avoiding any form of violence on television, in movies, or in newspaper reports of violent occurrences. Seeing her therapist driving his car one day led her to talk in the next session about her early childhood memories of having been molested on the beach, and of having been "looked at" in the woods. Her associations were to a fantasy in which the therapist/driver might damage her body in an accident. She spoke of having wondered for a long time after these early incidents whether her body was strange, or in some way damaged. It was in this session that she recalled her worries about her legs.

She said that she felt inferior because she was a woman; that she felt out of place and deprived of parental attention and affection. She said that she kept trying to remember what life had been like for her as a child, and attempting to understand it. She felt somehow "stuck" along the way, and hoped that the therapist would be the "good" parent who would help release her, although she was also afraid that his help would cause a repetition of the traumas she had suffered from others in the past. She dreamed of trying to climb a ladder and of failing from it when the rungs broke away beneath her feet. She remembered having been punished for sexual strivings, and having been called a "sex pot" by her mother when she had wanted to make her skirt a more fashionable length.

In her fourth month of therapy, it became increasingly clear that there was a link between her early perception of having been damaged and her relationship with her dead brother. She recalled how interested she had been in his body in the shared room of their early childhood. She had a cowboy suit at the time, which she associated with manliness and valued highly. She had once gotten up in the middle of the night while everyone else was asleep and taken the suit out to look at it and admire it, wishing fervently that she might be a cowboy. Based on these revelations, her therapist initially formulated her case in terms of penis envy.

At this point in her treatment, she dreamed of being pregnant and of knowing that because she was pregnant she would stop doing all the "bad" things that she was accustomed to doing, such as drinking and smoking. She had a wonderful feeling of "completion" in this dream that encouraged her to believe not only that she no longer needed her therapist, but that she no longer depended on anyone. She could survive without him, she suggested, and told of her fantasies of moving far away and living in the woods by herself. Her therapist thought that the feeling of completeness experienced in the dream was a response to her feeling of having been damaged; that the implicit fetus in the dream of pregnancy represented the penis that would have made her feel "complete."

At the start of her fifth month of therapy, she told her therapist that she thought she really was pregnant. She was afraid that he would be angry and would tell her not to talk to him again. Instead, he told her that he suspected that as a child she had felt insecure and incomplete and that since visiting her childhood memories in treatment these feelings had given her increasing discomfort. He added that the dream of being pregnant was a dream of being complete without him and of not having to remember uncomfortable thoughts and feelings. He made no suggestions as to what she might do to determine whether or not she was pregnant.

In following sessions, she seemed flooded with dream images, some relating to her childhood fantasy that eating led to pregnancy, and some including symbolic references to womb-like objects, to clutching a penis, and to seeing bloody injuries and abortions. As she talked about these dreams, she recalled her father's watching her urinate and questioning whether the urine came from the right hole in a way that had encouraged her fantasies about her anatomy. Hastings speculated that one of these fantasies may have been of having lost a penis. She then spontaneously offered her feeling that a part of her was missing after her brother had died. She was sad on the day she spoke of this because she realized that she was not, in fact, pregnant. She spoke of a connection between her "losing" the (fantasied) baby, her fear of losing her boyfriend, and the loss of her brother. As a matter of fact, she added, having a baby would have made up for the loss of Kenny—would have relieved her sorrow about his death. She had had a fantasy that if she had been pregnant, her child would have been a boy, and that she would have given him the middle name of Kenneth.

In subsequent sessions she told her therapist that she sometimes felt very distant and cut off from him. He replied that this feeling might be connected with her wish to be pregnant and "complete" without him.

She told her therapist that she felt he was withholding the "good stuff" from her, although she acknowledged that he was also the only person in her life who didn't "cut her off."

She spoke again about feeling "stuck" in her life and finding it hard to make progress in her job and in her relationship with her boyfriend. She became preoccupied with the thought of cutting herself, in connection with her fear of being "cut off" by her therapist.

During the sixth month of her therapy she spoke about how obnoxious one of her brothers had been on a recent visit to her—a "real prick." She said that talking with her therapist about all her fears would leave her with only a "gaping hole"; an image expressive of her fury about not having a penis. Being afraid and envious of the therapist, she found a female version of him who was less threatening, a woman nicknamed "Brian" (her therapist's real name), to whom she could talk about the feelings she had had about her body. She had dreams of being the powerful person herself; in one of these dreams, she was driving at excessive speed in a car belonging to her brother (the "prick"), clocking 110 miles an hour and accelerating. She "accidentally" pulled the doorknob off the therapist's door on several occasions as she left his office, and asserted that by being quiet she would make him powerless.

One night she dreamed of seeing her dead brother's foot sticking out from a pile of dead leaves in a graveyard. This was followed by another dream in which she saw her female cat with holes in its belly made by worms that crawled in and out. She also dreamed of a baby with its limbs and torso pruned away so that it was nothing more than a living head. She was uncertain whether or not to put the living head into the oven. It turned into a hot cross bun, and then into a baby's head once again, with blood and pus oozing from it.

Her therapist told her that there might be a common theme in much of what she had told him. She had had thoughts and dreams about bodies, blood, and babies, and had had vivid memories of uncertainty as a child about the state of her body. The loss of her brother, he said, was experienced by her as being like the loss of a part of her body, the loss of a penis. She responded to this interpretation in the next session, which came in the seventh month of therapy, by reporting dreams that again denied her fantasied state of castration. In one, she felt that her boyfriend's penis belonged to her as she sat beside him on a fence and complacently held it. In another, she was riding through the country on a great white horse whose neck went up and up in front of her and whose mane was of unusual curly black hair. Her therapist interpreted the horse as representing her fantasied penis. She then reported that at the end of this dream she had fallen off the horse (separating herself from the phallus) and found herself facing a house (a symbol of female genitalia). In the next session she reported dreaming of riding an old-fashioned bicycle, bright red with balloon tires (once more there was a swollen penis between her legs), and her therapist had appeared in the dream, trying to persuade her to dismount so that she could talk to him. She had refused to get off the bicycle and had compromised by talking to him as he walked along beside her.

She recalled one day how she had competed with boys as a child, but said that she no longer desired to do that because she would rather have babies. In the next session, however, she again felt something unacceptable in her castrated condition and defensively declared that she was not the one that was incomplete—that her therapist could make her talk if he were truly powerful. She spurned her father by failing to send him cards on his birthday and on Father's Day, and she spoke of "cutting off" her therapist by failing to pay his bill on time.

In her eighth month of therapy she appeared at the door of the therapist's office with a knife in her hand. Giggling, she reassured the therapist that the knife was not intended for him, but for gathering mushrooms; she carried it with her everywhere in case she came across an edible mushroom. She then recalled the "Bonnie and Clyde" fantasies that she had had as an adolescent, in which separation and sexual behavior had been the cause of terrible punishment. Her therapist's upcoming brief vacation had been perceived by her as a kind of punishment, and possibly as a form of castration; the evidence of the knife suggests that Carol wanted to take her therapist's penis, like the edible mushroom perhaps, inside her during his absence.

Now more confident and womanly, Carol became interested in solidifying her relations with her boyfriend, and wondered if it might be possible for the two of them to live together successfully. Still, her dreams reflected her uncertainty about her ability to do this as a "real woman." In one, for example, she and her boyfriend were playing baseball, and she was next at bat. She suddenly realized that she had forgotten how to hold the bat (a phallic symbol, of course), nor did she understand anymore how to use it. She wanted to avoid her turn at bat, but her only escape seemed to be to assume the stereotyped role of the weak and scatterbrained female. The therapist interpreted, telling her that as a child she might have fantasized that to be without a penis was to be weak.

Carol then began to allow her erotic feelings about her therapist to surface in full force. These were reflected in her silences, and also in a dream in which she and her therapist were engaged in yoga exercises with their legs intertwined. These feelings were counterbalanced by others expressed in dreams, reflecting abiding fear of being despised, inferior, and weak.

She began testing the reality of her family situation; she now gave serious thought to the ways in which her upbringing had contributed to her feelings of inferiority. She experienced an urge to "fix" her family by making her parents love each other more. At the approach of the fourth anniversary of her brother's death she wore a black dress to her session with the therapist. Since this was the first time she had appeared in black, he suggested that her choice had something to do with the anniversary, but she insisted angrily that her being dressed in black was only a coincidence, and complained that the therapist tried to involve Kenny in things with which he was not concerned. However, she spent most of this session talking about funerals and her memories of the circumstances surrounding her brother's funeral.

Soon she reported a dream about a "bad man" who had approached her just before a therapeutic session in which she had asked the therapist to help her get rid of him; before the dream was over she had succeeded in throwing the "bad man" out herself. Presently the symbolic meaning of this intruder became clear. While on a visit to her parents' home, she had slept for the first time in the bed that had been Kenny's. Awakening during the night with a dream of masturbation and orgasm that reminded her vividly of similar dreams she had had as an adolescent, she re-experienced her fear that Kenny would see her as she dreamed. This event was the beginning of her "throwing away" the disruptive representation of Kenny that she had been harboring. Her efforts to observe and to understand herself in her work with the therapist increased, and she became better able to realize that it was possible to accept the death of her brother: he was neither a missing part of herself, nor was she responsible for his having died.

The completion of her work of mourning was openly crystallized in a dream she brought to her therapist about a year after the start of their work together. Its first portion, as her associations showed, was a kind of review of her first year in therapy, and the second part represented a sort of farewell to her brother. She dreamed of seeing him—looking remarkably like her therapist in appearance and manner—and talking to him. In reply to a question, he told her that from where he had gone he could no longer see what was happening on earth. She hugged him, and sadly told him goodbye.

Carol's second year of psychoanalytic therapy

I believe that the detailed material drawn from this patient's first year in therapy provides ample evidence of her alternation between feeling "damaged" (lacking a penis) and denying that she was damaged; and that this was condensed with her alternating between letting her brother "die" and keeping him alive. The resolution of one set of opposing possibilities was necessary for the resolution of the other. Carol's psychoanalytic therapy dealt mainly with the effort to effect such resolution, although other areas were not altogether neglected. Some work was done, for example, on the condensation of the decision to let her brother die (or not) with her childhood conflict of letting her feces go (or not). The equation of feces, phallus, and corpse eventually became clear to her.

In the middle of the second year of therapy, Carol and her therapist began to refer to the possibility of termination, whereupon Carol started missing her appointments. Investigation of this led to the reactivation of her old "habit" of denying losses. Skipping her hours was a way of denying his importance to her, as well as an attempt to "wean" herself from him. She then alternated between exaggerated anger at and love for her therapist; in one dream, she heard noisy fire-crackers and shouted so loudly above them that the universe was shaken; in another, she saw herself romantically involved with someone representing her therapist. Her ambivalence toward him as well as her reaction to her impending loss was clarified, and she began looking radiant and feminine. She was reassured in a dream about her girlfriend nicknamed Brian that they would not be separated. She began coming to her hours without wearing her watch, and in due course, this was interpreted to her as her attempt to deny the passing of time with its inevitable move toward separation. This interpretation elicited reports of more dreams and fantasies of romantic and sexual love between herself and her therapist. When it was pointed out to her that such ideas partly served to shore up her illusion of keeping him, she accused him in one dream of being a homosexual, and she became more aggressively sexual toward her boyfriend.

As the theme of separation, and her reactions to separation were interpreted and clarified, a date for termination was arrived at; it marked the close of two years of treatment. When the date was set, Carol dreamed of driving a car and being seized with the fear of killing someone. She was using her brother's death as a symbol of the "death" of her relationship with her therapist; she was able to make this interpretation unaided. She then feverishly tried to consolidate and integrate the insights she had gained from her treatment; as treatment drew to a close, she put her financial affairs in order in consultation with an accountant, and began studying for a career she felt would in the long run offer her expanded opportunities. She took stock of her relationship with her boyfriend, making a realistic assessment of what it meant to her. By the time of termination, she had sufficient ego strength to be able to give up an important other.

Conclusion

Carol's case illustrates the long-term psychoanalytic psychotherapy of certain infantile conflicts highly condensed with complications in the work of mourning. The interdependence of these infantile conflicts with established pathological mourning is demonstrated. In the following chapter, two more examples of the psychoanalytic psychotherapy of complications in the work of mourning are given, with the focus this time on reactive depression.

CHAPTER 8

The daughters of Goodbar

This chapter describes the psychoanalytic psychotherapy of two more patients with complications in the work of mourning, complications that led to reactive depression in each case. The patients were sisters, and each was mourning the death of their mother by murder. By a coincidence, their physicians were both members of the Charlottesville Psychoanalytic Psychotherapy Study Group, so it became possible for the membership of this group to monitor their progress through treatment. The discussion centers on the similarities and dissimilarities of responses to death of different members of the same family.

The Charlottesville psychoanalytic psychotherapy study group

For the past five years, six young psychiatrists, all of whom have undergone personal psychoanalysis, have been meeting weekly with me for psychoanalytic investigations of different aspects of therapeutic technique as well as different theoretical issues. When the group learned that two of its number were treating two members of the same family, and that these patients had both sought help in dealing with their mother's murder, we spent a considerable amount of time discussing their cases and the process of their therapy. We were highly interested in the similarities and differences in the reactions of the two sisters to the murder of their mother. From the disclosures that both patients made to their therapists, it was evident that other siblings in their family had also developed severe symptoms like theirs. Moreover, we learned that a third sister was in psychotherapy in a city some distance away, although, for therapeutic reasons, neither of the Charlottesville therapists made any effort to get in touch with her therapist. Although the treatment of the two sisters has not yet been concluded, they have been in therapy for some time, and there is ample material for a useful discussion of their cases. What follows is adapted from the case reports of J. Anderson Thomson, Jr., and Salman Akhtar.

Introduction

For reasons of confidentiality, the members of the Study Group did not know the actual identity of the patients under discussion. We called them Debra and Heather, and came to refer to them as "the daughters of Goodbar." The book *Looking for Mr. Goodbar* (Judith Rossner, 1975) is a fictional account of the real murder of a lonely woman who frequented the singles' bars of New York City; a motion picture was based on it.

The mother of Debra and Heather was at the time of her death an overweight and possibly depressed divorcee. She was often drunk, especially at night, and frequented the local bars. She was probably sexually promiscuous. She was murdered in a car after leaving a bar in the company of a man she did not know. During his trial, the man claimed that her death had been accidental, that he had hit her on the face and unintentionally broken her cervical spine. He had apparently been infuriated over her urinating on the seat of his car. His attorney alleged later that, after the death, he had become frightened by her lack of response, and, realizing that she was dead, had sexually abused her, and bitten her body and thrown it by the side of the road in order to make her death seem the act of a sadistic psychopath.

Her daughters, as will become evident, held different fears about the way in which their mother had perished, and their perceptions were on several levels. Heather, the younger of the two sisters, had been living with her mother at the time of the murder. She was then 15 years old. Debra, the elder, was married, and lived in a city at some distance from the site of the crime. She was 25 when her mother died, 35 when she began her treatment with Thomson about two years before Heather consulted Akhtar. Both were seen in psychoanalytic therapy three times a week. Thomson and Akhtar came to the conclusion that the strikingly similar symptoms both exhibited were evidence of disruptive identification with their dead mother. They had become "living memorials" to her.

Debra

Debra was the second daughter in her family, and the third of seven children. She described her father as "a John Wayne type" very much concerned with seeming manly and virile. Her mother appeared to her to have been a submissive woman who tolerated considerable emotional abuse from her husband. Debra's early memories were pleasant, and reflected the emotional and material comfort of the family of her youth. The father worked for the government and, as a result, the family moved often. They spent a dozen years or so in Europe during the post-war period, with a living standard considerably above what it would have been had they lived in the States.

Sexuality was early a major and overt issue in Debra's life. She remembered sensing that her mother had had her last three children in rapid succession many years after the first four, as a way of keeping her marriage together. Debra felt that she had played a role apart from her siblings; when her father was away from home (and possibly with another woman) she had slept with her mother. She had reconstructed from the confidences of other siblings that she was the only one among them to receive sex education from their mother. She also had to sleep with an elder brother when she was a child, and remembered waking often to find that he had put her hand around his penis. She remembered several comments from her father about her appearance that had unmistakable sexual implications, and she thought he had singled her out sexually from among her sisters. He had shared male magazines with her, and often liked to dance with her while she was a young adolescent. Once the mother's jealousy had broken out, and in a drunken rage she had allegedly screamed at Debra to "just go ahead and get in bed with your father." When her father heard that Debra had slept with a high school coach, he believed it despite her denials; he then seemed to her to be more concerned with his own reputation than with the welfare of his daughter.

On the family's return to the United States when Debra was in her late teens, she became aware of family problems. A sudden reduction in the family's standard of living had perhaps brought them to the surface. More and more often both parents drank to excess. The father became openly involved with another woman. Debra went away to college, but was only briefly independent; she soon married a student to whom she was masochistically compliant and submissive. She was responsible for all the housework in addition to carrying a full academic load. When her husband blamed her for his poor grades, she accepted the blame. In retrospect, she compared her behavior to her mother's—a blind acceptance of blame and complete subordination to her husband.

A few years after the return from Europe her parents were divorced, and her father quickly remarried. During the family upheaval, Debra sided with her father and saw her mother as being responsible for the failure of the marriage. She was angry at her mother for having acted victimized, helpless, and pitiful in the wake of the divorce. Resentment grew with each late-night call she received from her mother, who remained in the family home with Debra's youngest sister Heather.

Debra said that when an early morning call from her father brought news of the murder, her husband merely got out of bed to unload the gun they kept at their bedside, as if to protect her from killing herself, and went back to sleep. Debra shed few tears at first. Her eldest brother had reportedly identified the body, so Debra never saw her mother dead, either at the morgue or in her casket. Her memories of the funeral centered around her father's flaunting his new wife and drinking heavily. His behavior made her feel guilty for having taken his side at the time of the divorce. While cleaning out her mother's possessions, Debra found a number of letters her mother had written to her but had never mailed. She impulsively destroyed them, feeling unable to read them. It is possible that the letters might have functioned as a linking object, but the guilt she felt for not having taken her mother's side in the divorce made it necessary for her to deny their existence. Without the benefit of a linking object, her feelings of guilt increased.

She returned from the funeral to her own failing marriage. Soon after the funeral her husband took her to see a film about a woman who was raped and murdered. Debra then began to experience anxiety attacks and sought psychiatric help. Her therapist allegedly failed to pursue the issue of her mother's recent death, and focused on her marriage problems. Debra terminated treatment after he made what she saw as a sexual overture.

She cared for Heather during the next two years, during which Heather had an illegitimate child. Debra's husband divorced her, and her father died from the results of alcohol abuse. By the time he died she had changed her opinion of him, coming to hold him largely responsible for the discord in his marriage to her mother. Nevertheless, she reported having felt grief over his death. For several years she led a driven, promiscuous sex life, and even worked at night as a waitress in a bar. This clearly represented an attempt to identify with the promiscuous mother, as well as being a counterphobic gesture aimed at trying to master and simultaneously deny what had happened to her mother. After marrying again, she settled with her new husband into an old house in the city of her mother's birth. She soon became symptomatic again, experiencing depressive affect, gaining weight, becoming frigid, and using alcohol more and more often. She formed an intense friendship with a woman very much like herself and like her mother—depressed, fat, and alcoholic. It is interesting to note that Debra's identification with her mother changed with her marital status. Single following her divorce, she was promiscuous in the service of denial. Remarried, she quickly lost interest in sex, becoming frigid—again in the service of denial, but this time in the service of denying her (repressed) perception that her mother had been sexually assaulted before being murdered.

She again sought psychiatric help, this time consulting a woman psychiatrist. Her presenting symptoms were depression and alcohol abuse. She worked for two years with this psychiatrist, who suffered from cervical disc problems and had to wear a cervical collar. (You will remember that the mother's cervical spine had been broken in the murder.) When her psychiatrist moved away, Debra was referred to Thomson, who was thus her third psychiatrist. In due time, Thomson came to understand that Debra's intense relationship with her second psychiatrist had, through transference, involved Debra in an effort to protect and save her. The fact that the woman physician had disc problems, and physically resembled Debra's mother as she had looked before becoming obese, made it difficult to work through and resolve her transference manifestations. It can be said that because the mother was recreated in the person of the woman psychiatrist, and because her "reappearance" was not resolved in the transference, the therapy had become a way for Debra to deny her mother's death and thus avoid the pain of grieving; therapeutic movement was thus effectively blocked in spite of the "trusting and good" relationship between Debra and her psychiatrist. Since reaction to the mother's murder could be denied as a result of this "good therapeutic relationship," Debra's depression was relieved—although obviously not worked through. Both therapist and patient tried to work on ways in which the latter could shake off her husband's domination. The sleeping tiger—which usually wakes up sooner or later—was left untouched in the service of playing with a kitten.

Debra's mourning

Debra embarked on treatment with Thomson preoccupied with the belief that work with a male therapist would inevitably be hindered by the issue of sexuality. She had split the representation of her mother, so that the "good mother" image—deposited with her previous therapist—was no longer available to her. This left her with what she called "the filth fairy," in comparison to which Thomson was seen as "Mr. Clean." Debra lamented her continued infertility, seeing it as punishment for her promiscuity. She granted enormous power to men, submitting to their wishes even while resenting her submission. Although she consciously denied her angry resentment, she acted on it in passive fashion. To her, any expression of affection or closeness offered by a man had sexual implications. The transference then developed around the paradigm of the seductive father and the submissive but stimulated daughter.

During her first five months in treatment, she seemed preoccupied with oedipal issues, but the oedipal reference was far too open. Although she had as a child been stimulated by her father, the therapist felt that the oedipal material she offered was not genuine; when he tried to explore the affective aspects of the transference manifestations of these issues, nothing happened, and he began to form the idea that such manifestations were in fact a screen over other conflicts. When Debra complained of her depression, her gain in weight, her resort to alcohol, her early rising with an urge to urinate, and her fear of death, her therapist systematically brought to her attention that these symptoms included those suffered by her mother just before her death. Debra's complaint of frigidity was also linked to her mother as a form of denial of the sexual assault that had accompanied her mother's murder. Slowly her resistance to recognizing her reactions to her mother's murder, and the fantasies that she had had about it, were brought to Debra's attention. She reacted with intense anxiety, anger, and stubborn refusal. She dreamed of tornadoes killing her mother, and associated them with penises. She openly stated her fear that it would overwhelm her to experience her feelings about her mother. She wore a beautiful summer dress to one session, proudly telling how she had spent many hours making it during the previous week, but suddenly, near the end of the hour, became aware, that there was something wrong with it—that it was black, the color of mourning.

In the sixth month of Debra's psychoanalytic psychotherapy, Thomson sensed her willingness to give up her resistance and to set aside the oedipal material. She reported one dream in which she had returned to the family home in which her mother had lived at the time of the murder. She found her mother living there in abject poverty. Associations produced the insight that Debra had been living during the ten years after the murder as though she were waiting for her mother to return. She felt that she had ignored her mother's plight, and that she could have done much more than she had done to alleviate the despair and loneliness she imagined her mother had suffered. In another dream, Debra found herself in a field with other women. They were all being shot but Debra escaped to make love with the "friendly assassin." She believed that since she had been so angry with her mother at the time of her death she should not be permitted to love her, and therefore to grieve. Now both Debra and her therapist could see that her pattern of drinking and obesity was identical to that of her mother. The excess weight and alcoholism evidenced a disruptive identification with her mother's representation that served to keep the mother alive within her daughter. It served further to hinder her sexual life with her husband, and reduced the possibility of happiness and sexual fulfillment in her marriage. This understanding led her to say that she thought her mother would be happy knowing that her daughter was not enjoying sex.

She dreamed of separating a "pussy cat" and a "tomcat" that were fighting. Tom was her father's name, and she connected this dream with feelings of being the arbitrator of her parents' discord and sexual conflicts.

The treatment process did not go smoothly, however. Debra continued to present resistance in the form of oedipal transference material, such as dreams alluding to sex with her therapist. Hysterical character pathology was reflected in her dreams of penis envy and masochistic submission. To be sure, these were important aspects of her psychopathology, but at this point in her treatment they were in the service of resistance rather than of working through.

Throughout her therapy she had denied that her mother had been raped at the time of her murder. She would become furious whenever this possibility was mentioned, or when its likelihood was linked to her own promiscuous period after the murder and her current sexual dysfunction. Denial ended only when her equation of sex with death was unmasked. Unconsciously, Debra had believed that becoming emotionally and sexually intimate with a man would lead her down a road from which there was no escape. Way stations on this road were abandonment by the man in favor of another woman; rejection; separation; and divorce. The end of the road was death. The expression of these feelings allowed her to experience the buried emotions attached to her mother's death.

This new phase of her treatment was heralded by a critical dream in which Debra drove across a bridge to see her burned mother in a hospital. Debra had complained of a bridge phobia when she first consulted her female therapist, and one may speculate that this phobia may have had to do with Debra's fear of retaining a link between her dead mother and herself. (Recall the destruction of the letters that had linked her to her mother.) While Debra's primary mode of dealing with her mother's death was disruptive identification, there were also elements of the externalization that is characteristic of established pathological mourning. She had externalized the "good mother" onto her female therapist, for example. In the same way, the "bridge dream" may have been evidence of externalization. In any case, after seeing her mother in the dream, Debra felt that "It's all right for my mother to die now."

Other dreams were equally important. One evening, when her husband made a casual sexual approach, Debra panicked, feeling trapped, convinced that she was about to be raped and murdered. Several nights later, she dreamed that she and her mother were standing outdoors when two tornadoes passed over; she ran to retrieve her mother's empty purse (symbolic of the female genitals) and a large storm passed over her mother who nevertheless remained alive, soaked by a "cleansing rain." Debra's associations equated the two tornadoes with her parents, whom she felt obligated to protect from each other. The large storm had a sexual quality, and she saw it as her mother's death after being sexually molested. The "cleansing rain" and the fact that her mother remained alive despite the large storm expressed her wish that her mother was now in heaven and that she herself had been absolved of guilt by her therapist.

The next session marked the turning point in her treatment. Her sister Heather had kept their mother's autopsy report in an envelope in a closet with the transcript of the murderer's trial. Debra came into the crucial session carrying an envelope that she laid on a footstool before the therapist. She was extremely agitated. After a long silence, she asked him to open the envelope and read the autopsy report aloud to her. He did not, but, by way of exploring her resistance, asked her to read it aloud herself, and assured her that he would stand by her while she did. After much hesitation she opened the envelope and began reading the report. Only a few of the medical terms had to be explained to her. The rest was gruesomely clear.

A dam broke. In the end of that session and in all of her hours for the next several weeks she was filled with grief. She repeatedly imagined what her mother's last hour of life must have been like. She had her sister read the trial transcript to her. At his trial, her mother's killer had declared that she had been drunk, and had urinated on the front seat of his car. He claimed to have exploded with fury and to have broken her neck. After sexually abusing her, he scattered the contents of her purse, just as Debra's dream had indicated, and fled. The feelings she had had at the time of the funeral also poured out. The intense responsibility she had felt for her mother's death had caused her to shut out all emotions at the time it occurred, as it had caused her to destroy all her mother's unmailed letters to her. Her denial ended, Debra raged against the murderer and acknowledged all the anger her mother had provoked during the year before her murder. For the first time, Debra openly reviewed her life with her mother, with all the extremes of feeling such a review involved: joy and sorrow, anger and pity, hope and disappointment, frustration and guilt.

This phase ended with a dream in which Debra was riding in an automobile, seated on the front seat between her father, who was at the wheel, and her mother, sitting on the passenger side. Her father reached over and began fondling her leg, whereupon Debra insisted that he stop the car and let her mother and herself get out. When the car stopped, her mother refused to get out with her daughter, who pleaded with her at first and then made it clear that if she did not come she, Debra, would not be responsible for the consequences. The mother stayed in the car and was driven away by her husband. Debra walked down the road alone, feeling content in the knowledge that she had done all she could do to save her mother.

With her buried grief unearthed, Debra quickly moved into a genuine transference neurosis. She worried about her therapist's power and sexuality. Her spontaneous associations, fantasies, and dreams showed the dynamics of a classical hysterical neurosis, and treatment followed this path. Her grief continued to ebb and flow, usually in response to anniversaries, or dreams of her mother. Its full affective expression was not resisted, and it almost always led to deeper insights.

Heather

At the time Heather began psychoanalytic psychotherapy with Akhtar she was an attractive though mildly obese woman in her mid-twenties with many inhibitions. She could not bring herself to exercise, and kept putting on excess weight. Like her sister, she had low self-esteem. She did not enjoy having sex with her husband, and often made excuses to avoid it. She could not dress well, play her piano, or visit museums and art galleries; she consciously wanted to do all these things but, much to her annoyance, never actually did. Her marital difficulties arose from her lack of sexual responsiveness as well as from her ruthless and sadistic attacks upon a husband she insisted was a decent and considerate man. She was afraid that she was driving him away, but she could not stop herself.

She was the fifth child in the family, and remembered their life in Europe as pleasant, although she admitted that her mother had been given to drinking and that her father had often been away. She was 13 when her parents separated after their return to the States. Since the other siblings had already left home, Heather and her younger brother remained with their mother, whose drinking became more and more of a problem. Soon the younger brother left to live with their father, and Heather was left alone with her mother, who by then was an alcoholic and often obnoxious during her spells of hard drinking, which usually came at night. Heather recalled, "Mother was a mean drunk ... a lady during the day and a devil at night." She then reported, as had Debra, that her mother had found a loving and considerate friend and had begun to lose weight and to take better care of her appearance.

Her initial report of the murder was brief and to the point. One evening, as Heather was leaving home to go to a party, her mother asked her if she would be back soon. Heather said that she would, but later decided not to go home at all. The next morning she learned that her mother had been murdered during the night. Her version of the story was that her mother had apparently gone out to buy liquor, and on her way home had accepted a ride from a stranger, who had killed her. She also reported the familiar version of the mother's allegedly urinating in the man's car, and his killing her accidentally.

Her recall of the events immediately following her mother's murder was fragmentary and vague. She did say, however, that it had changed the course of her life. She became very much involved with Jim, with whom she had been partying the night her mother had died. He was a playboy who attracted—and was attracted to—many young women, but he did remain supportive of Heather for two or three years, making one condition of their relationship that she not get pregnant. Although she was aware that a pregnancy might rupture her relationship with Jim, Heather did get pregnant, and bore a son she named after Jim. The couple parted, and Heather then moved to the city where Debra lived. Debra provided much-needed emotional support, and it was on her suggestion that Heather gave up her son for adoption. The sisters stayed very close during the following three years; for all practical purposes Debra was her sister's surrogate mother. Then Heather married, and bore a daughter in the first year of her marriage. It was around this time that her psychological state worsened. By then Debra had gone into psychotherapy, and Heather gradually began disengaging herself from her sister. After about a year of suffering, Heather decided to seek professional help as well.

When psychoanalytic psychotherapy was suggested to Heather after her initial evaluation, she suddenly became resistant and dropped out, insisting, not very convincingly, that she could not afford the treatment financially. After about a year and a half, however, she returned to the same therapist and began treatment with him. Her reasons for returning were unclear, although it was soon learned that the day she went back to the therapist was the tenth anniversary of her mother's death. It also became apparent somewhat later in therapy that the considerable clinical improvement Debra had made in her treatment had been a source of encouragement to Heather.

Heather's mourning

Heather began treatment with detailed elaborations of her current limitations. She emphasized especially her lack of sexual desire, and her inability to lose weight. She wondered aloud about her reasons for maltreating herself, and quickly made the connection with the feeling of guilt she had had over her mother's death. This understanding seemed largely intellectual, however, and in its own right defensive. Session after session found her enumerating her inhibitions and wrapping up the discussion by pointing to her guilt over her mother's murder as the underlying cause of it all. "I know I feel guilty. ... If I had come back home that night, mother would not have gone out and gotten killed. She never used to go out at night alone." It was only later that she came to modify this last statement, as will be seen. With her guilt openly admitted, albeit in intellectual fashion, Heather was "hiding in the open."

During this phase of treatment, Akhtar's attempts to get her to talk about the circumstances of her mother's death and funeral were met with strong resistance. She would wave such efforts off, summarily announcing that she "knew" she felt guilty, and adding, "So what?" Or she would complain about the slowness of the psychotherapeutic work, and insist on quick removal of her symptoms. She would insist on talking about her sexual inhibitions as being her main difficulty, but her disclosures seldom led to any new association.

Because she seemed so resistant to. talking about her mother's death, Akhtar encouraged her to talk more generally about their relationship. She started with her childhood and recalled the warmth and love her mother had had toward her. Prominent among various memories of this time were recollections of their going together to art galleries and museums, and of her mother's explaining to her what they were seeing. Again resistance took over, and her associations became flooded with her flamboyant father. She would endlessly present material suggestive of a thinly disguised erotic relationship with him. He used to take her out alone on his golf trips; he made her a small golf club of her own; they often slept together when she was ten years old; and so on. She also recalled one of her brothers fondling her genitals when she was about eight or nine. (The same brother who had made Debra fondle his penis.) Then her associations led her to Jim, her first significant lover, and her descriptions of him made him seem remarkably like her father.

Instead of pointing out the oedipal issues in this object choice, Akhtar suggested that she must have badly needed to have emotional support after her mother's murder, and that this need may have consolidated her relationship with Jim. This conjecture led to the disclosure of more meaningful material; she recalled how obnoxious and even frightening her mother had been in her drunkenness. Once her mother had chased her around the block with a naked sword in her hand, and on another occasion she had run after her daughter with a golf club, threatening to hurt her. On many occasions, Heather now recalled, her mother had snatched the telephone on which Heather had been talking to a friend, calling her daughter and her daughter's friends dirty names. "Mother was a real bitch," Heather said. It was then pointed out to her that she often called herself a bitch, too. This was intended to be a gentle indication that she was identifying with her mother, and the reply was the intellectualized statement, "Oh, yeah. I know I have become like my mother. So what?" During the following session she enumerated her symptoms all over again, and insisted that the therapist do something about them and "not just keep talking." When it was pointed out to her how difficult it seemed to be for her to talk about her mother's last days, significant emotional flooding took place, and she began telling the story of her mother's death once again, this time in greater detail, and with genuine affect.

When Heather had returned home the morning after the party, she had been met by a neighbor who reported that someone wanted her on the telephone. It was the police, who asked her to go to the police station but gave her no further information. When she got to the police station she was taken to the morgue, where she (not one of her brothers, as the rest of the family, including Debra, had always believed) was asked to identify her mother's body. With many tears she reported her memories of what she had seen; her mother lying there with her neck broken and her hair matted with dirt and blood. Her eyes were open and there were bite marks on her face, neck, and shoulders. Heather recalled her state of shock; she had thought, "No! This is not happening! It's all an awful joke! It's a movie!"

After identification procedures were completed, arrangements for the funeral were made. By this time, all of the other family members had arrived, including her father and his new wife. Since nobody else knew the household well, Heather was asked to find a dress for her mother to be buried in. She chose a certain white dress that was actually one of her own. A few sessions later, Heather recalled that on the day of the funeral she herself had worn a black dress that had belonged to her mother. The distinction between the representations of the two women—one dead and one living—was thus blurred; the dead mother carried with her part of the living daughter, and the daughter symbolically wrapped her mother around herself. A Mother's Day card that Heather had planned to give her mother two days later was buried with her mother at her insistence.

Heather told about her mother's murder and funeral with appropriate emotions and pain, but soon turned her associations toward Jim, who stood for the seductive father. Openly oedipal material poured out, and in the transference Akhtar became the object of Heather's sexual attention. What had happened after the murder was being repeated in treatment. Heather was escaping from the pain brought about by the murder by seeking shelter in an activated relationship with the oedipal father. In due time, Akhtar interpreted to her the nature of her resistance against mourning.

Heather was now able to talk about how her mother had begun to lose weight and had begun looking prettier just before her murder. She also associated her own inability to lose weight with a fear of dying. Like Debra, she suffered reactive depression in disruptive identification with her mother. As therapy helped her to understand such identification and the emotions that accompanied it, she revealed the presence of linking objects that she used in a somewhat different way from that of a person in typical established pathological mourning; that is, she was able to touch them and to feel peaceful and guilt-free as she did so. Her mother's children had divided her possessions among themselves, but from her mother's considerable estate Heather had kept only her cold cream and her toothbrush. Her guilt would not permit her to claim anything expensive, but her desire to remain in contact with her mother led her to choose these seemingly insignificant items for their intimacy. After some years, however, she abandoned these objects and obtained a diary that her mother had kept during her last years, and the autopsy report and transcript of her murderer's trial.

During one of her sessions, Heather remarked in passing that she often got traffic tickets for parking in "the wrong place," and she added that she had recently caught herself driving rather recklessly. Associations to this behavior led her to confide that she had often told acquaintances that her mother had died in an auto accident—had been killed in a car parked in a "wrong place." She gained insight about her counterphobic attempt to master danger at "the wrong place"; about paying her dues (parking tickets) for her guilt; and keeping contact with the dead woman by identifying with her activity. This insight was followed by her revelation that she herself was "ladylike" by day but "a bitch" during evenings at home. She felt as if part of her were dead—had died along with her mother.

At this point she became greatly concerned over her daughter, and declared that if she resigned her job and spent more time with her daughter all her problems would be solved. She reported having had a dream in which she was with a graceful woman wearing a "white dress" and standing near a stream. Everything was safe and blissful in the dream. Attempts to interpret it as evidence of regressive longing to keep her mother alive met with resistance. Heather insisted that it reflected her desire to be closer to her daughter; the drama of mother–daughter reunion was thus being played out in reverse. She began to entertain fantasies of leaving her job, separating from her husband, and dropping out of treatment in order to relax and spend all her time with her two-year-old daughter.

Further inquiry revealed, however, that the fantasy of separating from her husband included her subsequently becoming "fat, miserable, and lonely." Similarities between this and her mother's fate after her divorce were pointed out. More associations led to the reconstruction of Heather's first "divorce"—from Jim after having Jim, Jr. Other important lost objects were thus cathected. She remembered further that after meeting her present and rather thin husband for the first time a thought had occurred to her: "God! Has no one fed this child?" He seemed to have become a replacement for Jim, Jr., the child she had not nourished but had surrendered instead. When she had a female child, the stage was set for the reenactment of the mother–daughter melodrama left unfinished by the sudden death of her mother.

As she uncovered this material, her associations once again led up to her sexual inhibitions. Exploration of these now revealed that when sexually approached by her husband she felt as if a "criminal" were touching her. This feeling was connected with the overt sexuality of her mother's murder. Her story of the murder now became more elaborate. She revealed that she had learned from the court transcripts that her mother had gone out to drink and was in a neighborhood tavern for two or three hours socializing with the men there, and being playful and seductive toward one much younger man. Then she had left in a drunken state with the man who was to be her murderer. Heather's fantasies now permitted her to believe that her mother may have been sexually aroused at the time, and that she may have been sexually assaulted before she was killed. She expressed surprise at her having taken at face value the testimony of her mother's killer; it seemed likely to her (as well as to Debra and to their therapists) that the statement about the sexual assault's having been an afterthought was an invention of a clever attorney and not a fact. She recalled that the murderer had been accused before of sadistic sexual assault on a woman, and had once been committed to a state hospital.

These realizations made it possible for her to feel angry at her mother for being in the bar in the first place. She then repeated her account of her mother's drunken and obnoxious behavior in greater detail, with genuine fear and anger. She also recalled that the night of the murder was *not* the first time her mother had gone out drinking, as she had previously insisted. Apparently her mother had been in the habit of dressing flamboyantly "in a red velvet dress with her hair loosened—looking like a whore," and going out at night alone.

A "second look"

Around this time there was a big family celebration for Thanksgiving. Heather reported that she, Debra, and the other two sisters had driven by the house in which their mother reportedly had spent her childhood. It was a kind of "second look" (Novey, 1968). With their car parked across the street from this house the four sisters looked at it and wept. Heather had fantasies of going in and touching the banister of the staircase that was visible from behind an open front door. "Mother must have slid down that banister as a child," she thought. She felt simultaneously in touch with and somewhat removed from her mother. Filled with sad feelings, the sisters drove home. During this time together it had become clear to them all that they had had quite similar responses to their mother's murder. All had become "depressed," and all had had episodes of being indifferent toward sex. Three were in treatment.

Some time later Heather's therapist took a six-week vacation overseas. She took this calmly enough, but in his absence, resigned from her job, thus seriously reducing her income and the insurance coverage for her psychotherapy. When her therapist returned, she insisted that he keep on seeing her without her making any payment. She was intellectually aware that this demand represented resistance to further treatment, but she doggedly refused to seek another job or to explore other means of payment. Soon she declared openly that she did not want to be in therapy any longer, and that spending more time with her daughter would be enough relief for her. Although significant and helpful work had been done with Heather, she seems to have reacted to separation from Akhtar in a symptomatic way with false bravado and denial of his importance to her. At the time of writing, a few months after Akhtar returned from his long trip abroad, she had not resumed therapy.

Conclusion

The "daughters of Goodbar" had disruptively identified with their mother's representation. Clinically depressed, they had used the mechanism of denial as a means of reducing their feelings of guilt. Both reported feeling as though a repulsive stranger was about to touch them whenever their husbands approached them sexually. Both held a deep-seated fear of sex, and equated it with death. Their sexual inhibition seemed directly related to the erotic overtones of the mother's murder, condensed with incestuous guilt based on childhood interaction with a seductive father and/or brother.

It is evident that both sisters failed to mourn their mother's terrible death. Each used her character neurosis as a defense against confronting her grief. Character pathology "contained" their grief, so that initial attempts to analyze the character neurosis failed until it was approached as a resistance to grieving. Both seemed to defend against two aspects of the mother's murder that they especially feared, and that their therapist reasonably assumed were true: that the mother *had* been sexually interested in her murderer and had knowingly placed herself in a vulnerable position; and that he *had* raped and sexually abused her while she was still alive and conscious. The daughters feared their grief; in their minds, it would mean coming face-to-face with the terror both imagined their mother to have felt in her last moments.

Their treatment, one continuing, the other finally "terminated" prematurely, shows how for ten years after the murder they used all kinds of maneuvers to deal with the tragic event. Debra had managed to avoid grieving in her two earlier therapies by hiding her reaction to death behind a smoke screen. Heather, who went into therapy a year and a half after her initial contact with Akhtar, seemed unable later to tolerate another meaningful separation—this time one from her therapist—by acknowledging pain or other emotion.

CHAPTER 9

Re-grief therapy

This chapter describes a short-term psychotherapy called re-grief therapy. The clinical research that led to its development was conducted with patients who had been hospitalized with established pathological grief or reactive depression after the death of someone important to them; it was based on a psychoanalytic understanding of the phases through which a mourner must pass in order to complete the mourning process. Research was focused on what dominated the condition of these mourners—the complication that had arisen in the course of their mourning.

I examine here the way in which re-grief therapy fits into the general classification of psychotherapies, and clarify what re-grief therapy can and cannot accomplish for the patient.

The case reported in this chapter serves to illustrate how the clinical study of re-griefing was conducted, and how an attempt was made to evaluate its benefit to the patient. Since the patient in question underwent psychoanalysis after completing his re-grief therapy, it was possible to see through the psychoanalytic microscope how he perceived his "re-griefing."

Brief psychotherapy

Both psychoanalysis proper and psychoanalytic psychotherapy are of necessity lengthy processes. In the first, the aim is to analyze systematically all of the patient's unconscious conflicts by encouraging the development and resolution of a transference neurosis, resolution being accomplished primarily by interpreting the forces that oppose it. The general aim of psychoanalysis proper is to help the patient make the best possible adaptation to both his inner and outer world.

The routine way of conducting the psychoanalysis of an analyzable patient is well established. The same routine is employed when the patient has initially undertaken psychoanalysis as a result of complications in the mourning process, however idiosyncratic his responses to his loss may be, however much obstruction to analytic progress his loss might represent. But while psychoanalysis proper deals comprehensively with impulse–defense constellations, internalized object relations conflicts, and developmental and psychosexual issues, I have not attempted in this volume to present all of the details of a pathological mourner's psychoanalysis, but have focused instead on bereavement-related issues of patients in analysis.

In previous chapters, I have given examples of the psychoanalytic psychotherapy of one case of established pathological mourning and two cases of reactive depression, all being associated with a loss by death. I have examined how some of the patients' unconscious conflicts relating to the complication of mourning were resolved, how they stemmed from childhood experience, and how the psychotherapist focused on the relation of the patients' difficulties to complications in the work of mourning.

The specific aim of re-grief therapy is to stimulate the resumption of the work of mourning. It is based on an understanding of the mourning process, on the use of all the therapeutic instrumentalities Bibring (1954) has described (see Chapter 7), and on the value of the linking object, a characteristic possession of this kind of patient, as a therapeutic tool. It may come about in certain cases that the patient not only becomes able to grieve as a result of re-grief therapy, but becomes interested as well in the possibilities for further emotional growth.

I should like at the outset to place re-grief therapy in the general classification of brief or short-term psychotherapy. A number of therapists have developed psychotherapies of no more than short duration based on psychodynamic insight (Sifneos, 1972; Malan, 1979). Sifneos selects as patients for brief psychotherapy those who exhibit acute neurotic symptoms, have a structural conflict and the ability to bear anxiety, and are psychologically-minded. He mobilizes anxiety in such patients against a background of manipulated positive transference. His therapy is, in other words, anxiety-suppressive, inasmuch as it requires the surrender of defenses (symptoms) erected against the (signal) anxiety. With the therapist's help, the patient finds a resolution that is more adaptive. I am in agreement with Gray's (1978) evaluation of Sifneos's method. She writes that while Sifneos's treatment

> ... does assuage the suffering caused by the patient's emotional crises, it does not aim to offer an opportunity for emotional growth through the development of insight. Although it is based on psychoanalytic theory, it is technically inconsonant with psychoanalysis. (p. 39)

Gray herself proposes a model for brief psychotherapy It

> ... uses the forces of change inherent in normal development to enable the patient to complete a developmental task which may have been insufficiently mastered at the appropriate time. (p. 29)

In Gray's opinion, the patient's present illness can often be correlated with this developmental failure, whether it occurred with respect to an oedipal task or one of an earlier or later stage in development. She holds that the clinical objective of her form of brief therapy is to help the patient take this one neglected step. As her clinical examples clearly show, she clarifies a single developmental issue in the context of a positive transference (working alliance). Since her technique is consonant with psychoanalytic technique, brief psychotherapy like hers can serve to introduce the patient to psychoanalysis proper should he choose to undertake it at some later date. I agree with her impression that it is usually futile to take a patient through more than one course of brief psychotherapy if the first is not profitable. If the patient cannot learn enough or effect enough change to maintain a good long-term adjustment, some other psychotherapy—one focusing on working through in the service of a major character change—is indicated.

Re-grief therapy is relatively brief in terms of the overall time involved but, given the nature of the material confronted, quite intense. Its objective is to help the patient complete the mourning process. The developmental issue affecting the patient's inability to mourn is identified, whether it pertains to the oedipal level or the level of separation/individuation. With the knowledge of this issue, which he may or may not share with his patient, the therapist helps the patient take the one step beyond the phase of mourning at which he has been arrested, a step that will enable him to bring the work of mourning to its practical completion. Although anxiety and pain appear when mourning has been (re-)initiated (as the patient faces his dependency needs or his murderous oedipal rage), these affects usually are utilized to gain further insight and not to erect more defenses. I believe that after the evolution of re-grief therapy from its crude beginnings (explained in the Introduction of this book) it became consonant with psychoanalytic technique itself, and that, thus, it is helpful in acquainting the patient with the nature of psychoanalysis proper, paving the way for him to embark on long-term psychoanalytic psychotherapy if that is his desire. When I report the termination dreams of Mike (following) and Roberta (Chapter 10), both of whom went through re-grief work, it will be evident that these patients perceived their re-grief therapy as focused mini-analytic work designed to help them understand and resolve limited conflicts, and that they understood their options about undertaking a "major operation" to help them resolve conflictual issues of a more general nature.

Re-grief therapy described

While elements of disruptive identification may sometimes be present in the clinical pictures of patients undergoing re-grief therapy, their use of a linking object clearly identifies them as suffering primarily from established pathological mourning. For all practical purposes, therefore, it is established pathological mourning that re-grief therapy attempts to relieve.

The therapist's initial task is the development of a formulation to explain his patient's complicated mourning. Although interpretation of the formulated issues is not initially shared with the patient, some clarification concerning them will help set the stage for therapeutic work. The patient is told that his dominant psychological state arises from his inability to mourn; he is offered a treatment (re-griefing) that will address this inability.

The patient in re-grief therapy is preoccupied with remaining in psychological contact with the representation of the person he has lost. He may perceive this representation as an introject, or he may be able to fully externalize the representation onto his linking object, so that he does not feel an inner presence. In any event, the assumption is that the patient continues to relate ambivalently to an unassimilated representation of the one he has lost. He longs for the person's return, at the same time as he wants to finally "kill" him, so as to complete the work of mourning.

During the initial phase of re-grief therapy, the therapist helps his patient to become aware of the distinction between what properly belongs to him, and what belongs to the representation of the dead person. When I first conceptualized re-grief therapy, I developed a rather mechanical means, which Showalter and I (1968) called *demarcation exercises*, to help the patient make such distinctions. For example, one patient referred to a letter he had received from his father shortly before his death, and was clearly preoccupied with certain statements it contained in which the father had expressed criticism of his son. The therapist could sense that his patient's feelings of guilt were such that he felt the criticisms to be his own self-criticisms. By means of various suggestions, the patient was directed to examine the handwriting in the letter and to recognize it as his father's. Thus his secondary process thinking was stimulated to help him distinguish his own representation from his parent's. I have moved away from the use of such mechanical devices, but I believe a detailed and empathic eliciting of the patient's history can serve as an exercise in demarcation, enabling the patient to begin differentiating his own thoughts, attitudes, and feelings from those under the influence of his introject. The therapist is well advised to refrain from questioning his patient while taking the history, which is best elicited in non-directive exchange.

The demarcation of the introject should focus not only on the history but also on the free associations pertaining to the relationship that had existed between the patient and the one he has lost. Such a focus enables the therapist to help his patient see what he has taken in, and thus helps the patient understand his feelings about the introject or the externalized representation of the dead. It is important here to note that although the patient himself may employ the kind of physical terminology we use in referring to his introject (as an inner presence), it is actually an affective-dynamic process. In this respect, the therapist who shares with his patient too quickly his formulation of the reasons for his fixation may find that he has retarded the affective-cognitive process involved in the activation of mourning. Conversely, the therapist should not encourage an outpouring of intense emotions, but help his patient into a state of preparedness for such an outpouring. If the patient senses emotion building up in himself, and feels frustrated at being unable to allow himself yet to feel its full impact, the therapist may say, "What is your hurry? We are still trying to learn all about the circumstances of the death and the reasons why you cannot grieve. When the time comes you may allow yourself to grieve."

During this time the therapist will have learned more of the reasons for his patient's having become fixated and unable to work out his grief, reasons that will later guide his clarifications and interpretations. At this point, however, he encourages the patient to repeat his accounts of the past pertaining to the deceased, to recall the circumstances of the final illness (or the fatal accident), the conditions under which he learned of the death, his reaction to seeing the body, the events of the funeral, etc. Again, instead of asking question after question to elicit this information, the experienced therapist will get better results by indirectly stimulating the patient to offer these topics, and allowing the verbalization of such material to blend with appropriate feelings.

The ambivalence felt toward the dead person is clarified. The therapist accepts such ambivalence not by reassuring his patient that it is normal, but by his therapeutic neutrality and his empathy. He wants to pique his patient's curiosity and promote his understanding that this ambivalence is largely responsible for his being torn between wanting to "save" the one he has lost and wanting to "kill" him. When the patient becomes able to alternate easily between the negative and positive aspects of his ambivalence, he usually becomes angry. Such anger may be diffused and directed toward others, but it authenticates the reality of the death, much as though the patient had gone back to the initial stage of his grief. Using his understanding of the psychodynamics involved in the patient's need to keep the dead alive, the therapist slowly clarifies and interprets the relationship to the lost one, and the reason why anger is an expectable emotion. Abreaction—"emotional reliving" (Bibring, 1954)—concerning certain past experiences connected with the dead one or with his death may occur at this point if everything goes well. Such abreactions reflect a recurrence of the initial reaction to death and a (re-)commencement of the work of mourning; the patient has started to re-grieve. It can be assumed that certain impulses su.ch as death wishes are now surfacing, and the patient's readiness to have these interpreted, and his readiness to confront his guilt feelings, can be assessed.

The patient with established pathological mourning typically uses the mechanism of (high-level) splitting in the initial stage of grief, and continues to use it thereafter. His use of it is brought to his attention by helping him focus on how he became aware that the dead person was in fact no longer living. This focus will obtain good results if attempted at an emotionally suitable time, and not as an intellectual exercise. The patient may show genuine surprise, and blurt out something like: "I thought he was not breathing anymore. But I didn't really look!" The therapist has helped him revisit the point at which splitting first took place. Now he can re-evaluate the reality of the death.

It is characteristic of our patients' experience that the funeral rite did not go well. The patient often did not see the coffin lowered into the ground. Asked at an appropriate time, "How do you know that he is buried?" the patient will surprise himself by realizing that one part of his awareness never did accept that the burial had been accomplished. He is then likely to feel anger at those who stood in the way of his participation at the funeral ceremony. The therapist has clarified for him that while he felt, and indeed knew, that death had occurred, he had paradoxically continued to behave as though nothing had happened.

The most important part of this phase of confrontation, clarification, and interpretation of death-related impulses, fantasies, and wishes—and the defenses against them—is the focus on the linking object. Because it has physical existence, with properties that reach the senses, it has greater impact as "magical" than does the introject. (It is assumed that where there is no introject, it is because the linking object substitutes for one through externalization.) Once the patient grasps how he has been using the linking object to maintain his absolute control over contact with the image of the dead person, as well as to postpone mourning, he will use it to activate his mourning. It will be suggested to him that he bring the linking object to a therapy session, where, typically, he carefully avoids it at first. With the patient's permission, the therapist may keep it in the therapy room, saying that its magical properties exist only in the patient's own perception of it. Introduced into the therapy process at last, it is placed between patient and therapist long enough for the patient to feel its spell. He may even be asked to touch it and to report anything that comes to his mind. I am even now astonished at what intense emotion is invested in the linking object. The emotion that is now generated serves to unlock the psychological processes that, until now, have been contained in the linking object itself. Emotional storms may continue for weeks; at first diffuse, they later become differentiated, and with the therapist, the patient can identify anger, guilt, sadness, and so on. The linking object will then at last lose its power, whether the patient chooses to discard it altogether or not.

Clarifications and interpretations concerned with death and the deceased, and the sharper focus on these subjects effected by the introduction of the linking object into treatment, lead to the treatment's final phase—disorganization, which is followed by re-organization, in which sadness appears. A graft, as it were, of secondary process thought is needed to help heal the wound that this experience has torn open. Patients who had never before visited the grave of the dead person now do so, as if to say goodbye; some who had not had a tombstone put in place are now able to make the appropriate arrangements. The mourner feels sad without experiencing guilt. Many patients spontaneously plan some kind of memorial ritual for the one they have lost. Many consult priests, ministers, or rabbis for religious consolation as they begin to accept the death. Patients have a sense of the introject's having left them in peace. They feel free, even excited, with the lifting of their burden, and begin to look for new objects for their love. It is my experience that the manifest content of the serial dreams of patients throughout their therapy is a useful indicator of where they are in re-griefing. Indeed, the fact of there being serial dreams, and not the repeating dreams of fixated mourning, suggests that progress is being made. Re-grief therapy can be completed in about two to four months with frequent sessions—three or four times a week.

Transference, insight, and working through in re-grief therapy

To elucidate the important meanings of the patient's loss would not be beneficial if done purely as an intellectual exercise. Throughout their treatment, patients should experience a variety of emotions as they gain insight into their inability to let the dead person die; re-grief therapy is designed to reactivate emotions frozen in the arrested mourning process.

Conversely, the use of the linking object—a non-analytic maneuver—brings about special emotional storms that are not curative without interpretation designed to engage the close scrutiny of the patient's observing ego. Thus, the link to the representation of the dead, externalized onto the linking object, is brought into the realm of the patient's inner experience. It should be noted finally that the patient's resistance to acknowledging his fixation in the work of mourning is interpreted on such levels that the interpretations made do not necessarily bring about a resolution of the infantile conflicts that underlie the fixation. One can assume that the patient may repress such conflicts even further as he frees himself of the conflicts of a higher level.

In spite of the use of a special device (the linking object) in re-grief therapy, the transference relationship is the vehicle whereby insight into ambivalence and the conflict between longing and dread is gained, and resolution effected. As in all other therapies whether psychoanalytic or not, the therapist must convey his non-exploitative desire to heal, and encourage his patient to express himself directly without any fear of hostile, punitive, engulfing, or abandoning responses. The therapist should actively, directly, and instructively oppose any initial shame or excessive control with which the patient may conceal the complications of his grief, and encourage his head on exploration of feelings and fantasies about the person he has lost, and the internal and external relationship he has with him. Through his activity, the therapist offers himself as a new object for the patient's consideration, aiming, as in psychoanalytic therapy, to develop a therapeutic alliance. But unlike psychoanalysis proper, re-grief therapy does not encourage the development of a full infantile transference neurosis. With modifications I have made for my own use, Rado's (1956) term "interceptive interpretations" accurately describes the therapist's interception of the development of an infantile transference neurosis in re-grief therapy by premature interpretation of the transference phenomenon. Thus, when it appears that an infantile transference neurosis may be developing, the therapist will interfere with *full* displacement of the representation of the dead person onto himself. The patient is thereby kept aware of the complications in his mourning for the original lost one. Still, the patient's reactions to parallel situations of loss involving the therapist—separations at weekends, for example—*are* interpreted in due time, and such interpretation makes it possible to work through past conflicts with the dead person in a focal way. (And, of course, the fresh grief caused by separation from the therapist at termination can also be put to appropriate use.) Transference reactions are inevitable, but infantile transference is not; selected references to and interpretations of transference reactions are therapeutically useful for providing close and intimate contact within the therapeutic setting as the patient's conflicts are understood.

Thus, although re-grief therapy is brief, lasting for months instead of years, it is intense, intimate, and certainly not superficial. Josephthal and I (1980) have written about how it is a type of therapy consonant with psychoanalysis, in spite of its avoidance of a ripened transference neurosis. It can be described as

> ... "mini-focal analysis" since it leads to the activating of certain areas of intrapsychic process, however focalized, and effects intrapsychic change in areas under treatment by means of "working through." Thus it is not recommended for therapists inexperienced in listening to the flow of unconscious process. It requires adherence to a therapeutic position and expert handling of transference and countertransference. (p. 135)

An example of re-grief therapy

Mike, a 23-year-old Jewish man, was the subject of an early effort to apply re-griefing techniques (Volkan, 1971). Seen from May 1st to July 1st—exactly two months—he had 25 sessions altogether. Although he had already manifested symptoms typical of established pathological mourning, it was not until the first anniversary of the death that an exacerbation of these symptoms brought him to the hospital's emergency room. He was at this time exhausted by his preoccupation with the image of his father, and had anxiety attacks and increases in heart rhythm that alarmed him about his physical health.

His parents had been vacationing at a resort when his father died. The couple was in bed after a day of swimming and snorkeling when Mike's mother awakened and noticed that her husband had thrust one of his legs out from beneath the covers. In the dim light, it looked bluish, and the thought occurred to her that he should have some attention for varicose veins. In trying to cover him, she felt how cold his flesh was, and screamed for help, realizing that he was dead. The mother's account of her grim discovery was repeated in detail to her son, to whom she somehow conveyed the notion that it was the swimming and snorkeling that were responsible for his father's death.

On the night his father died, Mike was far away, in the town in which he attended college. He had taken his girlfriend, who was visiting him, to a motel, feeling some constraint in doing this because his mother disapproved of their fervid relationship. He received word of his father's death from friends, who after taking the telephone call from his mother, banged on the door of his motel room with the news.

Mike had a sister a few years his junior. His father had been a surgeon. In giving his history, Mike referred to his mother as having been "manic-depressive" during his childhood. This may or may not have been an accurate statement, but she had spent time in a hospital when he was very young, and her absence had sensitized him to separations. When "manic," she had acted in a seductive way toward him in childhood and puberty. He recalled her preening before him in a tiger-skin bikini. Such sexual stimulation frightened him. His father was often away from home because of his career. Mike made it a point to appear extremely self-reliant, but his basic dependency needs persisted. He had a cohesive self-concept.

At times, Mike's father, who had been dominated by his own father, and overshadowed by an elder brother, had seemed bewildered by his wife's behavior. It was only after his elder brother's death "liberated" him toward the end of his life that he had presented a model for his son, in whom he then began to take an active interest, preparing him for medical school and supporting his plans for marriage. It seems that both father and son had tried to make up for the lost positive oedipal relationship, and that Mike had responded on his own part with constructive attempts to identify with his father. When Mike started dating, his father was the only family member who supported his choice of the girl who interested him most. Mike had long talks with his father about the earlier behavior of his mother, and the father now gave his son "permission" to redefine his mother's role, and to replace her with his own woman.

At Mike's puberty, his father checked his testicles to be sure that both had descended so that he could one day beget a child. This act made the boy anxious about his manhood, and in spite of his father's reassurances, he felt that only by impregnating a woman could he prove himself. When Mike was 22, just after his father's death, he made his girlfriend pregnant. He kept his father's image alive in order to convey this triumph to him, as well as to deal with other oedipally tinged issues.

Mike's re-grief therapy

After his diagnostic interview, Mike was told that his symptoms had a great deal to do with his unfinished mourning for his father, and a goal-limited treatment to help him complete his mourning was offered. During his first three hours, he talked spontaneously about death and his dead father, and was preoccupied with the business of death. He anxiously made jokes and "unintentional" remarks openly referring to "death wishes" about "killing" his father in order to complete his mourning for him. From time to time he referred to feelings of reunion and merging with his father's image, speaking of the strange feelings that seized him when he handled things the dead man had handled. He treasured his father's electric razor, for example, but when he used it he was obsessed with the idea that his whiskers would "merge" with those of his father in the instrument. He could not bring himself to clean it for six months after the death.

He indicated that in recent years he had come to depend upon his father. "When he died, a rug was pulled out from under my feet. Where will I turn now?" He felt as if he had contributed to his father's death. In describing a dispute they had once had, he spoke of his father as having been "mortally hurt" by something he had said. While wishing his father were alive, he disclosed unconscious fears that his father would come back and hurt him. He joked, "I can't talk against the dead so much, because if you knock them down they come back." He felt that his father was both dead and not dead, and he had repeated dreams of seeing him struggling for life as a hospital patient. He recalled sensing complications in his grief reaction: "Suddenly I was the head of the family. My uncle said I should take care of the women. No one thought of my shock!"

During his fourth hour, Mike told about how, soon after the news of the death had come, he had felt compelled to eat a beefsteak that his father had bought, and which was still in the refrigerator in his apartment. I understood this as a symbolic attempt to internalize his father, but this formulation was not shared with the patient at the time.

I must emphasize that Mike was treated at a rather early stage in my investigation of the complications of adult reactions to death, and that my ideas about the linking object were not then fully formulated. But I had been impressed by the value such patients placed on "magical" inanimate objects, which I initially referred to as "symbolized objects" (Volkan, 1970). Mike's very early reference to his father's electric razor piqued my curiosity again about these symbolized objects in which patients merge with and touch the image of the dead. At the end of his first week of therapy I explored with him the possibility that he had other inanimate objects that held unique meaning for him. He did have them, as I will report, and my work with him contributed greatly to the formulation of my ideas about linking objects.

The first item Mike referred to in this connection was a letter from his father in which his father blamed him for buying a motorcycle. Free association elicited an account of its purchase and its subsequent sale at the insistence of both parents, who had thought it dangerous. Mike felt his manly pride had been injured by this episode, and the negative aspect of his ambivalence toward his father surfaced.

It was in the third week of his treatment that he directed my attention to his most important "symbolized object." After his father's death, his mother had enlargements of her husband's photograph made, and had given one to each of her children in a folder. This picture became magical for Mike. I asked him to bring it to his hour, but when he did so, he hesitated to open the folder. When he finally did open it, he anxiously closed it again after one brief glance at the picture inside. I noticed that the folder was wrinkled, and when I commented on this, I uncovered a highly symbolic story. Mike had taken the picture to the basement of his apartment building, and had "accidentally" placed it under a dripping water pipe. His further associations to this made it clear that (1) he had been unable to weep over his father's death, and the dripping water was associated with his desire to do so; (2) he wanted to drown his father. Drowning, of course, was associated with the actual circumstance of the death, the snorkeling of the previous day that had caused his father to take in considerable amounts of sea water. It was then that Mike told me how his mother had conveyed to him the idea that water sports had killed his father by putting an insupportable strain on his heart. Mike's act of putting the photograph under dripping water may thus be said to represent an attempt to "kill" his father. This magical act supported his illusion that he could choose between "killing" or "saving" him.

After talking about the picture Mike said that in fact he was afraid of crying. I asked him if he felt, in view of his mother's report that his father had nearly drowned while snorkeling, that if he shed tears they would drown him. We were both aware of the many times he had experienced "merging" with his father. I reassured him that I would stand by him if he wept. When he understood my suggestion that looking at the photograph might make him cry, he took off his glasses. I told him he need not look at the magical photograph until he was ready. During one of his later hours he did open the folder, which I had kept in my office. On doing so he felt shock, and stated that the picture was not exactly like the image of his dead father that had appeared to him in a dream, which he later told me about. Touching the folder, and then his face, he recalled the razor and began crying aloud. The tears ran down his cheeks for 15 minutes before he gave a narcissistic cry: How could his father have died and left him? Who was going to look after him?

Returning to the dream, Mike reported:

> I was with my father at a shopping center. I was being prepared to have an operation on my leg. Then I looked at my father and I knew that he was about to die.

This dream was reported on May 23rd. Mike's first association was to his father's attempts to be friendly with him and to help him follow in his own footsteps and go to medical school. He had once invited his son to watch him operate, trying to promote his identification with him as a physician. Mike had regarded watching his father perform surgery as highly significant, and symbolized it as an initiation into manhood.

I told him that he had identified with his dead father in his dream. His mother had emphasized how she had noted the blue look of her husband's leg before she realized that he was dead, and had spoken of her immediate thought that he needed an operation for varicose veins. In his dream, Mike's identification had led him to become the live father in need of an operation on his leg. I used the manifest content of this dream to clarify for Mike how he was maintaining contact with his dead father, but I made no attempt to convey to the patient the latent content of the dream.

We used the photograph in the next session as well. This time Mike did not cry openly, but his eyes watered and he sneezed, attributing all this to "a cold." He recalled the night when news of the death had reached him in the motel room he was occupying with his future wife. He remembered a dream he had had that night after intercourse with his girlfriend. In it, his father had punished him for driving his car too fast. The recollection of this oedipally significant dream led to an angry outburst against his mother and uncle, who had treated him as a child while burdening him with the adult responsibility of making the arrangements necessary for the funeral. They had, of course, been trying to "protect" him from his grief. On the night of the death, his uncle had warned him over the telephone not to try to drive home alone. At the same time, however, he had given Mike the responsibility for the legal affairs that now needed attention.

Toward the end of the first month of his re-griefing, Mike brought in another symbolized object, a key chain. It lacked the magical impact of the photograph, but there was confusion in Mike's mind as to whether it belonged to him or to his father. As a typical linking object, it had become a meeting ground for his representation and his father's. When he associated to its somewhat limited magic, he was able to differentiate himself further from his father

On May 31st, he reported dreaming of receiving a birthday gift, which, when he unwrapped it, turned out to be a telephone that came in pieces like a puzzle to be put together. I reminded him that the telephone call in which his mother had tried to notify him of his father's death had come from a great distance, and she had been unable to reach him directly since he was not in his room. I told him that he felt guilty about being in the motel room with his girlfriend. And since the dream about the birthday gift came when he was learning in his therapeutic work to distinguish what was his from what was his father's, I suggested to him that it represented his putting together bits of reality—solving a puzzle. He responded by reporting that he had been for some time assembling the components of a hi-fi set, and that the telephone in the dream stood for the communication with me that had given him hope to believe that he could learn to bring together the scattered pieces of his psychological processes.

There were further associations to the "birthday dream," now more indirect ones. After it, Mike reported that he had stopped seeing his father's body as it had been when flown home for burial. He felt that he had now achieved a "spiritual merging" with his father that he did not want to spoil. He continued to assess his father's own life at the end. He recalled that his father had at last escaped paternal and filial domination after the death of his own father and his elder brother, experiencing what Mike called a "re-birth." This "rebirth" had permitted Mike's father to become close to his own son and to initiate him into manhood.

Mike continued to relate memories of his father's death. At the funeral, he had left the cemetery before the interment. Since he insisted that he had been unable to look into the coffin, I asked him how he could be sure that his father lay within it and thus had been buried with it. My question was designed to bring to the surface his suspicion that his father was not dead. He became bewildered at this, and seemed uncertain as to whether his father were dead or alive. At home he had once cried out, "Get out! Get out!" to the introject of the dead father he felt within himself.

He had married his pregnant girlfriend a few months after his father's death. Husband and wife seemed to be close, and I felt that his wife had supported his efforts to complete grieving. She became concerned about him in therapy, and with his permission, I saw her as well, in order to support her efforts to stand by him during his difficult hours.

External events often have profound internal meanings for our patients. Robert Kennedy's assassination was such an event for Mike, helping him to examine his splitting. He said, "It is so absurd! It was so sudden!" He refused to watch the televised funeral until I suggested that he do so. The sight of a Kennedy son acting as pallbearer reminded him that he had been "an errand boy" at his father's services, and had been unable to participate fully in them or to express his feelings. He remembered being angry at those who wept. He had wanted to say, "Don't cry! *I* want to cry. After all, he was *my* father!" I asked him to name his emotion as he told me this with tears in his eyes. "Grief—Okay," he replied, and once again I introduced his father's picture. This time his emotional response was different—silent, and genuinely sad.

While, typically, he had not visited his father's grave since the funeral, he now became interested in doing this. I suggested that we talk about it first. He was uncertain about being able to locate the grave, even doubted its existence. He commented disapprovingly on burial in sealed coffins of the kind selected for his father, and gave his view that immediate decomposition should be allowed to occur. I interpreted these thoughts as doubts about the reality of the death, and fears that the dead man might rise. Since he had friends who were medical students and he himself had worked part time in a hospital in anticipation of entering medical school, he had access to a medical center and decided to make arrangements to see a cadaver there because he had never had the experience of seeing a dead body. Although his plan sounded macabre, I did not interfere, since I knew that this was something he wanted to do in the service of testing reality.

His preparation during early June to visit the grave evoked two temporary symptoms—tube vision, which made him feel as though he were "sinking into a grave," and stomach trouble with loss of appetite, which is a symptom of the initial stage of grief. Eating is then sexualized and defended against; I recalled Mike's eating the beef steak after learning of his father's death. His reluctance to visit the grave was conscious. He postponed the visit for three days, first doing something to his car that delayed his departure so that he arrived at the family home after the cemetery was closed for the night. He also "forgot" his camera, and was obliged to use his father's to take pictures of the grave to show me. On the second day at home, he visited a rabbi to go through the Jewish burial ritual. Instead of going to the graveyard that afternoon, he went to an ophthalmologist for treatment of a stye that had caused his eye to fill with tears, which he also understood were caused by his emotion.

He did go to the cemetery on the third day, and was virtually on top of his father's grave before he was aware of it. "For all practical purposes I was *in* it—I mean I was *on* it!" He knew that his father was buried six feet below, but at the graveside he felt him to be nearer; he was apparently not ready to bury his father completely. He reported that at the last minute he had taken the caretaker's dog with him to the grave in spite of his determination to make this difficult pilgrimage alone. The companionship of the dog seemed to have helped him deal with his anxiety. In telling about this, he began to weep, and reported a new dream he had had on the night after visiting his father's grave on June 17th.

> I was driving some type of vehicle on the sidewalk as I had done when I was a child. My dream took place in the downtown area of the town I live in. I was going toward the University Medical Center [where his therapist's office is located], and after I passed the Safeway Store I found myself at a place that looked like a slaughterhouse. [In reality, between the downtown area and the Medical Center there is a Safeway Store, next to which is a funeral home.] I saw a big dead cow and a newborn calf. Someone had slit open the cow's belly and then wrapped up the newborn calf and placed it in the belly of the cow.

This dream, which we called his "Safeway dream" and which followed the visit to the grave, might represent, I told him, the "safety" he now felt in examining the disturbing unconscious processes. In direct association to this dream, Mike himself suggested that he was the calf that had been placed in the dead cow and thus forced to merge with it. Further associations were to his remark at the grave: "For all practical purposes I was *in* it—I mean *on* it."

At the end of this hour, Mike spontaneously announced that he was ready to take back the magical photograph of his father in its folder, which I had been keeping in my office. He took it and later had it framed and put on his desk. Its magic had disappeared and there was no longer any need to distance it.

Within a few days he returned to the cemetery, this time without the dog. By now all of the pictures he had taken at the grave had been developed. The film included some pictures his father had taken on the vacation trip on which he had died. I felt that Mike had known all along about these pictures so poignantly reflecting the closing days of his father's life, and that he had wanted to test reality with them. He included them with the series of 24 pictures taken at the cemetery, which he asked me to view in order. He had taken them according to his memories of the funeral, beginning with the approach to the cemetery and continuing with pictures of the gate and views from both sides of the road. He had managed to include his shadow in all of the pictures of the grave, and interpreted this maneuver himself as evidence of his wish to "go in." He laughed at the notion, and denied that it still made him nervous. I could now see a welling up of humor in his ready smile.

The termination of Mike's re-grief therapy

On his second visit to the cemetery, Mike actually walked on the grave and convinced himself that his father was indeed dead. This was toward the end of the second month of re-griefing, at about the time he reported having gone to see a cadaver and not being afraid of it. After he viewed the cadaver, he had a dream that he reported during his next hour with me on June 24th.

> I saw many of my classmates, and was getting ready to take an examination. I was anxious. Then the thought occurred to me that, after all, I was not in school anymore and there was no need for me to be anxious. I felt relieved.

I felt that this "examination dream" in many ways resembled Freud's (1900) description of examination dreams. Freud held that such dreams occur only when someone has successfully passed some test. They convey to the dreamer the message, " 'Don't be afraid of tomorrow! Just think how anxious you were before your Matriculation, and yet nothing happened to you' " (p. 274). The dream suggests to the dreamer that he has already succeeded in what he has had to tackle. The part of the dream in which Mike rationalizes his anxiety may be viewed as representing his understanding that there was no longer any reason to fear death or dead bodies, just as there had been no reason to fear the viewing of the cadaver. Mike had taken a sick leave from the university just before beginning his re-grief therapy, and after reporting his examination dream, he went to register at the university once again.

During his hours now, he did not refer to his father but talked excitedly about his own daughter. Suddenly he announced that the child's name began with the same initial as his father's. He had found a link between the living and the dead On June 27th he reported: "I had a dream about my father, but this one was different. In this dream my father was *dead*." We then talked about how our task of helping him to complete his work of mourning was coming to an end·

On July 1st he reported the following dream: "I felt that I had had a minor operation on my chest, performed recently. I also felt that I had the option of undergoing a major operation." On this day, we both agreed that the "minor operation" referred to our goal-limited therapy. Mike then told me that he had become increasingly interested in the unconscious psychological processes that we had observed and understood in therapy. Recalling his childhood amid his mother's "depressed" and "manic" episodes, he had become curious about his general characterological makeup, and thought of going into analysis. I offered neither encouragement nor discouragement. He said that he had an "option" to go into analysis but that he wanted to wait to see what would develop after his "minor surgery" was concluded. With this we mutually terminated his re-grief therapy.

Sequential psychological examinations

Mike's re-grief therapy was included in a project devoted to the study of established pathological mourning and its treatment, and all the patients involved were given psychological tests just before and just after undergoing re-griefing. A carefully selected series of Thematic Apperception Tests (TAT) and Make-a-Picture-Story Tests (MAPS) was used to supplement the standard administration of Rorschach, Minnesota Multiphasic Personality Inventory (MMPI), Bender Gestalt, and Draw-a-Person (OAP) tests. The MMPI was also given at the midpoint of therapy because it is more sensitive to symptomatic changes than the other tests in the battery. The midpoint became clinically evident when the patient's "frozen" mourning process began to thaw, so to speak, and disorganization appeared as antecedent to the anticipated reorganization that would permit firmer reality testing of the death.

The psychologist and the therapist had agreed not to exchange information about test results or the progress of therapy until the conclusion of the study. While the psychotherapist was aware of characterological problems and psychopathology other than that centered on unfinished mourning, the presence of which was confirmed on the psychological tests, the emphasis remained on established pathological mourning, and the effect of re-grief work on this constellation. Mike's test results are given here as an example of the usual test responses over time of re-griefing patients. Figure 1 is a summary of Mike's MMPI tests,[1] given to him on May 1, June 3, and July 1.

Mike's interim MMPI (June 3) shows a peak on scale 2 (referred to as the Depression Scale), which was also seen on May 1. But his interim test gave evidence of decompensation of his obsessive–compulsive defense system, and the occasional appearance of disorganized ideation. The time of the second MMPI, as indicated, corresponded to that phase in the treatment during which Mike's reality testing was being challenged by evidence of splitting and by the unacceptable thought and feeling about his father's death that he was being made conscious of for the first time. The test results are thus consistent with the clinical picture at that time. The final MMPI profile showed little change in Mike's basic personality structure, but indicated a marked reduction of his symptoms, particularly those of depression and anxiety.

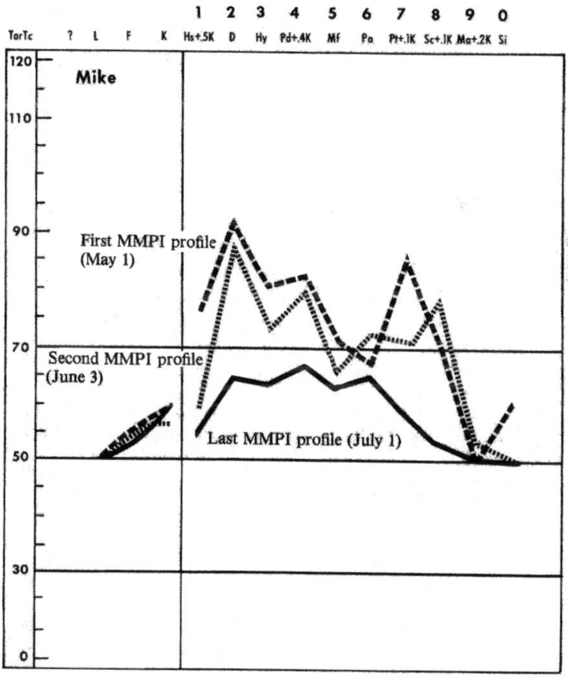

Figure 1 Summary of Mike's MMPI tests

[1] These tests and others referred to were given to Mike by psychologists Burke Smith and Nancy Phillips, who also helped prepare this section of the chapter.

In general, all data from post-therapy testing showed that Mike's intellectual controls had strengthened and enabled him to cope more adequately with environmental stress. His defensive use of somatization and obsessive–compulsive behavior decreased significantly. His scores in the MMPI were consistent with the composite MMPI scores of five patients in a pilot study of re-griefing (Volkan, 1971).

It is noteworthy that the MMPI is not only an effective self-rating measurement of change during re-grief therapy, but also offers promise for the selection of patients for this type of treatment (Volkan, Cilluffo, and Sarvay, 1975). Patients treated by re-grief therapy generally exhibit underlying personality traits of hysteria and dependence, and tend to show

> ... an elevation of scales 1, 2, 3, 7 and 8, and, to a lesser extent, of scales 4 and 6. Peaks generally came in scales 2 and 7, and the pilot data suggest that elevation of scales 2 and 7 to a point in excess of the showing on scale 8 is predictive of maximum benefit from re-griefing. (Volkan, Cilluffo, & Sarvay, 1975, pp. 190-191)

Sequential MMPI tests given to patients in re-grief therapy show that there is an increase in emotionality in the first part of re-grief therapy that is subsequently resolved in the later stages of treatment.

In other tests Mike took at the end of treatment, he showed an advance in control and organization on the Bender Gestalt and DAP, and dropped some of his poor response on the Rorschach test, particularly uncontrolled color responses. On the TAT and MAPS, he showed an increase in self-acceptance, along with a reduction of guilt feelings. He was less preoccupied with himself and his problems than he had been at the start of treatment, and felt better able to interact effectively with others and to pursue constructive aims, as shown by his responses to the blank TAT card. On May 1 he stated:

> Well, right now this card looks like my future .... I really don't know where to go, or what to do. I'm trying my damnedest to make decisions that are strictly up to me and I don't feel able .... But then this whiteness—is like a mass—it is like a block—it's like a large—almost like you see in a bad dream or nightmare—an intolerable weight that overpowers and paralyzes. ... It will represent the amount of work I have to do in order to catch up after not doing a damn thing for a year .... I have no answers. I find that

> I am in the position of having to make my own future and the pressure is on me and I can't stand the pressure.

His July 1 response was:

> Well, again I got not a particular image in mind—sort of using the idea "blank." Before, I thought that it was me, rather monolithic; this time it looks like a clean sheet of paper—as a future. I have absolutely no idea what's going to happen; at least, I don't feel superly impressed .... It is, you know, that I have a chance. I have more control over what is going to happen in the future than vice versa, than the future having control over me. Well, the idea of the future really oppressed me; completely weighed down, sort of like locked in—with everything. Like the future was almost too much to think about and I didn't feel capable of doing anything. I don't feel exactly capable of doing a lot of things now, but I think that I'll find something. ... I can sort of take the blows of fate and, you know, not get crushed.

Although Mike continued to be excessively dependent and attention-seeking, an increased willingness to deal with some of his dependency needs was suggested on the tests. Difficulty in the direct expression of aggression was demonstrated, but there was evidence of an increased conscious awareness of his hostile feelings. Acceptance of his father's death was shown by a comparison of his MAP responses to the Graveyard Stimulus card. (The subject has the option of placing different figures around the pictured grave to make a story.) His initial response (May 1) had described his mother grieving over her dead husband.

> The figure on the right is my mother, grieving. Her husband is dead, her marriage is dead—and all she has left is the grave. ... I'm on the left. ... I don't feel that I can help. I'm shocked and still stunned—over what's happened. That's it.

His final response (July 1) dramatically reflects his acceptance of the death:

> Reminds me of my fath er's grave as it appeared a few weeks ago, and I went and sort of stood there, almost exactly like that, contemplated my dead father, so to speak, except this time he was dead—very dead—never to rise again—and he would not help, cannot help, will not help—you know, I just came to grips with—the reality of it. He [the figure representing the patient] feels very tired, like he's sort of reached the end of a road, feels relieved, though he's tired. He doesn't feel like he has to worry about this anymore.

What ultimately happened to Mike

Three months after terminating his re-grief therapy Mike called for an appointment; when he appeared, he showed no symptoms of established pathological mourning. He felt subjectively at this time that his problems over his father's death had been solved. He was no longer bothered by the death, but had become curious about himself and aware of certain personal characteristics that he wanted to do something about. The "minor operation" was over, and he was ready to undertake the major one. Thus we began his analytic treatment. A year later he was admitted to medical school elsewhere and had to leave me, so I transferred him to an analyst practicing near his medical school. In due time I learned from him that his analysis had been completed.

Throughout his analytic work with me, the basic core constellation of established pathological mourning—the consistent search for reunion with the representation of the dead and the concomitant dread of such reunion—did not appear, nor did it appear during his work with his second analyst, from the reports he gave me. A father transference occurred in the usual analytic sense, but although the father was "alive" in the transference neurosis, he was "dead" in Mike's daily life.

As I noted, Mike's father had created in his 13-year-old son anxiety about the boy's ability to beget children when he was grown, dying before the son had an opportunity to prove his manhood to him. It became evident during his analysis that throughout his re-grief work Mike had thought of me as his benign oedipal father, and one of the determinants in his undertaking analysis was his desire to tell me about his child. The actual father was kept as the representative of the father of the oedipal age. Mike had been acutely involved with his father just before his death, had tried to identify positively with him, and had seen this identification as a solution for the separation–individuation problems presented by his early engulfing mother. Since the death had been so ill-timed for Mike, it was necessary for him to keep his father, and what he represented, alive, and this conflicted with his aggressive impulses against the oedipal father. During the year following the death, he had not only impregnated his future wife and married her, but had purchased a flashy car in continuing rebellion against his father's opposition to the motorcycle. In his analysis, it became clear that these accomplishments and possessions intrapsychically represented an oedipal triumph, by which he bypassed the necessary oedipal struggle, and which inevitably produced guilt feelings. Guilt was manifested in his aimlessness, the loss of his car, the near loss of his wife.

During re-grief work he saw me as someone who would teach him how to let go, how to learn to separate so as to achieve individuality. In an effort to identify with me, he became a psychology major shortly after his re-grief work terminated, and was later accepted into medical school.

Mike was in analysis with me at the time of the second anniversary of his father's death. Anxiety and other incapacitating symptoms exhibited at the first anniversary were by then absent. Only one symptom appeared, the meaning of which had been repressed and was brought into his awareness only during analysis. On the anniversary night, Mike had quarreled with his wife and had gone to a motel to sleep, the same environment in which he had received the news of his father's death.

On the third anniversary of the death, no incapacitating symptoms appeared, and he told his new analyst about his night in the motel on the occasion of the second anniversary. The approach of the third anniversary prompted him to consider the possibility of taking a holiday at the vacation spot in which his father had died, but he devoted himself to his medical studies instead, demonstrating the increased independence and self-assertiveness he now brought to his life.

Some years ago, many years after I last saw Mike, I received a brief but polite note from him, asking me to fill out a form to help him obtain life insurance. I noticed with delight that he had indeed followed in his father's footsteps and had obtained his medical degree. I do not know whether or not he became a psychiatrist, although I suspect that he followed his father's specialty, surgery, completing a process begun between him and his father in the years before the death.

CHAPTER 10

Three more examples of re-grief therapy

In this chapter I offer the details of the re-grief therapy of three more patients. The first was treated by me, the second by Thomas L. Sarvay, a psychoanalytically oriented psychotherapist, and the third by Daniel Josephthal, a practicing psychoanalyst. I think it important to demonstrate that the technique is useful in other hands, and does not depend on my way of responding to established pathological mourning, nor on any idiosyncratic aspect of my personality.

The case of a magical red robe

Julia began re-grief therapy a little more than six months after her mother's death, her clinical picture then being one of established pathological mourning. It is perhaps because she entered treatment so soon after the death that the resolution of her mourning took only a short time—less than a month and a half, from the beginning of July into mid-August. She was hospitalized in the psychiatric unit of a general hospital throughout her treatment.

She was a single black woman in her mid-thirties, the youngest of six children in her family. Her mother had been severely burned when Julia was six months old. Bedridden for a year, the mother had been unable to carry out many of her mothering functions, although the availability of mother substitutes prevented the child from experiencing severe deprivation. Nevertheless, the early mother–daughter relationship contained elements of unresolved separation–individuation conflicts, manifested in later years as sadomasochism.

Although her siblings all left home, Julia stayed with her widowed mother in the last ten years of her life, when she became an amputee as a result of diabetes. Since she spent most of her time in bed or seated in an armchair, Julia brought her food, cleaned her, and literally became her slave. Julia had surrendered all independent social life, a college scholarship, and opportunities for marriage so as to care for her mother. Although she sometimes was conscious of a wish for her mother's death, she kept in touch with her night and day at regular intervals "to see if she was all right." She phoned her several times a day from the place where she worked as a secretary, and slept at the foot of her bed, checking her state periodically during the night.

A little over six months after her mother's death Julia was flooded with different images of her mother, to which she related with ambivalence. Dreams of "saving" and "killing" her mother awakened her with anxiety each night, and she suffered from the loss of sleep. By day she was so greatly preoccupied with her mother that she was unable to carry on her secretarial work, and was in danger of losing her job. After her employer insisted that she "get herself straightened out," she was admitted to the psychiatric ward with the chief complaint that her mother was driving her crazy.

During her diagnostic interviews, I made the formulation that Julia was unable to get on with her work of mourning because she needed to keep her dead mother alive so as to make her "good" by her own efforts and attention. Once her mother had become "good," Julia could achieve psychological freedom from her—could separate from her without guilt. This wish to "save" her mother conflicted with her wish to "kill" the woman she had been a slave to. At the time of the death, Julia had disruptively identified with her mother's representation, though only incompletely. She had complained of weakness in the legs and difficulty in walking, a reflection of her mother's incapacity. She had also lain abed during the daytime "like a corpse," in an attempt to identify with—or at least imitate—the dead mother's representation. She did not exhibit low self-esteem, however.

Diagnostic interviews revealed the existence of a linking object, a red robe that Julia said had belonged to both her mother and herself. Several years earlier, a sibling had relieved Julia in caring for their mother, and she had been able to take a pleasure trip to a city, where she had bought what she thought "or as a "sexy" red robe. On her return, her mother had expressed a desire for it, and Julia had given it to her. What had once symbolized her freedom from her mother now symbolized her submission to an "abusing" mother. The women alternated in wearing it. Finally, the mother's condition grew so alarming that an ambulance had to be called; she wanted to wear the red robe on her trip to the hospital, and indeed, was wearing it in the hospital when she died.

After the funeral, Julia's siblings gathered in her home and busied themselves "protecting Julia" from confronting the sad reminders of the dead woman, taking away almost all of the mother's belongings. But Julia kept the red robe. She put it away in a brown grocery bag which she sealed shut and hid in a corner of a closet. As time went on, she realized that it had come to have magical properties and that she was afraid to touch it. It gave her eerie spells; she had to reassure herself about its whereabouts but she also had to distance it. Julia did not break with reality except for certain fantasies and visual hallucinations in which she seemed to see different images of her mother in the air, and dreams in which her mother appeared in the red robe.

Treatment

I told Julia that she had complications in her mourning process and that I would meet with her daily (except for weekends) to help her put her chaotic memories, surfacing in fantasies, dreams, and hallucinations, in order. We would talk about her mental processes and try to make sense of them; and we would also use such devices as the red robe to help facilitate her grieving.

She was initially concerned about her disturbing dreams, which she said were "killing her." Her hallucinations stopped during the first week of treatment. In one of her dreams, her mother lay in her coffin but was attempting to get out of it. Julia then called the undertaker to give her mother "a shot of something to calm her down." From the start of her treatment, I tried to use the manifest content of her sequential dreams to show her that she was engaged in a struggle to decide whether to rescue her mother or let her die. The goal here was to clarify the complications that obstructed her mourning, and to help her deal with them; no deeper understanding of her dreams was attempted. I collected data about Julia's relationship with her mother from childhood on, and attempted to develop a therapeutic alliance with her by suggesting that all the "bizarre" dreams, hallucinations, and fantasies would start being less bothersome for her once her grieving got on the right track.

I asked her to bring a picture of her mother, and she did, during her fifth hour, although she refused to look at it until later. After three more hours had been concluded, she did look at it, screaming "That's her!" and starting to cry. She refused to face the picture while she cried, since "Mother never cried, not even when Daddy died." (Her father had died some ten years earlier.) The next three sessions saw the outpouring of more memories. Julia's preoccupation with her mother changed from the reality of her abuse at her mother's hands to transient sadness about her death. She was even able to verbalize having wished from time to time that her mother were dead. In order to indicate my acceptance of her conflicting views of her mother, I told her that from what she had told me she had had a good reason for having had opposing perceptions of her mother.

At this point Julia's dreams about her mother were primarily concerned with running away and attempting to escape the powerful vindictive parent. When her linking object, the robe, was brought to therapy in its paper bag, she postponed touching it, finally doing so with panic and screams of "Let me out of here! I can't stand it!" During later sessions in which she was asked to examine the robe, to describe it, and to verbalize all of the feelings it evoked, she was flooded with emotions of anger and sadness, and wept, giving more details about the day of her mother's death, particularly details connected with her linking object.

I learned that when she had gone forward to look at her mother's corpse, Julia had fainted, and, as a result, had never seen the corpse. She had left the cemetery before the coffin was lowered into the ground. I told her that these circumstances supported her attempt to deny that her mother was dead. She discussed the funeral in detail, and recalled the sermon the minister had preached during the services. As she did this, she had further emotional storms. She confessed how she had wanted praise at the funeral, and how the minister had applauded her masochistic devotion and wished her luck and happiness in her new freedom. Since she was at the time fully aware of her anger toward her mother, these remarks had evoked intense feelings of guilt.

Again her dreams altered. Now her mother was shrunken, small, and powerless in the dreams. On July 24th she reported having dreamed of her mother in a casket: “The casket is small now, like a box. My mother is also small. She is shrunken!” I told her that her unresolved guilt was keeping her mother “big” ‘and that with the lessening of her guilt her mother would shrink further. On July 28th she dreamed of a cemetery in which mourners, her mother among them, looked disappointed at the absence of a grave. “I was able to look in my dream at the site where my mother was buried,” Julia said. “But there was no grave; the ground was all covered with grass!” This dream had been followed on the same night by one in which I performed “eye surgery” on her. Again connecting the manifest content of the dream to the grieving process, I suggested that she was perceiving me as an “eye opener” who would help her see the reality of her mother’s death, and that she was still caught between “seeing” and “not seeing” “killing” and “not killing”—her mother. In a third dream on the same night, she saw a nurse erase an image of her mother that had been drawn on a blackboard.

On the next evening (July 29th) she dreamed of seeing her mother. “This time she looked ‘like a ghost, and she could go in and out of a wall. In the dream she retreated into a wall.” Julia talked further about the funeral, and expressed more anger at the minister’s praise of her masochistic behavior. On July 30th she dreamed of her mother in a wheelchair; Julia pushed her chair off a cliff and noticed that her mother did not seem to object. After reporting this dream, she talked again about the funeral, with tears in her eyes.

She then dreamed of her mother sitting on the porch of their home. She said to her, “You are dead,” and when the older woman refused to believe her, Julia called a mortician, who carried her mother away in a casket. The photograph and the robe, which had been left in my office and had continued to be available to her whenever she had a session, now seemed to lose their magic. She asked if she could have them back, and when I offered no objection, she took them away with her. She told me that she had been looking at advertisements for tombstones. Although she had arranged for a marker to be placed on her father’s grave within a month of his death, she had been unable eight months after her mother's death to order one for her. She could now talk much more realistically than before about the death, and was no longer intensely preoccupied with thoughts of her mother. She began to leave the hospital for weekends out of town, and reported enjoying herself "for the first time in my life." Two sessions later she announced that she had burned the red robe, and ordered a tombstone. She said that the burning of her linking object was appropriate, and reviewed once more the history of her mother's having been burned and having been made unable to give her adequate mothering during her childhood. Now she was symbolically trying to get rid of the "burned mother" representation. She elaborated further, with affect, on the remembered problems of being the child of a burned woman.

She had been afraid to return to the cemetery since the burial, and was anxious at first over a proposed visit, the possibility of which had first been raised in her therapy. She doubted that she would be able to go through with it. On August 8th she dreamed of being at her mother's grave with two women patients who had in reality been present when she had burned the red robe. "I was able to see the grave this time, and there was a marker on it, but I kept digging into it. I wanted to reach my mother to give her flowers, but I never reached her." Julia wept aloud while reporting this dream, and displayed genuine sadness. The next day, without my suggestion, she took a brief trip as a tourist to the city where she had bought the red robe, and had a "wonderful time." I thought that she was repeating her attempt to achieve "freedom" from her mother. I interpreted this to her at the time. Unlike her mother, I made no demands on her to see or "steal" the items she had purchased in the city. She reported being proud of herself, proud of being able to go through grieving.

On August 15th she dreamed of buying new shoes. Her associations were to visiting the city and having fun in doing so, and finding herself actually going to visit her mother's grave. When she did make her visit to the graveside, she was accompanied by one of my assistants whom she had come to know while in the hospital. After making this visit, she was able to talk more realistically about her mother's death. While it is possible that the event helped to strengthen repression of some of her negative impulses toward her mother's representation, Julia did allow herself to review once again in treatment the reasons why she could not let her mother "die." The abuse she had suffered at her mother's hands and the anger this had aroused were posed on one side of the conflict, while her desires to save her mother and to cling to the image of an idealized mother were posed on the other. Her therapy was then terminated.

Follow-up

I had a three-year follow-up with Julia after the completion of her re-grief therapy. Since she lived at a distance, this was necessarily accomplished by mail. In the first letter, written a year after her treatment had ended, Julia reported working and "feeling simply wonderful." She went on to thank me, saying, "I am no longer afraid of the dark, of being alone, of expressing my true feelings." In a wry reference to the "burning" that had played such a part in her life, she continued, "I feel most energetic and have a *burning* [she underlined the word] desire to go places and do things." She concluded by saying that she had made plans to go to New York, which she had never seen, for a forthcoming national holiday.

Her last letter also gave testimony to her well-being. She reported that she was living with one of her sisters in the same small town from which she had come to me as a patient, but that she now had plans to move to a big city within two months. "As a matter of fact," she added, "everything is going fine for me these days—no bad dreams anymore—only a little nervous at times."

Psychological tests

Julia was given the MMPI on three occasions while in treatment: at the start of re-grief therapy; in mid-course, after the introduction of the linking object had produced emotional storms and some disorganization; and very near the completion of my work with her. She had other psychological tests as well: Bender Gestalt, OAP, MAPS, TAT, and Rorschach, all given at the beginning and end of her treatment.[2]

Figure 2 reflects Julia's three MMPIs. Cilluffo (Volkan, Cilluffo, & Sarvay, 1975) used a procedure recommended by Schofield (1966) to determine whether the magnitude of change in her scores from one MMPI testing to another was clinically significant. The degree of T-score change necessary for clinical "significance" is 14 points

[2] These tests were administered by Burke Smith, with the assistance of W. B. Fletcher.

for scale 2; 12 points for scale 6; 10 points for scales 3, 4, and 9; and 8 points for scales 1, 5, 7, 8.

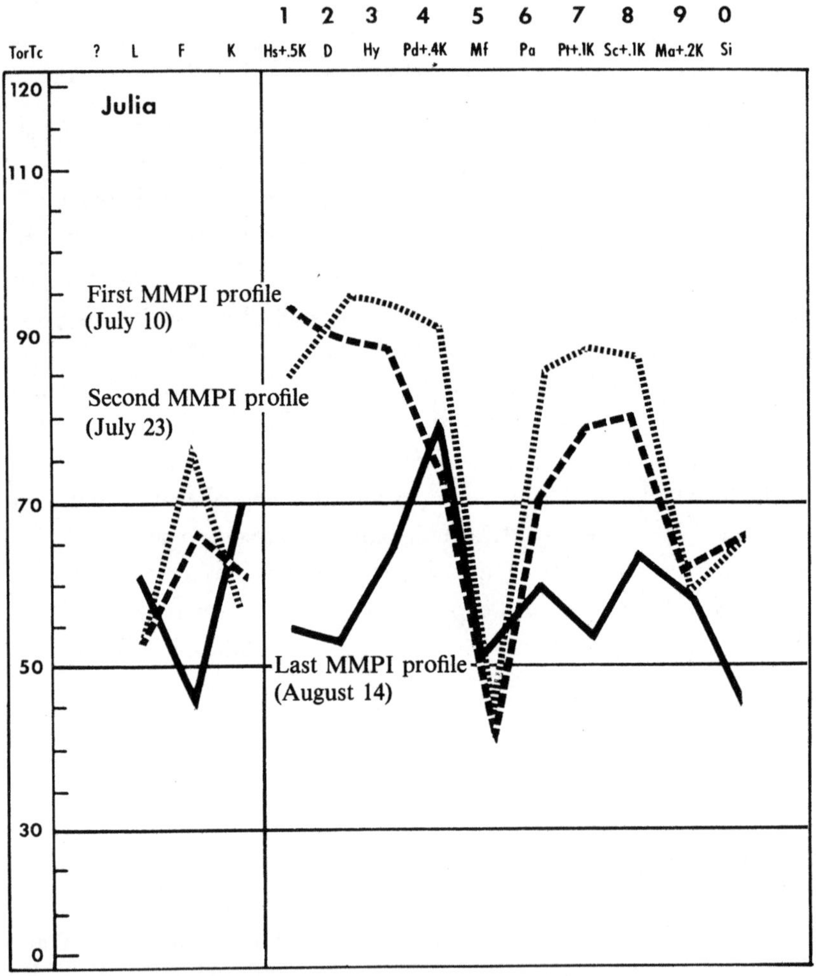

Figure 2 Julia's three MMPIs

These are based on estimations of the standard error of measurement of each scale and provide a way to measure the clinically significant change in each patient by comparison of his MMPI scores. It was expected that Julia's second MMPI profile would reflect her emotional storms and disorganization, and that the final test would reflect reorganization—the completion of the grieving process.

Julia's first MMPI profile showed marked elevation on scales 2, 3, 4, 1, 6, 7, and 8 in that order, with peaks at 2 (T = 94) and 7 (T = 88). The second profile showed a significant decrease in scale 1 and a significant increase in scales 4, 6, 7, and 8, reflecting ongoing emotional storms in the first half of re-grief therapy. Between the second and third MMPI testing, there was a decrease in scales 1, 2, 3, 6, 7, and 8, as predicted. This reflected a successful resolution of the emotional storming and re-griefing process. Finally, the comparison between the first and last testing scores showed significant decrease in scales 1, 2, 3, 6, 7, and 8.

Cilluffo then compared Julia's MMPI results with those of Mike (see Chapter 9) and concluded that the two patterns were similar. Smith and Fletcher wrote up their analysis of all of Julia's test results and compared those given at different times, stating:

> Julia's current conflict seemed to have been precipitated by the death of her mother, for whom she had strong feelings of ambivalence. This clearly emerges in the projective tests where the mother is alternately described as a "monster" and as a very "sweet" person. Although she acknowledged the fact of her mother's death intellectually, Julia's references to her were usually in the present tense.
>
> Failure to resolve the conflicts surrounding her mother's death is illustrated by her response to the cemetery stimulus card of the MAPS test. When the card was presented, Julia chose two figures, those of a ghost and an old lady. Holding them in her hand and looking first at the figures and then at the scene, Julia responded:
>
>> I don't know what to put there .... This lady sort of resembles my mother, you know? And I couldn't put her there along with the ghost because that wouldn't be right. I know it wouldn't be right, but my mother looks somewhat like that. She's an old lady. That sort of reminds me of [pause] ... but I couldn't do that to her. That wouldn't be right. I'll put the ghost here—this is the way I see cemeteries.

The interim MMPI results (July 23) indicate an intensification of symptoms previously reported with further decompensation of defensive structure. There appears to have been a significant decrease in repression accompanied by an increase in obsessional ideation suggesting agitated rumination, fearfulness, and strong feelings of guilt. The evidence suggests that, at this point in treatment, Julia was experiencing moderate disturbance of thought processes.

Results of the post-treatment examination revealed a dramatic remission of symptoms associated with established pathological mourning. There appears to have been a reorganization of defensive structure permitting effective emotional and intellectual control. Depression and anxiety were within normal limits, and there was improvement in reality testing.

Julia appears to have successfully resolved much of the conflict related to her mother's death. When the cemetery stimulus card was presented in the readministration of the MAPS test, she remarked, "Before, I put the ghost there but I don't see it that way now." Selecting the figure of a young girl, she placed it on the card, stating, "I'll construct it this way and I'll have her represent me." The following are excerpts of her response to this card:

> This figure that I have selected here seems to be of someone expressing grief or sadness and this is the only way I see the cemetery now. ... I have no further use for this ghost. ... I think that once this person leaves this cemetery she will realize that this is the end. And she won't forget the loved one but I think she will realize that she is buried there and that the marker is certainly bearing the name of the person who is buried there. There is nothing phony about that marker that is placed there to identify the person in the grave there. And I think after she leaves there she will lead a normal and happy life, I hope.

Smith and Fletcher finished their report by saying that although Julia was capable of functioning "normally" at the end of her re-grief therapy, and that she had resolved her complicated grieving, hers remained an unchanged personality, which they called the personality of a "burned child"—one with emotional shallowness, tenuous impulse control, and the inhibition of aggression.

A bloodstone ring used in re-grief therapy

Chip, a 20-year-old student, was treated by Thomas L. Sarvay (Volkan, Cilluffo, & Sarvay, 1975). He was eleven when his father began a struggle with lung cancer that lasted for two years. During the final two weeks of his father's life, Chip and his brother were sent to live with friends. He later learned that at the end of his life his father had been "out of his head" and had asked that his oxygen be cut off. His physician had allegedly complied, and within a few minutes, the father was dead.

Chip's initial response to the death was complicated. He felt numb and without much affect. He thought of the relief he felt now, not only from having to witness his father's agony, but also from having to endure his always ready criticism. He felt that his father was critical of him to the end, and that he had never measured up to what his father had expected of him.

Two weeks later he began feeling worthless and depressed, and felt so for some weeks, although. his depression finally lifted at the end of this time to appear only occasionally, and then not severely. He had become symptomatic two and a half years before coming to Sarvay's attention while he was a college student. The symptom that brought him to seek psychiatric help' was not his occasional depression, but a sense of his father's "continuing presence." His description of this phenomenon was vague, but he said there were times when he felt the presence within himself; he felt that his preoccupation with his father was unremitting. He was attending the same school his father had attended, and he paid his tuition from a fund his father had set aside for that purpose. Although he did well and received excellent grades, he thought of himself as failing, as though he needed to be in an inferior position, and kept comparing his grades with those he fantasied his father had received while a student. He was in a sense "castrating" himself with regret that he was not doing better, and fantasied his father's disappointment. This intense preoccupation was so bothersome that he finally sought psychiatric help.

Sarvay's initial formulation of his case pointed to an unresolved oedipal struggle. Chip was the eldest son. The arrival of a younger brother when he was five had initiated regression, and his longing for his mother had increased and become sexualized. This attachment led the child to see his father in an unrealistically harsh light, and the harsh, punitive, affectionless representation of the oedipal father had been kept alive in him throughout his latency.

When Chip reached puberty, his father's long illness and his death prevented the boy from resolving the oedipal struggle with him. Chip continued to behave as though he were still under the rigid domination of his father, and although the death represented an oedipal triumph, it was a triumph involving so much guilt that the father had to be kept alive. He competed with his father's achievement while in college, and no matter how well he did, he saw himself as inferior.

His struggle with his father's image had affected his approach to girls. For six months before he came into treatment he had been steadily dating a girl who had severe bronchial asthma that recalled his father's lung disease and depression. Chip fantasied rescuing her—symbolically rescuing his father. On the other hand, since his girlfriend was less desirable than. his childhood image of his mother, he was also putting himself in an inferior position in order to avoid becoming the target of his oedipal father's revenge. Sarvay noted that Chip continued to speak in the present tense about his parent, and referred to "my father's room" and "my father's house," in spite of the length of time his father had been dead. He continued to live in a world in which the father still lived; he was lost in the limbo of "killing" and "not killing" him.

Treatment

Sarvay told Chip at the outset that his treatment would focus on the father's death in an effort to bring him relief. The treatment took two months and five days—from March 4 to May 9—during which time Chip was seen as an outpatient for 26 therapeutic sessions. During the first hours, Chip readily talked of his need to keep his father alive in order to "acquire his love and approval." He felt—in a reflection of his sense of his father's presence in him (his introject)—"as if my father is part of me." He used the word "merge" in describing his total, albeit transient, identification with the dead man.

Chip brought to his first hour a dream typical of the dreams of person fixated in the work of mourning. Its manifest content illustrated the conflict between Chip's desire to kill his father and to keep him alive. In the dream, his father was in the hospital where he had been pronounced dead. The scene then changed and the dead father was coming home. Initially happy to see him, Chip then felt anger at his return. The father ignored his son and disrupted the household. Chip ran up to him and touched his face, which felt like soft clay and fell apart under his fingers. He then awakened in great anxiety.

Chip then talked about his father's asking that the oxygen be cut off, and the compliance of his physician. He became enraged as he described this, and cried, "He died like a dog!" He perceived his father's decision as selfish and cowardly, and felt that his father should have fought to stay alive rather than "copping out on him." He had refused to view the body at the funeral, and now confided, "I was afraid he would sit up." He saw only a glimpse of the coffin as it was carried from the church, and felt that perhaps his father was not inside.

At the next session, he described his father with ambivalence. He was in awe of him because of all he had accomplished, but he complained of his cold indifference and the violence of his disapproval. At last he said, "I think he almost said he loved me near the end but he couldn't—it would have killed him," and wept for the, first time since becoming a patient. The therapist then asked directly about any fantasy that Chip might have had about having contributed to his father's death. Chip then verbalized a fantasy of having murdered his father with his feelings. He had often wished for the death so that he might be free. When his mother told him that death was expected within a month, he had circled the date, which had been accurately predicted, on his calendar. The fact that he had done this added further weight to his fantasy.

After this disclosure, Chip began reporting more memories of his father's last days; he had seemed "gray and ghost-like" and "hollow and dead inside" during this time. Since Chip had described himself from time to time in much the same terms, his attempt at identification was pointed out to him. He brought to the eighth session an envelope containing several photographs of his father, as he had been instructed to do. At first he exhibited very little affect in looking at them, but then became anxious and turned them face down, crying, "I can't look any longer. I am afraid I will see myself in the pictures, and everything I am not." Sarvay's intent was to use these pictures as a demarcation exercise; he asked Chip to describe his father's features in the pictures, then to describe his own, and to verbalize what they had in common and where they were different. When Chip noticed a cigarette in his father's hand he began to cry, screaming that as a child he had often taken cigarettes to his father to please him, but that finally they had killed him. During the second session with the pictures, it was learned that Chip had a second set, pictures of his father showing the emaciation of his last year of life. He had avoided looking at them "because they look like pictures of a dead man." He was asked to bring them, however, along with his father's bloodstone ring, an heirloom from seven generations that had become his linking object. He kept it in a box rather than wear it, on the grounds that the stone might break if it were worn, and that this would mean the loss of "my last link" with his father. He brought the ring in a box to his therapist, who, with Chip's permission, kept it to use later.

Chip spoke of his father in health and in illness as though he were two persons. Looking at his father's youthful image in one of the photographs, he explained, "This is my father—vital, alive—everything I want to be." But when asked to touch the pictured face, he refused, saying he was afraid of blocking out his father's face. This fear was interpreted as fear of killing his father again, this time with his finger. His reaction to the second set of photographs was quite different; they aroused little affect. He said, "This picture is a lie. He is just a shell, a dead man. I feel like I should cry, but I can't. It is not real."

For the first five weeks Chip emphasized the negative aspects of his relationship with his father, speaking repeatedly of his lack of warmth and demonstrativeness. When evidence of warm moments surfaced in these sessions, Sarvay pointed them out to Chip. It appeared that father and son had spent considerable time together and that, during the summer before his death particularly, his father had done many things with his son. Family members told Chip how during the last two weeks of his life the dying man had spoken of his pride in his two sons and his love for them. Chip insisted on discounting and rationalizing this, saying, "I wish I could believe that, but I know it's a lie." Even when he remembered his father's direct expression of affection for him, he scoffed at its "phoniness." Interpretation suggested that in refusing to accept the positive aspects of the relationship Chip was trying to avoid feeling that he had killed someone who had loved him. Chip then had an emotional storm, saying, "I killed him because he wasn't there when I wanted him. Now he is always around and I can't get rid of him!" The narcissistic blow of his father's death was evident in this outcry.

The dichotomy of the "dead" and the "live" father was repeatedly pointed out to Chip. In order to work on his (higher-level) splitting, he was asked to examine a picture of the "dead" man alongside one of the "live" man and to contrast them, naming each as he did so. He called the "dead" father Daddy, but used his first name, Jim, in pointing to the "live" one, experiencing an emotional storm as he did so. At the end of the hour he cried out, "They are the same person. They are both dead. Now I have nothing!" He recalled in greater detail the pain of watching his father die. He had carefully avoided telling him goodbye on his last visit, thinking magically that if he failed to say goodbye his father would not die. He began recalling more and more of the warm moments with his father. For the first time in six months he dated someone other than his chronically ill girlfriend; during his second month of therapy he reported going on a blind date and greatly enjoying it, but on the following day he felt a depressive affect. It was suggested that he was feeling guilt over having enjoyed himself—and over having let down his ill friend (who represented his father). He became more confused than before about the boundaries between himself and his father, expressing uncertainty about whether his academic grades were his own or his father's. He said he was ashamed to speak of his A average because it might be clear that the grades were not his own but his father's. Sarvay told him that his preoccupation with the grades had a great deal to do with the complication of his mourning process; if his own grades were as good as or superior to his father's, it would mean, to him, that he no longer needed a loving father to hold his hand. In other words, it would mean "killing" his father. He was defending himself against doing this by feeling that his grades were inferior, or, at least, by sharing his good grades with his father. Sarvay clarified for him that the real issue was his acceptance of his own manhood, as opposed to his continuing to lean on his father's image. After listening to this, Chip reported on the following day that he felt himself "rotting inside." Sarvay interpreted this, saying the Chip was joining himself to the "sick rotten father" internally just as he had attempted to join himself externally in his grades. Sarvay suggested that he could let the "rotten part" of his father die without joining it himself.

Chip was angry as he told of having been excluded from the family's grieving. He had been sent to the home of friends and had not seen his mother again until the funeral, to which he rode with other children rather than with her. He had also been seated with the other children in the church. Remembering the ceremony, he screamed, "It was pagan—vultures from everywhere pretending how sorry they were—they just threw him in the ground!" A second MMPI was given as his impulses found expression and as he began to appear disorganized. He was angry at having to take the test again, and directed his anger toward the therapist, describing him in terms he had used earlier for his father. Interceptive interpretation regarding this displacement was made, and Chip sadly described his feeling that his father was now gone. "It hurts—I miss him. I have lost everything." When the therapist produced the bloodstone ring he had been keeping for Chip, Chip cried, "That is the link! It is a legacy. I'm not worthy of it!" and refused to open the box.

Two sessions later he showed signs of successful reorganization. He was now making active efforts to establish new emotional investments. He made new friends and began to take pride in himself and in his work. He made plans for the future enthusiastically, reporting that he had stopped being preoccupied with thoughts of his father; he began to accept credit for his own accomplishments. He decided to break off his relationship with his sickly girlfriend and to seek girls "with more life." The therapist returned the father's pictures he had been keeping, and Chip had one framed to stand on his dresser. After doing this he spoke of having a much greater sense of personal identity. "I look at the picture and I know that it is he, my dead father; and I am me." This time when the therapist put the ring box on his desk Chip readily picked it up, slipped the ring on his little finger as his father had worn it, and then put it on his ring finger, where he left it. "I like it better this way," he said. "After all, it is *my* ring."

In his next-to-last session Chip reported dreaming of his father as frozen, awaiting re-animation until a cure for his disease could be found. The father asked to be thawed out, although he knew this would mean his death. His request was honored, and he returned home for a final meal with his family. Although everyone in the family circle realized that the father was going to die, there was an atmosphere of acceptance and peace. Then the father arose and said goodbye to Chip. When Chip awakened from this dream he had a transient feeling of sadness that he described as his awareness of loss. After one more session therapy was terminated, the therapeutic aim having been fulfilled.

Figure 3 shows Chip's three MMPIs, which were given at the beginning, the midpoint, and the end of his treatment. His movement from disorganization toward reorganization seems to have been more direct than Julia's or Mike's. The change between his first and last MMPI testing showed significant decreases effected by therapy in scales 2, 3, 4, 6, 7, and 8. Unfortunately, no long-term follow-up on this patient is available.

A pterodactyl with a man's body

I am indebted to Daniel Josephthal for permission to include this case of a 30-year-old, highly respected, and extremely competent woman lawyer (Volkan & Josephthal, 1980). Josephthal, an analyst, saw this patient in re-grief therapy for six months, meeting with her once a week except for times when he felt that more hours were necessary to help her deal with highly charged affective-ideational outbursts. Her sessions were less frequent, and the course of her re-griefing somewhat more lengthy than that of the other cases cited.

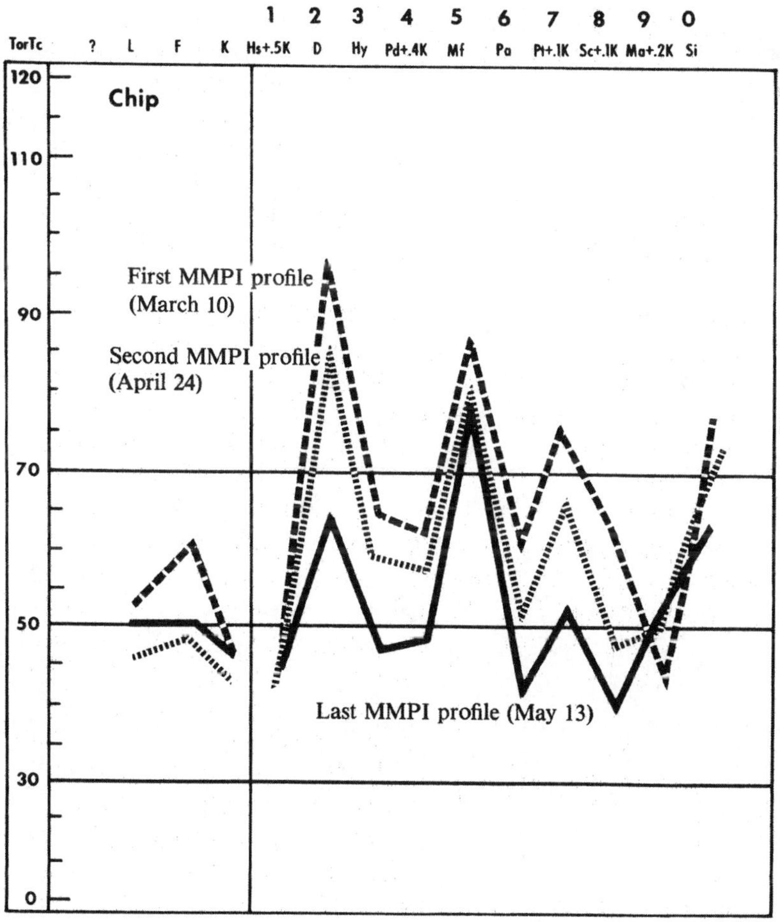

Figure 3 Chip's three MMPIs

This patient, Roberta, was aware of her inability to mourn, and sought treatment six months after the death of her husband in an airplane accident. Both the therapist and his patient agreed that the aim of treatment was to be limited to helping her complete her work of mourning. Although she showed some manifestations of what could be understood as prolonged initial grief, her case history revealed a basic picture of established pathological grief with typical psychodynamics underlying it. She continued to be unable to control the tears and weeping that came whenever she thought of him, was ashamed over losing her self-control in this way, and dismayed that the situation did not seem to improve as time went on. Her tears were accompanied by sad longing for her husband and for her own death so that they might be together again. She reported being especially upset on the tenth and twelfth of each month; she had identified her husband's body on the tenth day of the month in which he was killed, and she had arranged for its cremation on the twelfth.

Her history indicated no significant psychological or developmental trauma, no deprivation, overindulgence, or difficulties with object relations. She had come from a farm family that had honored self-reliance, and she had rejected signs of dependency within herself. Her social, educational, sexual, and vocational development had been smooth. She had married a dynamic, successful, and glamorous lawyer and real estate investor when she was 24; she spoke of their life together as having been full and exciting. They had traveled widely and had had many friends. She felt that her relationship with her husband—deep and intimate—had but one flaw, his propensity for transient connections with other women while on business trips. He had been candid with her about this, and while she had tried to view it as unimportant in the light of contemporary mores and because she thought that he had felt no real emotional commitment to these "other women," it had disturbed her, nevertheless, that her husband had betrayed the total commitment to their marriage that she had expected. She had tried to feel accepting and liberated, and not to be controlling, but however much she had struggled intellectually with her objections, she had resented his affairs emotionally. This was an unresolved issue at the time of his death. She thought of her marriage as having been very happy otherwise. Although she and her husband had chosen to postpone having children, Roberta was looking forward to having a child eventually. It was then that her husband died in the crash of a private plane while on a business trip abroad.

In her first sessions she went over the experiences she had had immediately after notification of her husband's death. She had felt shock and disbelief at first, and had continued to hope that the news was somehow false until she identified the body two days after the accident in the country where the crash had taken place. The identification had been traumatic; to her horror, she saw that his face was severely mutilated, that part of his jaw was gone, and what was left was bloated and discolored. His ruined face had kept appearing in her mind's eye in what she called a "flash," but as time went on, began returning to its normal appearance without any volition on her part. The missing area began to fill in and the swelling to subside. Such a gradual fading of horror is similar to what happens in the recurring dreams of traumatic neurosis.

Roberta kept her husband's ashes in her bedroom in a wooden box. She had made various plans to dispose of them in places where she had spent happy times with her husband, but she had kept postponing any action. She never had been able to open the box and look at the ashes. When she happened to see the Tutankhamen exhibit touring the country at the time, she had what she called a "weird experience." As she read the dates of the excavation of the Tutankhamen tomb, and made some mathematical calculations with her husband's birthdate, his age at death, his age at the excavation dates, etc., she had a sudden flash of insight that persuaded her for the moment that her husband had been the King's reincarnation. She quickly saw the absurdity of this, and understood that it expressed the wish that her husband could return through reincarnation. This "insight" was replaced by a search for meaning. Being of a philosophical turn of mind, and well read in Eastern philosophy, she began to try to understand what lessons or meaning her husband's death would reveal to her.

Except for visits on four consecutive days when she brought the wooden box with her husband's ashes to the therapist's office, Roberta came to therapy once a week. She started treatment with a well-developed capacity for therapeutic alliance, and with unusual insight and psychological-mindedness, and she seemed to bring to each session some fresh and absorbing material, toward which she exhibited deep and appropriate affect. She had shared her grief response with no one, and now seemed eager to unburden herself and to work on some of her difficulties. She began working through her problems very quickly while the therapist encouraged her, acting as an auxiliary superego to help her overcome initial resistance based on shame and fear over being what she thought of as weak, dependent, and vulnerable. After the first few visits she had fewer episodes of crying, and they seldom occurred now outside her sessions. Shortly after beginning treatment she took a previously arranged trip that included flying. This was preceded by a dream:

> Five pterodactyls fly over my property. I hide. One of them seems to have a man's body. He swoops down and carries me off. It felt pleasant.

Her immediate associations were that there had been five people in the plane crash, that the pterodactyl with a man's body was her husband, and that this was a dream of reunion. The therapist suggested that her husband had mastered what killed him by being able to fly, and she immediately added "and thus be immortal." She then reported a recurring thought, a quotation from T. S. Eliot's *Four Quartets*: "… the end of all our exploring will be to arrive where we started and know the place for the first time."

She then suggested—as the therapist had been about to do—that it might be therapeutic to open the box of ashes. Her wish for reunion, apparent in the dream, along with the attendant dread, was experienced and worked through in the following way. She had left the box of ashes in the care of her therapist while, together, they explored all of her fantasies about it. These included what she called her "terrible imaginings"; for example, she had not opened the box because she was afraid of feeling compelled to smear the ashes over her face and hug herself if she did so. Although clearly pointing to images of merger, the opening of the box also meant the final separation from her fantasied reunion and thus an act of "killing" her husband.

On the day Roberta opened the box she was dressed altogether in black without realizing the significance of this. She wore a necklace of seashells. When, with trembling and great trepidation, she opened the box, she gasped at unexpectedly seeing chips of bone. These she likened to seashells. She and her husband had enjoyed sailing, and had spent considerable time at the seashore. She ran her fingers through the ashes in an almost caressing manner, then unconsciously patted the side of her jaw. When this gesture was called to her attention she immediately realized that she was trying to "repair him." Then she relaxed, and examined the ashes with more detached interest.

She took the ashes home after that session, and went on to dispose of most of them, keeping some in the box, which she patted from time to time, engaging in fond reminiscence as she did this. The box of ashes continued to be a linking object, but further exploration disclosed that it no longer evoked anxiety and dread, that it now held a new meaning. At first she said, "I'd rather keep it and not think about it." She explained that if she thought about it she was afraid that she "would think angry thoughts and lose the fond memories." She also thought, "I'm keeping him in the box," and this came to mean that she was holding him as she had been unable to do altogether when he was alive. She was somewhat ashamed to realize that she was acting out this fantasy, but her shame gave way to greater interest in her motivation. She began to work in a more integrated way on the ambivalence she felt, trying to sort out and reconcile the anger she had been denying, and the affectionate feelings that had also contained an element of over-idealization of her husband. At this point, further "unfinished business" came to light as she described in greater detail her experience of mourning the death of her father when she had been in her early twenties. He had died of metastatic cancer, and had so used denial that she had not been able to discuss his impending death with him. Any approach to the subject disturbed him, and with tears in her eyes, she would have to turn the discussion to a more cheerful topic. She felt that she had never had "the chance to say goodbye," and she realized that this had also been true with her husband.

After six months, reference was made to terminating her treatment. Roberta was reluctant, recognizing spontaneously that termination would bring yet another separation and yet another experience of grief that she would have to resolve. She recognized also that the closeness and intimacy she had felt in her treatment had served at some level as a replacement for the closeness and sharing of her marriage. She reported what she called a termination dream in which she was a schoolgirl painting the portrait of a girl with great care and considerable attention to detail. She could not finish the portrait in the time allotted because when she applied the brush to one eye and one side of the mouth, no color showed, although she had been able to color the rest of the face easily. She thought, "Oh well, I can always come back and finish it later; besides, what I've done is beautiful." She saw the incomplete eye as evidence that there was more to see about herself, and the incomplete mouth as testimony that there was more to say.

The therapist offered the interpretation that the absence of color around the eye represented her tears, and wondered whether the incomplete mouth might represent her husband's jaw. This made her tearful, and she said, "I thought I had gotten over identifying with him." She went on to describe her feeling that a piece of her had died with him. Delineating a small square space with her hands, she spoke of "this space in me where he resides." However, there was now a boundary around her and around the dream; and the dream face, although a fusion of herself with her husband, was also separate from her, the dreamer. The suggestion in the dream that she could "finish the portrait later" represented her thinking that she might like to be analyzed at some future time. Characterological issues—some obsessional and superego features, and her concerns about dependency—had come under discussion. Roberta's dream at the termination of her re-grief work reminds one of Mike's (see Chapter 9), in which, faced with termination, he dreamed of having undergone minor surgery and acknowledging the presence of an option for major surgery. But it was agreed that analysis might well await fuller resolution of her grief. Her feeling in the dream that the rest of the painting was beautiful had to do, she surmised, with her feeling of being otherwise fairly hopeful and optimistic about herself and her life. Thus a termination date was set for a short time after the first anniversary of her husband's death.

During the termination period she presented what she called a "healing dream." It was introduced in association with her mention of a man she had been seeing toward whom she now felt it possible that she might come to respond deeply. Up to this time she had been judging men as, first, not her husband, and then, not like her husband.

> I was running in a marathon, a peculiar kind with a lot of obstacles, over a gorge. It was 26.2 miles. My husband was there encouraging me. In the first part of the dream it was as if I were running in slow motion. I thought I'd never do it. It got dark. I didn't want to stop but I was afraid I'd trip in the dark. My husband went into a store, bought me a flashlight, and gave it to me. I was able to run easily. The next morning I had finished the race. Getting the light was a great relief. At the finish, where I placed or what my time was didn't matter—it was a notable finish.

Roberta immediately connected this dream with her experience in therapy and the past year of dealing with her husband's death—how hard it had been, how slow and painful. In association to the flashlight, she felt that her husband's death had made her aware of troubles previously warded off, and that the therapist had given her the light of the therapeutic process to guide her way. She began that session with a radiant smile that reflected her relief and well-being—her delight at finishing the race after dreaming of feeling incomplete. She had not finished grieving, but the obstacles and complications of her grief were now gone. The gorge or chasm with its unfathomable black bottom represented her wish for union with her husband in death. She had surmounted that obstacle in therapy. The finish of the race, which, in the dream, came in the morning, transformed *mourning* into *morning*; she associated to this by saying that she had once again begun to enjoy the morning sunrise on her way to work. She wept as she said that although she had been eager to tell her therapist this dream, it also made her very sad because it was so evident that she was ready to leave him. He had appeared as her husband in the dream; with him, she had lived again through the loss of her husband. She felt that if she could set a date for terminating therapy she could prepare herself for losing her therapist and feel some control over the loss, which she had been unable to do when she lost her husband so unexpectedly. She was wearing a black dress, but with a white blouse and a gray jacket, and she commented that after getting dressed in this way she realized that she had finally become able to blend white and black.

CHAPTER 11

A yellow spot in the bottom of a coffee cup

When complications develop in the work of mourning, splitting of ego functions with respect to the death, natural in the initial stage, persists. It is usual, however, for the aspect of ego functions oriented to reality to dominate over functions that deny the death. Denial is nonetheless facilitated by the mechanisms by which the representation of the dead is internalized or externalized. The continued availability of this representation fosters the illusion that the bereaved remains in contact with the one he has lost.

While in some cases denial dominates, I do not believe that we should consider the individual so functioning as psychotic as long as his break with reality is not generalized, as long as it pertains, that is, only to the reality of the death in question. Of course, depending on personal history and symbolic expression, even this limited break with reality may appear ominous on the surface. The psychotic-like behavior such persons exhibit should be seen as part of the clinical picture of established pathological mourning or reactive depression.

This chapter emphasizes the importance of giving attention to death-related events and their psychological consequences when making a diagnosis. I offer here an example of a man considered psychotic who was successfully treated with re-grief therapy.

The mark of melanoma

In this chapter I will give a fifth example of the process of re-griefing. It differs from the others inasmuch as the patient, Clyde, was initially diagnosed as psychotic; his case provides an excellent example of the importance of postponing the diagnosis of severe conditions such as schizophrenia until it can be established that the disturbance in reality testing is based on more than denial of a loss by death. Clyde was by no means the only example encountered in our research of a patient who exhibited behavior that seemed psychotic but was in fact focalized and uniquely related to a fixation in the work of mourning.

A 36-year-old married man, Clyde "discovered" a dark yellow spot in his coffee cup after he drank it one morning, and concluded that his wife was trying to poison him, the yellow spot indicating to him the presence of poison. He then gave up coffee altogether. Two months later he became my patient.

Before his concern about the coffee had manifested itself, Clyde had noticed "wrinkles" on his feet, and had concluded that his wife had put poisonous powder on his socks. The suspicions of his wife had been awakened in a vague way about six months before the episode of the yellow spot, at a time when his wife had gone to work outside the home. He had become suspicious that this outside work had led her into an affair. His disquiet led to somatic complaints and changes in his sleep pattern.

His family sought psychiatric care for him after the episode of the yellow spot. His increasing suspiciousness was by then too much for them to tolerate. Diagnosed as a paranoid schizophrenic, Clyde was admitted to the hospital. Since the family had limited means, and since it was thought that he might need long-term hospitalization, arrangements were made to send him to a state institution. Before he left, however, an alert psychiatric resident, who had been involved in our clinical research on complicated mourning, noted a possible connection between his symptoms and the accidental drowning of his half-brother just prior to the appearance of his symptoms, and referred him to me.

In his diagnostic interviews with me, Clyde readily made associations that suggested a connection between his seemingly bizarre preoccupations and the recent death. His mother had died of melanoma after a lengthy illness when Clyde, the eldest of three siblings, was 13. Shortly thereafter his father had remarried and had had three more children. Clyde and a full sister had each undergone surgery for melanoma within eleven years of their mother's death, and had lost an aunt to the same disease. It was not surprising, then, that he had reacted to his half-brother's death with great anxiety; his own narrow brush with death had left its mark. His associations to the dark spot in the cup suggested strongly to me that it represented melanoma and those fateful skin tumors suffered by his family members, which had contained granules of melanoma, groups of dark yellow-brown pigments. The spot was thus the sign of death and anxiety. The coffee in the cup stood for the muddy waters in which his 15-year-old brother had died while fishing. Clyde thus attempted to identify with his drowning brother at the same time as he denied his death and/or his own anxiety about the death by refusing to drink the coffee.

Clyde had viewed his brother's body after its long immersion, and had been struck by the wrinkled condition of the skin on the hands. Although he had not seen the dead boy's feet, it was natural to assume that they too were wrinkled in this curious way, which would account for his worry over the supposedly significant "wrinkles" he had "seen" on his own feet. It happened that Clyde's wife had taken a job at just about the time of the death, and that she had begun paying less and less attention to Clyde and his needs. Her appearance of separating from him was one of the reasons she had become the target of his suspicions.

News that his brother had disappeared while fishing had reached Clyde when he was at home alone, putting a stack of records on his record player. It was several hours before the body was recovered, and during this interval Clyde had refused to believe that death had taken place. After the body had been found and identified, Clyde still could not accept the reality of what had happened.

Since the body had been so long in the water, it was necessary to arrange quickly for the burial. As the eldest man in the family (his father had died ten years earlier), Clyde was so much occupied with funeral plans that he had no opportunity to express his initial grief. He later described the funeral as a tearless, unemotional affair. He left the cemetery before the body was lowered into the grave, and did not return. Friends accepted the death as being God's will, but Clyde felt anger, which he suppressed. He was hypercritical of himself, saying that he had failed the youngster and that if he had accompanied him the drowning would not have occurred. Obsessed with the boy's image, he continued to speak of him in the present tense.

Treatment

Clyde's re-grief therapy took little more than two months.

Since he had come to the hospital from another state, he remained an inpatient during his treatment, and was seen four times a week. As the treatment got under way, he remembered the repeating dreams he had had after the death, which had involved his diving into muddy water to save his brother, and his searching for him unsuccessfully. He would awaken from these dreams with anxiety. Since the death, he had been preoccupied with teaching his children to swim lest they drown in a shallow brook on his property. I soon learned that after his own brush with death, Clyde had wanted to make sure that he could save himself, and had bargained with the threat of melanoma by becoming a "good" person—one who refrained from expressing anger, and who did not question God's will.

Encouraged to talk about his brother in the early sessions, he insisted that he had failed him, and expressed strong feelings of guilt about the accident. In an effort to keep his brother alive, he had signed up to study electronics with the idea of finishing a television set his brother had been putting together before his drowning. Severe headaches led him to abandon this work, however, reflecting the negative aspect of his ambivalence toward the dead boy.

Early in his treatment I tried to learn why Clyde's paranoid ideation was so greatly concerned with his wife; I looked for some reason other than her increasing unavailability. An interesting feature of the relationship between husband and wife was his high degree of dependency on her, and his sensitivity to separation from her. It came out that his brother had called Clyde on the telephone the day before his death to ask for a loan with which to buy a car. In Clyde's absence, his wife had talked to the boy and refused his request. The couple had already discussed his reckless driving. Displacement thus accounted for Clyde's anger, since he saw his wife as having failed the boy just before his death.

The family history of melanoma had led to a realistic and cautious self-protectiveness, as exemplified by Clyde's protecting his skin from sunlight. When his half-brother died, Clyde's anxiety about his own death was exacerbated, and his fear of being hurt by his wife had to be defended against. His "delusional system" was, in a sense, in the service of pushing his wife into a divorce. He kept assuring me that, although he did not want a divorce, he felt compelled to get one. He was forestalling the dereliction of the woman he depended on by paradoxically initiating separation from her on his own terms. These two interpretations of what was going on between husband and wife were adhered to throughout Clyde's re-griefing, and offered for his consideration each time he reintroduced his delusional ideas about her faithlessness.

He brought to the fourth session a picture of his brother that had held special significance for him. I took it from its envelope and placed it face down before him. This practice, customary in re-griefing, grants the patient the initiative in looking at the significant object only when he is ready to do so. Clyde made no immediate move to examine it. During this interview, he reported an incident that had helped him toward insight. On the previous day he had spilled coffee on his neck and on his shirt collar while talking to a medical student on the ward, and had jokingly but anxiously remarked that he was trying to drown himself. I complimented him on the astuteness of his observation and suggested that he felt the same way about his unexpressed emotions concerning his brother's death, fearing that their expression would end up drowning him. From this point on, Clyde showed an increasing ability to express his angry feelings, and by the end of the hour he stated that his brother had been a fat show-off who had been stupid in getting himself drowned and thereby making all kinds of complications for the patient.

While telling about a dream that had occurred at the end of the first week of re-griefing, Clyde had his first intense emotional storm. In it, he saw his eldest son, and the thought "Kill! Kill!" came to him. He spontaneously associated the dead brother with his son, and in so doing, consciously acknowledged his feelings of aggression toward his brother. Toward the end of the hour, he related another dream he had had shortly after agreeing to start re-grief therapy. In this dream, he had been in a dark valley, riding a bicycle. He rode on a wet and slippery road but was able to hurry along and escape an impending storm. At the end of this session I complimented him on his tolerance of the emotional discharge that had taken place, and warned him that the process was not yet over, encouraging him by saying that the experience of similar feelings might not be so frightening in the future. The manifest content of a dream was thus used to guide him in the process of mourning.

The next day he spoke of another dream in which he had seen a small man and a tall, dark one whose shoes were old, comfortable, and wrinkled. His association to this dream indicated that he was the little man, who had felt humble all his life, and who had tried not to provoke trouble, such as the melanoma that was God's will. The tall man represented the therapist, whose shoes indicated wide travel and had an easy fit. Clyde's shoes were uncomfortable, and they fit poorly; he longed for more comfortable ones. The tall figure also bore the condensation of the dead half-brother's image; its shoes were wrinkled, and Clyde thought of the dead boy's feet as having been wrinkled. After reporting this dream, Clyde described in detail his viewing of the boy's dead body. His peculiar belief that his wife had put itching powder in his socks to redden and wrinkle the soles of his feet and ultimately to kill him was interpreted, as was his concern about the dead boy's skin. His attempts to imitate the dead boy were then contrasted with his efforts to save himself by rejecting the socks that made his skin wrinkle. The establishment of this connection relaxed him. He then made his first attempt to look at the photograph, but was unable to do so. He felt cold. I told him that it was his half-brother, cold in death, whom he felt to be within himself. Sighing, he declared emotionally, "I wish I could start living again!" The wish to keep in contact with the dead boy by internalizing him was interpreted. He was reminded of his earlier dream of "Kill! Kill!" that demonstrated his wish to complete his grieving by "killing" his brother's representation within himself, and the guilt he felt regarding this.

During the next session he looked for the first time at the picture and exclaimed, "He's dead and I had nothing to do with it!" He began to cry, and talked about how handsome his brother had been and how sad it was that he had died on the threshold of manhood. About this time, Clyde's behavior on the ward changed considerably. He gave up reporting his "delusional ideas" to ward personnel and other patients. He went into what he called a state of grieving, weeping violently and suddenly becoming angry with the dead boy. In this agitated state, he shouted several times at the representation of his brother, now felt as an introject within his breast, using the same words Mike (Chapter 9) used in screaming at his father's introject, "Leave me alone! Get out! Get out!" On the following day, he commented that he felt better than at any time during the year just past.

At this point, after a month of therapy, he was asked to direct his attention to the receipt of the tragic news, and the funeral. He reported a dream in which he was relaxing comfortably in what might have been his own home. After a knock on the door, a woman entered. He explained to her that he was "just relaxing—waiting for my brother." The woman was associated with a next-door neighbor whose house his children had frequented. Finding himself alone at home after his brother's drowning, having taken some time off from work, he had been feeling uneasy, rejected, and emotionally separated from his wife, now at work, and the children who so often played next door. When this association was made, he was able to laugh and say, "Here I go again—sour grapes. Yes, I was very mad at my kids, who left me alone by going to the neighbor's house."

The records he was about to listen to when news of the death had arrived had become his linking object. He had not played them since the sad news came, but had kept them stacked up apart from the rest. It was as though he could, by never playing them, stop time at the last moment in which his brother had been a living person in his perception. He even refrained from touching them, thereby effectively keeping them at a distance. I suggested that he have his wife bring the records to the hospital, and during his next hour I joined him in his hospital room and we listened to them there instead of going to my office. The experience brought a flood of emotions, and he cried aloud for a long time. The next day he had abortive emotional spells, saying "ah-ah" without being able to continue. He finally described a "weight in his chest" that he wanted to remove. Then he voluntarily suggested that we talk about "that fellow"—the dead boy. He recalled how reckless the boy had been, and how unrealistically he had dreamed of the future. He kept asking me, "What do you do with a fellow like that? How do you advise him?" as though his brother were still alive and the questions actually awaited solution. At the height of this negative outburst I asked, "He was a big show-off, wasn't he?" to which Clyde replied by expressing anger and explaining that it was his brother's recklessness that had made it necessary to withhold money from him, and that had killed him in the end.

Clyde then spoke of something that had angered him at the funeral. The dead boy's friends had come from a distance for the funeral, and had spoken of seeing the town as soon as the services were over; it was a town of some interest as a tourist attraction. They had rationalized this proposal by saying that the dead boy had so often spoken of a certain part of town that he had awakened their interest in seeing it for themselves. Clyde felt that these mourners had behaved like casual tourists and that he had been pressed into service as a tour guide even before the coffin was finally put in the ground. I then asked him how he knew that his brother had actually been buried, and reminded him that he was so greatly preoccupied with his brother's image that he had in effect buried him in his own breast rather than in a grave. It was not surprising, then, that he talked to his brother as though he were resident in his chest.

I suggested to him that when he was ready he might visit the grave, and we discussed the possibility of getting photographs of it to bring for discussion to a therapy hour. This discussion created intense interest in various aspects of the burial—the depth of the grave, the efficacy of the concrete vault, the absence of a marker—all the preoccupations typical of established pathological mourning and indicative of anxiety that the dead might rise. Toward the end of the second month, Clyde reported a dream in which he had found himself alone at the grave. He had lowered the casket containing his brother's body into the vault and fastened the cover. He had started shoveling dirt into the grave when a second man—representing the therapist—appeared and joined him in this work.

During this time, Clyde began to reinvest in new objects the attachments withdrawn from the dead brother in the course of re-griefing. He was concerned about improving the relationship with his wife, returning to work, and assuming normal involvements and activities. A sportsman most of his life, he had given up sports after the drowning, but now once again expressed an interest in golf, fishing, and hunting. He reported feeling more relaxed, and his behavior during the interviews bore this out. He voluntarily brought a cup of coffee to one interview and drank it before the therapist. In the middle of this hour, he realized what he had done. His humor had returned, and he joked about it, finishing his coffee. Now there was no "yellow spot" in the cup!

The next day, although anxious, he went to a funeral home and asked about monuments. At the end of two months in the hospital, he spent a weekend at home with his family, and twice visited his brother's grave, which he had avoided doing since the funeral. He also visited his stepmother and, with her, decided on a marker to be put on the grave. A few days later he was discharged from the hospital, and his re-grief therapy was at an end.

Psychological tests

Clyde was given the MMPI at the outset of his treatment, at the midway point, and at termination (see Figure 4).

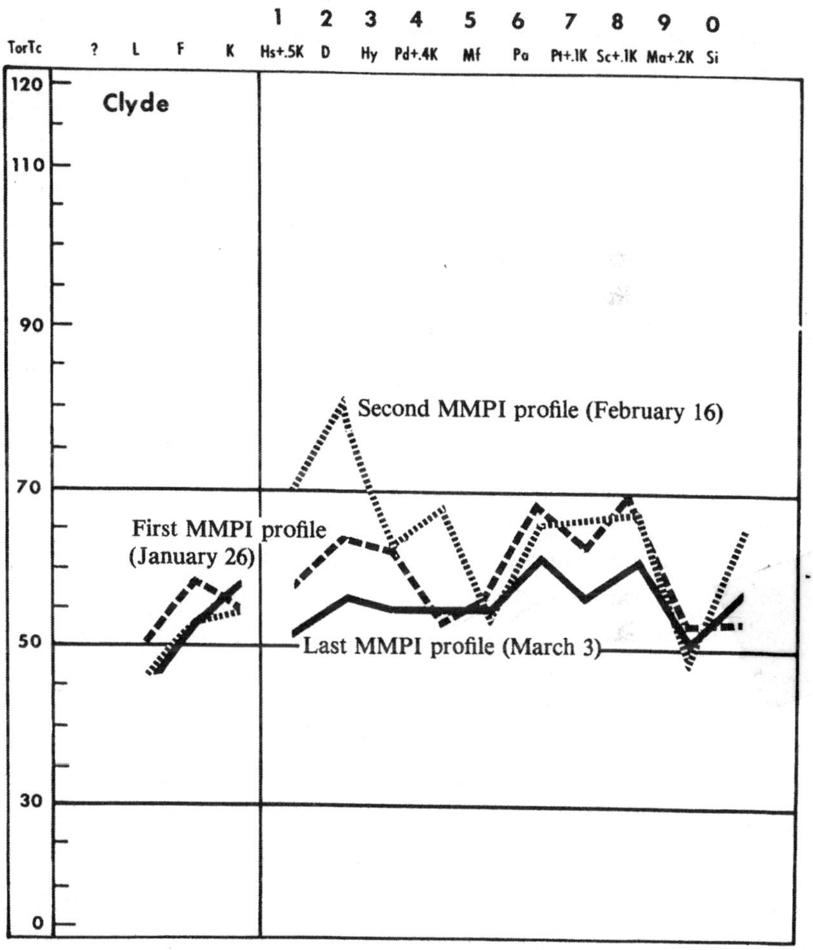

Figure 4 Clyde's three MMPIs

Despite his presenting symptoms (circumscribed paranoid ideation and numerous delusional somatic complaints), Clyde had a fairly flat pre-therapy MMPI profile. There were peaks at scales 8, 6, and 2; however, only 8 was above T = 70. The validity scales were within normal limits for Clyde. As I anticipated, scales 1, 2, and 4 increased significantly in the second MMPI testing. Patients often seem worse midway through their therapeutic course as they are picked up in the throes of the re-griefing process. There was significant decrease in scales 1, 2, 3, 4, and 7 between the second and third use of the MMPI. However, only one scale changed significantly between the first and final testing; this was scale 8. Other scales decreased slightly, below the level of significance. This may reflect the limited initial elevation on the MMPI scales displayed by Clyde in all but scale 8. The significant increase in "psychopathology" halfway through Clyde's re-griefing, and a corresponding decrease at the termination of therapy, as predicted, are striking. The fact that he showed significant improvement only on scale 8 remains to be accounted for. It is possible that, for this scale, the second MMPI testing gave a more accurate indication of the extent of established pathological mourning in the initial stages of re-griefing than did the first testing.

Clyde made six follow-up visits within—three years after completing re-grief therapy. He was seen three times during the first post-treatment year, twice during the second year, and once during the third. At the fifth follow-up interview, a year and nine months after termination, Clyde reported what I felt was a "review dream." In it, he was swimming with his ten-year-old son, who wrestled with him. Clyde disengaged himself by swimming away, but the son turned into someone large and dark who recommenced the struggle in the water. Although anxious, Clyde felt confident enough in his superior swimming ability to separate himself and swim to safety. His associations to this indicated that during his re-griefing he had associated his son with the lost brother, but that he now enjoyed a better relationship with the boy. The drowned brother had in a sense tried to draw Clyde under the water, but Clyde could now save himself, i.e., differentiate himself from the boy who had drowned. Nevertheless, he wondered whether he had left the door open once again to denial of the drowning: during this hour he could not recall its exact date. He was puzzled, and I learned later that after this interview he went to the county offices for a copy of the death certificate.

He talked during this fifth check-up about the past anniversary of the drowning, and also felt some anxiety which he connected with that date. With this insight, he had decided to visit the grave rather than to continue feeling anxious, and the visit did allay his anxiety. He was now able to use his linking objects simply as records to be played, and he resumed golf and hunting, diversions he had given up during his pathological period because of their "aggressive nature." He was no longer phobic about guns or hunting.

Clyde seemed to have accomplished a great deal by himself by the time of this check-up, although he was still rather markedly cautious. When he reviewed the symptoms he had had, he stated that one of the reasons his brother's death had so strongly affected him was that he had become sensitized toward loss at the age of 13 when his mother had died. At the time of this check-up, many of his fellow workers were being laid off and his job was also in jeopardy, but he seemed able to handle this threat in a reality-oriented way. By his final interview, during his third post-therapy year, he still had his job and was carrying on in his usual lifestyle without further preoccupation with his brother's image.

Part III

Living linking objects and related psychological states

CHAPTER 12

Children's reactions to death: "Negative" outcome—the case of the stone swan

This chapter opens with a brief review of the literature on children's reaction to death. I am in agreement with those analysts who hold that the child's internal process of mourning prior to the full development of object constancy differs from that of the adult. It may indeed be possible that adolescence, which provides a "natural" developmental model of mourning by necessitating the modification of the images and representations of the parents of one's childhood, must be accomplished before the adult type of grieving becomes possible.

When a child between the ages of three or three-and-a half (when object constancy becomes rather stable) and adolescence loses by death someone psychologically significant to him, he may cling to the lost object's representation in a way similar to that of the adult in established pathological mourning and/or adult reactive depression.

A child's reactions to death may establish inner organizations that will influence the individual's character traits and symptoms. Such developing character traits may follow either the course of negative adaptation or positive and creative adaptation. This chapter describes the case of a young woman with a maladaptive response to the early death of a sibling, and takes into account, as well, her response to her mother's grieving. The material relates to a study in the following chapters of the influence a mother's grief has on her child, even where the death had occurred before her child has developed full object constancy.

Children's reactions to death

Thus far I have considered only adult mourners—their uncomplicated and complicated mourning processes and the treatment of the latter. It seems obvious that the nature of adult mourning will depend to a great extent on the way in which the mourner learned in childhood to deal with loss, including the psychological loss involved in separation–individuation (Mahler, 1968), but I will review here only those responses of children to actual object loss. Such a review will help shed light on issues brought to our attention by adult patients who have experienced such a loss in childhood.

There is controversy among psychoanalysts as to when a child is capable of mourning. Bowlby (1960, 1963, 1969) emphasizes in his attachment theory (see Chapter 1) that mourning is possible in infancy, a view that has been widely criticized. Anna Freud (1960) states that the process of mourning includes "the individual's effort to accept a fact in the external world (the loss of the cathected object) and to effect corresponding changes in the inner world (withdrawal of libido from the lost object, identification with the lost object)" (p. 58).

> At least the former half of this task presupposes certain capacities of the mental apparatus such as reality testing, the acceptance of the reality principle, partial control of id tendencies by the ego, etc., i.e., capacities which are still undeveloped in the infant according to all other evidence. We have hesitated therefore to apply the term mourning in its technical sense to the bereavement reactions of the infant. (A. Freud, 1960, p. 58)

Anna Freud goes on to state that prior to the development of object constancy—that is, prior to the time when the image of a cathected person can be maintained internally—the pleasure–pain principle governs the child's response to a loss. Thus the chronological age is important: "The nearer to object constancy, the longer the duration of grief reactions with corresponding approximation to the adult internal process of mourning" (p. 59).

Schur (1960) and Spitz (1960) also question Bowlby's belief that the reactions of an infant separated from a significant other are identical with those of the mourning adult. Furman (1964) states that, in general, it is not until a child is between three-and-a-half and four years of age that he can mourn. Wolfenstein (1966, 1969) goes even further: she hypothesizes that passage through adolescence is a necessary precondition for the ability to mourn, as mourning is described by Freud (1917a). A gradual and somewhat painful decathexis of one's living parents (never totally achieved) is accomplished during one's adolescence and serves as an initiation into what mourning in the adult sense involves. My own experience supports her view that the experience of adolescence provides a model for the adult type of grieving. I agree with her that, whereas the bereaved adult who has not encountered complications in his mourning decathects the representation of the lost love object, children and adolescents hypercathect the lost object's representation whenever a suitable substitute person is not available. And they cling to this representation in a way similar to what I have seen in adults in established pathological mourning and/or adult reactive depression.

Barbara, a 22-year-old, came to treatment because of recent difficulties with a married lover she described as "old enough to be my father." She recalled identical problems in the past with other men, all of whom had been much older than she, and married. Her presenting problems were not unlike Linda's (see Chapter 2), except that Linda's lovers were not invariably chosen from among much older men. But Barbara's problems stemmed from genetic events unlike Linda's.

"Elation" attended Barbara's establishment of relations with each older married lover, but anxiety and disappointment soon followed. At the outset of her therapy, she called herself "a searcher for something in men," although she could not identify the object of her search. It soon became evident that she was searching for her dead father, an F.B.I. agent killed when she was three, when the plane in which he was flying to Chicago crashed. She recalled having denied his death and having at different times fantasied his continued existence. As time went on, and she learned more about the F.B.I., she convinced herself that he was living incognito as a crime-fighter in Chicago. Her therapy later revealed that each of her men represented him for a while, until guilt over "incestuous" behavior would surface, and she would become anxious over and disappointed in their "fatherliness" (Volkan, 1970).

In his review of children's reactions to the death of someone important to them, Nagera (1970) concludes that such losses interfere with development, and that such children may not only have overt or insidious symptoms but character disorders as well. Such character distortions are not always maladaptive; they may, indeed, give direction to a high degree of creativity. Children differ constitutionally, and may fantasy different roles for themselves in connection with the loss, e.g., being responsible for the death of a sibling in order to have sole access to the mother. Such fantasies and those that counteract them may have an *organizing* effect on the developing character structure of these children.

Berman (1978) tells how sibling loss was the organizing core of a profound, enduring, but unconscious sense of guilt that afflicted one of his analysands, a 46-year-old physician. This patient's sister had died shortly after birth in the hospital in which she had been born, so that the three-year-old patient had never seen her. Berman identifies several factors that accounted for the profound impression her death had made on the patient; these included his developmental state at the time, the circumstances of the sister's death, and the way in which these combined to enhance his belief in magical, omnipotent thinking. Berman also points out how the mother's sadistic impulses and her own magical thinking were taken in by her son's primitive superego.

The way in which the mother, or mother substitute, mourns and the way in which she seeks to tame the child's fantasies about death is most important in determining how the child will adapt to loss internally. Sometimes the mothering person passes on her own fantasies to her child, perhaps even "depositing" in her child's self-system the concept that he is the dead person's representative; then the child becomes the mother's "living linking object." I will examine a few such living linking objects in the following chapters. Here I will present the case of a young woman who, not unlike Berman's patient, was influenced by the death of a baby sister she never saw. The sister had died ten days after birth, of hydrocephalus or meningomyelocele, in the hospital where she had been born. The patient was two-and-a-half at the time.

This young woman, a physician, was analyzed by Robert King. Her case was striking inasmuch as, although she mentioned the dead sibling in the first year of her analysis, the influence of this childhood loss was not clearly understood until the third year of analysis when she dramatically referred to an unassimilated composite representation of the dead baby sister and her grieving mother that was lodged in her breast, so to speak. She had up to that point worked through important constellations of childhood wishes, frustrations, and fantasies, and the defenses against them. After the introject of the sibling/mother made its appearance, it became possible to analyze the influence it exerted over the patient.

King's case is presented here to illustrate how a childhood loss can leave its mark—a guilt-provoking internal organization—on the psychological makeup of the surviving child, and to point out that one is well advised to pay close attention to any account of such occurrences in obtaining a patient's history. There may be no initial clue to the importance of a past event of this kind in the patient's symptoms or behavior patterns, and it may indeed take analytic treatment for a connection to become clear.

Polly's background

What follows is taken from King's extensive notes on the treatment of the young physician he called Polly. Polly was 26 when she sought analysis with a presenting problem she described as having something wrong with her "internal identity," a "feeling that the inner tapestry of my life is dull." She felt discontented in spite of her achievements and her professional competence, and remained deeply dissatisfied with herself. This state alternated with periods of her being "perfect Polly"—witty, bright, and desirable with men whom she ultimately came to regard as unsuitable. In general, she had difficulty relating to men, and regarded sexual intercourse as dangerous. As she began her analysis, she spoke of having a cold sensation and a blank state of mind, which may have resulted from an identification with the dead sister/grieving mother, although this connection did not become apparent until she had been in analysis for some time. Interestingly enough, when King suggested analysis as the treatment of choice for her, she spoke of feeling "as if I had been told that I have a cancer within me." It would take some years to learn the significance of this "cancer," which, lodged in "the inner tapestry" of her life, had caused a confusion of "internal identity."

Polly came from a lower-middle-class Catholic family. When she was two-and-a-half, the congenitally defective sister, who was named Molly, died in the hospital. A year later *to the day* of Molly's birth, another sister was born, and there were indications that this latter sister became a replacement child (Poznanski, 1972), an idealized version of the one who had lived so briefly. This child was considered a "perfect angel," and Polly was jealous of her into adult life.

The father, a charming ne'er-do-well, abandoned his family when Polly was about seven, and saw his daughters only sporadically for a few years after his departure, disappearing completely until Polly was 21. Her only contact with him during the intervening time had been through cards and mysteriously left presents. Polly felt angry with her mother for driving her father away, but also felt that she must not display her anger for fear that her mother might abandon her as well. She responded to the loss of her father by throwing herself into her school work. Later, after being disappointed in a man, she would throw herself into her work. She felt that she had to look after her depressed mother, whom she viewed as needy and incompetent, and become the man of the house to replace her father. When she finished high school, without any emotional or financial support from her family she obtained a scholarship to go away to college and then graduate school.

Polly's analysis

Polly began her analysis with a strong positive oedipal transference, experiencing her analyst as a perfect man who would cure her and give her everything. The analyst's abstinence soon precipitated the kind of "seduced and abandoned" feelings with which she had reacted to her father's departure from her life. It was not until the second half of this year of analysis that her ambivalent preoedipal relationship with her mother was elaborated in the transference. At work, Polly said that she feared being taken over by strong women friends, or by her female boss, another physician. Rage at the abandoning father/ analyst was now linked to "being abandoned and relegated to the world of women." Polly expressed curiosity, jealousy, and angry fantasies about the analyst's wife, child patients, and women colleagues. Analytic work on all this led to the recovery of explicit primal scene memories—Polly had shared a bedroom with her parents until she was three—and a jealous memory of her mother departing for the hospital to have a baby. These feelings were dramatically paralleled at work, where her boss, who explicitly, although ambivalently, regarded Polly as a daughter, put another young woman above her in the chain of command, giving her a position Polly coveted. Furious and jealous, Polly felt displaced and unable to please her boss by any means at her command. At the same time, she sniped at her, and made provocative efforts to assert her independence of the mother/doctor. Her intense jealousy of her new superior recalled the death wishes she had entertained toward her sisters, as well as the horror and guilt awakened by the death of the first sister. Polly began to recognize for the first time previously repressed but intense fantasies she had had regarding the death of the infant she had never seen, and the affect dispositions that had accompanied them. She was now able to recall feeling close to her mother and being the favored "perfect Polly" until the hated sisters arrived. (In reconstructing the past, it seemed likely that the mother had been not only deeply depressed by Molly's death, but preoccupied with her pregnancies and marital difficulties.) Since little Polly had been unable to regain her mother by being good, she had become as bad as possible, kicking and screaming on the potty, for example, and as "independent" as she could manage, often wandering several blocks from home by the time she was four. As a preschooler, she had often taunted the living sister and had thrown things in her crib. Until she was nine, she had been regarded at home as a hellion.

As her analysis entered the second year, the deepening of the ambivalent early maternal transference was paralleled by new and alarming symptoms. During the fall of this year, Polly revealed reluctantly that she had often had trouble eating because of tormenting fears that she might be poisoned by dirt or toxic substances on her hands. Sometimes she was compelled to check her food to see if it was spoiled. Associations led her to recall an anorectic period when she was about three when she had refused food her mother had prepared, accepting only that prepared by a neighbor whom the mother had disliked. This rejection of the mother's food, and the fear of being poisoned, pointed to an early retaliatory rejection of the mother and a hostile, counterdependent assertion of autonomy that was tinged with fear of retaliation and the projection onto the mother of Polly's rage. Polly felt she deserved to be punished for having (successfully) wished her sister to die.

Around this time in her analysis, she began having episodes of tachycardia. The first such episode occurred—probably as a result of epinephrine sensitivity—after a woman dentist had given her an injection of Novocain.

She recalled a frightening penicillin injection she had had when she was three; she saw this as both a sexual assault and a murderous punishment for her own angry wishes toward her sister (as well as for her sexual longings for her father). As a physician, Polly had herself always felt inhibited about giving injections.

Other associations to Polly's two new symptoms—her difficulty in eating and her tachycardia—are not reported here, since my emphasis is on those associations to her guilt connected with her baby sister's death. However, it should be noted that these symptoms were reflected in the transference neurosis; for example, dental work—the genesis of Polly's tachycardia—was a metaphor for the analysis by which she hoped to be cured of her oral rage. Furthermore, there was a strong parallel between her refusal to take food from her mother and the content of the transference neurosis. Her symptoms lessened when King suggested that she could not take in anything good from the analyst either; that his food was unwholesome and would only make her worse; that unless he took complete care of her she would fall ill and die, and it would all be his fault. Prior to her analysis, Polly's rage over oedipal disappointment, and her frustrated longings for her mother, had had to be dealt with either by reaction formation or projection. She came to see that much of her difficulty with her work, which was heavily involved with infant and maternal health and with child abuse, stemmed from her conflictual attempts to undo or to deny her rage at the birth of a sister. Moreover, King helped her to see how the issues of autonomy were suffused with concern about aggression. To be independent at work, in the transference, or as a child, was equated with hostile rejection by the disappointing boss, the analyst, or the mother, and was seen as the only alternative to desperate dependence. True autonomy was impossible, since her extremely strict superego punished her rage-contaminated strivings for independence. King also interpreted the reason for her tending to reject men in spite of her desire to marry and have children; she was afraid of being abandoned by them. Polly then recovered a childhood fantasy that, if she had been a boy, her father would have stayed—or, at least, she would have been a man for her mother. By the time she had been in analysis for two full years, much work had been done on her guilt over her baby sister's death, her oral rage at being abandoned by the preoedipal mother, the frustrations of her oedipal longings, and her general confusion.

The swan of white stone bearing a picture in its breast

Polly entered her third year of analysis feeling greatly improved and less panicky. She functioned better at work, and tentatively started to date for the first time in a year. What is interesting in this third year in analysis is the persistence of something in her that could still induce symptoms associated with depressive affect and feelings of hopelessness, in spite of the analytic work accomplished. Just when things seemed to be getting better for her, it seemed that full progress toward inner comfort and fulfillment was suddenly inhibited. This inhibition came from an inner organization associated with the early childhood loss—an organization that had autonomous existence, as it were. Just as Alice (see Chapter 1) had had to understand what her "little man" stood for, Polly had to come face to face with her inner "enemy." It is only when our enemies are out in the open that their influence and domination over us can be assessed and tamed!

Feeling improved, Polly had made plans to move from the previous monastic isolation of her apartment far out of town to a location that had seemed to promise more social stimulation and gratification of her cultural interests. It had become clear that to be independent, to begin enjoying herself, and to give up her angry, reproachful dependence on her analyst was experienced not only as involving loss and separation but as an angry attack on him as well. It was as though she were saying (as she had said to her parent when a child), "I don't need you, I can live without you!" But now, contemplating the move to town, she had become panicky again, fearing some sort of financial and somatic catastrophe. More important, thc anticipated physical change symbolized a major psychological changc toward inner independence that caused a dramatic surfacing of the guilt-provoking "frozen introject" lodged in her breast. Before she signed the lease on her new apartment, Polly reported the following dream:

> I was working in a public health field unit. I was told [by a doctor] that they were sending me as a student to study migrant health in the field—I thought it was silly, a way of killing time. Then I was in the house of a Spanish woman. There was a white stone swan on the table with a picture in its breast of a mother and child looking at each other. I asked it if was "Jorge Rojas," who had been referred to me but had

> committed suicide and killed her baby. I told the woman in the dream that I had tried so hard to find and stop her. I tried so hard to reach her. I woke up with my fists clenched.

Polly went on, "The white swan, that's me, carrying in me my dead sister and my grieving mother. Maybe I felt like she was dead too. I looked all over for her; I couldn't prevent it. Looked all over for my mother, but she was at the hospital. By the time I found her she was dead. It wasn't my fault, I tried so hard to get through, to save her."

Polly began to sob and laugh uncontrollably at the same time; she suddenly had a pain in her chest. With the help of her analyst, she now understood that her fears of moving toward independence were linked to guilt over her sister's death and her mother's depression. The combined representations of these two had turned into an inner organization within her, influencing her throughout all of her adult life. It was now possible to identify the "cancer" she had spoken of having in her "inner tapestry." The persistence of the representation of the baby sister/grieving mother within her, and its dominion over her, could now be acknowledged. She told King that she felt she was bound to this frozen introject and thus unable to invest herself in the world around her. For her, actual independence meant to "kill" the introject. To give up her depression meant becoming separate from her depressed mother. Her analysis had come to a new depth of understanding in the service of resolving a pathological structure from her very early life. It was only then, after the introject had surfaced, that it began to lose its power over her.

CHAPTER 13

Children's reactions to death: "Positive" outcome—the case of "Immortal Atatürk"

It is obvious that there is no one typical response to the childhood loss of a sibling, parent, or other important person. Children are different from one another constitutionally, and fantasy different roles for themselves in connection with the loss; parents differ in how they operate as external ego–superegos in taming the influence of pathogenic fantasies and paving the way for useful or destructive adaptation. The impact of having been made a living link to the dead (see also the following chapter) can lead to a fantasy of the self as having been reincarnated, and a self-concept that either competes with or adjusts to other self-concepts uncontaminated by reincarnation fantasies. Considerable interest has been shown among psychoanalysts in the influence of early object loss in giving direction to successful creativity. Such losses are certainly not solely productive of developmental arrest and protracted immaturity of object relations.

This chapter briefly reviews the psychoanalytic literature on the "positive outcome" of a childhood experience with death. I then offer the case of Atatürk, the founder of modern Turkey, who was not only used by his mother as a link to his dead siblings (and thus made "immortal" in a sense) but who also organized his own self-concept as that of the savior of his grieving mother—and later of a grieving nation.

Review of the literature

Early attempts at psychoanalytic psychobiography indicate an appreciation of the "positive outcomes" of a childhood colored by death. Abraham (1911b) concluded that Segantini's painting reflected the death of his mother when he was five years old. Freud (1917b) referred to Goethe's childhood belief that "destiny preserved my life," although removing his brother and grandmother, and that he was thus "a child of fortune" (p. 156). Since Goethe did not have to share his mother's love with a brother, he became her unchallenged darling. Freud commented that "if a man has been his mother's undisputed darling he retains throughout life the triumphant feeling, the confidence in success, which not seldom brings actual success along with it" (p. 156). Hamilton's (1976) work on the concept of the death instinct suggests that these remarks of Freud may reflect the influence upon him of specific intra psychic issues deriving from the death of his brother Julius when Freud was 19 months old, and the subsequent disruption in his relationship with his nursemaid and his mother. Hamilton states that

> One must ... consider the likelihood that Freud's mother was depressed and withdrawn after Julius's death and thus not as readily available to her son, causing him possibly to be concerned that she had contracted a fatal illness. (p. 160)

Hamilton reminds us of Freud's concern with the possibility that the dead return to life. In 1907, Freud stated that "the belief in spirits and ghosts and the return of the dead, which finds so much support in the religions to which we have all been attached, at least in our childhood, is far from having disappeared among educated people, and that many who are sensible in other respects find it possible to combine spiritualism with reason" (p. 71). He described how a physician (probably himself) mistook the sister of a patient who had died for the patient herself and felt momentarily that "it's true that the dead can come back to life" (p. 71) and felt shame when he realized his error.

Like Hamilton, Pollock (1968) indicates that Freud's childhood loss of his next younger sibling may have been a significant factor in his life. Bonaparte (1933) notes the importance of a child's loss of a parent in the creations of Edgar Allen Poe, whose works so fascinated my patient Frances (see the following chapter). Niederland's (1965) study of Schliemann shows how a surviving child may represent his dead sibling in what is close to being an example of my "living linking object" concept; he points out that "all through his life Schliemann never was fully sure whether he was the *dead* brother inside or the *living* one outside the grave" (p. 375); and how he sublimated this dynamic process in his great archeological work. Niederland concludes that many creative people have early problems of body image, and explains that because important others contribute to early body and self-images, their disappearance can produce a feeling of body loss. He notes that creativeness can be in the service of survival, citing the case of a contemporary sculptress who turned to art as her salvation after many losses, claiming that this was the one thing she would never have to lose.

My formulations about Atatürk, whose career will be described, receive support from Pollock (1975b), who also has written on the relationship between childhood in a world colored by death and positive outcomes in adult life. His paper refers to the work of others on similar formulations, and earlier explorations of his own on this subject. He is impressed by the connection between childhood mourning and the unconscious intimation of immortality that arises from grappling with it psychologically. Although his paper on the subject concerns Lenin, he had gathered data on artists, scientists, and political leaders and pundits concerning their childhood experiences with death, examining the life stories of 1200 writers with such backgrounds. He is quick to say that loss does not necessarily account for the creative act or the creative product, but that the creative act may be given direction by childhood loss, as the Planks (1978) and Wolfenstein (1973) also indicate in statements with which I agree. Pollock suggests that conceptions of an after-life parallel the fantasies of the ideal Utopian secular existence sought by some political leaders, maintaining that

> ... immortality, actual or symbolic, appears to play an important role in the construction of Utopias. Studying Utopian and revolutionary leaders reveals a possible connection of childhood object death with subsequent political activity. ... I wish to emphasize that when one studies the lives of political leaders who had had childhood losses through death, one can ascertain certain evidence

> of psychopathology. These disturbances are not necessarily explanatory of the political leader's adult activities, but they cannot be overlooked. (p. 336)

I believe that what Pollock describes here is applicable to the history of Atatürk.

A most convincing series of papers by Hamilton (1975, 1979a, 1979b) on Joseph Conrad shows the relationship between Conrad's creativity and his loss of a parent as a child.

The last of these papers states that the reason for a Doppelgänger kind of relationship between Conrad and Bertrand Russell was the effect on each man of early bereavement. Hamilton reports that Conrad kept with him a picture of his mother's grave as well as an album of photographs of his parents and other relatives, which he referred to as "the graveyard," and which he did not allow others to view except on rare occasions. Hamilton considers the possibility that these photographs were Conrad's linking objects as I describe the term. They served to keep his parents alive symbolically while forestalling any adequate working through of the loss. Hamilton states:

> For Conrad, it appears that the creative process itself involved regression and a temporary, transient, or partial fusion with a dead introject. This would help account for the plethora of somatic symptoms, the hypochondriacal concerns, and the agony he complained of while working. (1975, p. 627)

Hamilton (1969) proposes a similar formulation to account for the creativity of John Keats, exposed as a child to repeated losses. Hamilton holds that object loss leads to regressive fusion with the lost object, and that the dream becomes an integral part of the process, having originally been utilized by the infant to cope with the loss of direct oral gratification. He points out how Keats turned to poetry after finding his initial choice of a medical career too conflictual. He did so

> ... in an attempt to complete the mourning process and to make restitution for the lost object, most importantly his mother, by externalizing his dreams in the form of poems. Because of the intense ambivalence and hypercathexis of the introject, this method was

> only partially successful and, having to be repeated over and over again, led to one of the richest, most profuse creative efforts in all of literature. (Hamilton, 1969, p. 529)

A psychohistorical research project

In 1973 I began a psychohistorical research project (Volkan, 1980; Volkan, 1981b) in collaboration with historian Norman Itzkowitz, professor of Middle Eastern studies at Princeton University; the subject of the project, Mustafa Kemal Atatürk, was the founder of modern Turkey. During the 1974–75 academic year I went to Turkey to do fieldwork on this project, chiefly to interview people who had known Atatürk before his death in 1938. Although it would be inappropriate here to report in detail all we learned about him and his interaction with history—Itzkowitz and I are preparing a volume devoted exclusively to our findings in this connection—Atatürk does exemplify a "positive outcome" of a childhood colored by death.

Like most Turks of my generation, I grew up regarding Atatürk in almost mythological terms, as a sort of god figure. His reduction to human size during the course of my study, the revelation of his inner sufferings and his loneliness, the burden of "immortality" that linked him to long dead siblings, and his self-concept as a "savior" of a grieving mother, all affected me profoundly. Here I will not try to identify all the reasons why he may have been a creative and successful political leader, but, rather, the psychological determinants that gave *direction* to his creativity and leadership.

Much has been written about the problems of writing sophisticated psychobiographies of historical figures (Beres, 1959; Greenacre, 1955; Kohut, 1960; Niederland, 1965; Erikson, 1968, 1969; Mack, 1971; Bergmann, 1973). There has been debate about both the type of data that can substitute for the associations and transference reactions of actual analysands, and the validity of the substitutes adopted. Nevertheless, psychogenetic factors that have contributed to the personality makeup of someone no longer living can be inferred with some confidence from autobiographical and biographical information that identifies consistent behavioral patterns in the life of the one under study. In the case of Atatürk, the literature about him has been supplemented by information obtained from people who knew him. Data from these several sources give ample evidence from which a reliable picture of his life can be drawn—his actions, belief systems, and primary process imagery.

I am, of course, fully aware that over and above psychological factors that mark the career of a national leader are political, economic, historical, and social circumstances that combine to determine its course. Nevertheless, I hope to demonstrate, within the limitations of this chapter, how certain *psychological* realities so influenced Atatürk's adult behavior that the environment—in this case, the arena of history itself—was made to correspond to those psychological realities.

A child born in the house of death

Atatürk, whose name means "Father Turk," emerged as a charismatic leader after the collapse of the 600-year-old Turkish Ottoman Empire at the end of the First World War. In typically charismatic fashion, he appeared at a time of national crisis (Abse & Jessner, 1961; Tucker, 1970; Abse & Ulman, 1977), and was perceived as someone who could deliver the populace from widespread distress by virtue of his unusual personal qualities.

At birth he was named Mustafa after an uncle who had died in infancy in an accident for which Atatürk's father had been in some way responsible (Kinross, 1965). Although there is some uncertainty about the date of his birth, it is probably 1881. Salonika, the city of his birth, is now in Greece but at that time lay within Ottoman territory. His parents had only recently gone there from the customs outpost on the Turkish–Greek border near Mount Olympus where the father had been a minor customs official. Their home at the border had been a harsh environment, and the couple had lost three children—two boys and a girl—one after the other. It seems likely that none had reached the age of seven. The body of one son buried on the sandy shore had been uncovered by rising water and torn by jackals, according to a family story (Aydemir, 1969, Vol. I). Whether or not the tale is true in all its grim detail, it speaks poignantly of parental anguish and the hardship of their lives. Mustafa, the fourth child, came during an all-too-brief interval of family prosperity and confidence. The move to Salonika had taken place because a wealthy lumber merchant had taken the father into partnership for his knowledge of the forests around Mount Olympus.

The mother had been beautiful as a child bride, a fair-skinned peasant with blue eyes and amber hair, uneducated but bright. Her husband called her his "dream girl" and his "heavenly rose." At the time of Mustafa's birth he was 40, his wife only 20; she bore him two daughters after Mustafa's birth, but Mustafa and a younger sister were the only children out of six to survive into adulthood. She had to provide for these children when she became a widow at 27. Her husband had lost his partnership when bandits burned the forests for which he was responsible, and he had lapsed into drink and despair, dying when his son was seven. It is likely that little Mustafa's world was full of fearful images of dead siblings and a dead father. Not only did death stalk the household, but memories of the harsh life at the border and of the somber, bandit-ridden forest cast a shadow over it. The father's stories of bandit border raids and their threat remained for many years in the memory of Mustafa's sister (Aydemir, 1969, Vol. I).

In spite of having been born during the family's brief flirtation with prosperity, at a time when they had been able to employ a wet nurse for Mustafa, and a black housemaid, Atatürk wrote, in 1930, an essay that reflected a far from happy early home. His preoccupation with freedom seems to have risen as much from a need for personal freedom (individuation) as from a political concern that his country should be free. This 1930 essay on freedom, which can be seen in his handwriting today, opens with a discussion of the relationship between man and nature:

> Man does not decide whether or not to be born. At the moment of his birth he is at the mercy of nature and a host of creatures other than himself. He needs to be protected, to be fed, to be looked after, to be helped to grow. (Atatürk, 1930, pp. 77–78)

Reference to his dead siblings and to the concern that both he and his mother felt about safety are evident in this passage. Elsewhere in the same essay he speaks of "primitive people," probably representative of his childhood, who live in fear of the thunder, the darkness of the night, floods, wild animals, and even one another. One catches an echo of the jackals tearing at the child's body.

It is likely that Mustafa's mother turned more and more to religion as she lost one after another of her four doomed children and, finally, her husband. Some of the people I interviewed remembered her as a kind of "merry widow," but it is clear that, either simultaneously or alternately, she was a religious devotee with an acid disposition; she was called *Molla*, a title given to the religious person seeking mystic union with God and his powers.

It was customary to speak of such tragedies as those that befell Mustafa's family as being the will of God, and the idea of the God his mother acknowledged frightened little Mustafa, who may have regarded his mother as God's agent. Atatürk's 1930 essay notes that the fear of one's parents becomes the fear of God, which sets up many prohibitions and restrictive traditions militating against the freedom of the individual: "Those who are heads of communities ... run the communities in the name of God" (p. 78). Such pious people seemed to him to represent his religious mother.

From Mustafa to Mustafa Kemal

Just before the death of Mustafa's father, he had directed that his son have a modern elementary school education rather than go to the religious school preferred by the mother. At that time, Turkish parents living in some big cities of the Ottoman Empire could select either kind of training for their children. His mother had wanted Mustafa eventually to make religion his career. Atatürk's earliest memory (Emin, 1922) was of the strong disagreement between his parents over what schooling he was to have. He recalled how skillfully his father had worked out a solution. First, the child was to enter the religious school with the traditional ceremony in which hymns were sung and a traditional garb worn. "Thus my mother's broken heart was made good," he noted. A few days later, however, he left this school and was registered by his father in a modern one: "Soon after this my father died." This theme of repairing his mother's "broken heart" before separating from her representation—or at least coming out from under its influence before identifying with the idealized "Westernizing" father—appears in Atatürk's adult life (Volkan, 1981b).

After the father's death, the family faced more hardship, and moved to the country to be looked after on an uncle's farm. Mustafa was sent to a nearby Christian church school, but disliked it, and his mother sent him back to Salonika to stay with a relative. She ultimately followed him there with her daughter. Her son was enrolled in the city in a civil secondary school where, he was to recall later (Emin, 1922), he was very badly beaten by a religious teacher who was a *hafız* (reciter of the Koran). The teacher had caught him quarreling with another boy and had punished him viciously, leaving him in a pool of blood. He had refused to remain any longer in this school.

It would appear that during these early years he was different from his peers, not only on account of having blond hair, blue eyes, and fair skin, all unusual in that part of the world, but in respect to his behavior as well. He was a vain loner much interested in his appearance, and "too proud" for childish games, omnipotent and aloof. In recalling these years he later told Emin (1922) of his jealousy of a neighboring major's son who wore a military uniform that he coveted for himself: "In order to do this [wear such a uniform] I knew that the only course to follow was to enroll in a military secondary school." Whatever other reasons there were for his choice of a military career, an already inflated self-concept, evidenced by absorption in personal appearance, played a part. Without telling his mother, he took an examination for a military school, passed it, and entered the school.

In military school he became interested in mathematics. His account of his relationship with his mathematics teacher reflects his glorified self-concept: "In a short time I had as much knowledge as the teacher who taught us—even more, perhaps" (Emin, 1922). Mustafa was the name of both teacher and pupil, and Atatürk remembered that "One day he said to me, 'My son, your name is Mustafa, mine too .... There should be a difference; from now on your name should be Mustafa Kemal, and from that time on, it was" (Emin, 1922). The name means maturity and perfection, and was well in accord with Mustafa's conception of himself. Accepting his new name, he pursued a military career as a "perfect" person, taking the necessary steps toward the convergence of his own history with that of his motherland.

From Mustafa Kemal to Atatürk

Since I am chiefly interested here in Atatürk's early life, I will give but a brief summary of his later career, highlighting aspects that demonstrate the psychological effects of a childhood colored by death.

As Mustafa Kemal climbed the ladder of military school to staff college, the Empire was collapsing; in his verbalized fantasies he appointed himself its savior. He was drawn to power and had the intellect to seize it, never surrendering his drive to be the nonpareil savior in spite of hardship. By his mid-thirties, however, he was only a division commander. He had already been sent to Bulgaria as a military attaché, and before this, to exile in Syria, because of his unacceptable political views. His mother moved to Istanbul just before the outbreak of the Balkan War, and lived there with her daughter, who was now married. Mustafa Kemal stayed at their house whenever he had the time. He seems to have grown close to his mother, now permanently separated from her second husband. The marriage to this man had enraged her son in his puberty. Reflecting his guilt over the oedipal triumph represented by her separation from this second husband, Mustafa Kemal now referred to a small boy adopted by his mother as "my son." Thus, the guilt of oedipal triumph was handled by "ritualizing" the attachment between Mustafa and his mother. She still represented piety and grief to him, and it is interesting to note that, for pleasure, he resorted to the company of Westernized women not marked by grief (Volkan, 1981b).

He vaulted into prominence at Gallipoli, where he exhibited uncanny military ability against the forces of the British and their allies. He was struck over the heart by a bit of shrapnel as he recklessly stood in the line of fire. The shot shattered a watch in his breast pocket without injuring him, and I believe it was at this moment that his conviction of being destined for immortality so as to expunge his mother's grief over her many losses crystallized and was transferred to the arena of history, becoming a mission to save his motherland. The incident certainly seems to have had an important psychological effect on him, reviving the omnipotent and immortal self-representation he had had in childhood, as the repository of the dead, impervious himself to death.

The defeat of the Ottomans in 1918 pushed the Empire toward disaster. Landing at various points, its enemies prepared to partition it, but against great odds the charismatic Mustafa Kemal was able to raise an army from among the ashes of his war-weary country, and by 1922, his nationalist troops prevailed in what came to be known as the War of Independence.

His mother remained in Istanbul during the war, and was taken to Ankara, the new political center of the country, only in the last months of the struggle. She and her son began observing a new ritual; each day when he arose, whether in the morning or, more often, in the afternoon (since he was a "night person" and often slept through the morning), Mustafa Kemal would enter his mother's quarters and kiss her hand before beginning his day's work. Thus, in a sense, he repeated daily a theme of his childhood, paying his respects to his religious mother. in an old-fashioned way, so as to mend her broken heart, before identifying with his idealized father.

Fifteen days after her death early in 1923—the same year in which he had been made the first president of the new Turkish Republic—he married a young Westernized Turkish girl as much his junior as his mother had been her husband's at the time of her first marriage. Three days before his marriage, he delivered a speech at his mother's grave, the clearly oedipal theme of which gives evidence of his displacing the representation of his mother onto his country (Rustow, 1970; Itzkowitz, 1974). Two years later, his marriage ended, being easily dissolved under the old Moslem custom some months before the institution of the new Civil Code. He never remarried but adopted a series of "daughters."

What interests us here is the cultural revolution he brought about after becoming president, and his attempt to purge religious or semi-religious influences from Turkish life. Religion had always colored daily life in the Ottoman Empire (Lewis, 1971), affecting laws, customs, medicine, etc. Atatürk proscribed education based on the Koran and the laws of Islam, with all their sacred values and symbols, and replaced Islamic law with the Swiss Civil Code, the Italian Penal Code, and German business law. He encouraged Western dress for both men and women, doing away with the fez, for example. He began to purge the Turkish language of its Arabic and Persian influences, actually creating new words in the process. Latin characters replaced the old Arabic ones, and where the Latin alphabet failed, he created a few new characters. Experts advised that it would take five years to change the alphabet in common use, but he granted only three months for the change, and took himself to the roadside with blackboards to give instruction to the people.

Rustow (1970) states:

> The criticism sometimes leveled at Kemal's reforms—that they dealt with such surface trivia as headgear, letters, and family names—does not stand up under closer examination. Kemal ... cared far more deeply about cultural matters than about social and economic problems as these are commonly defined in the post-Marxian world. But culture consists of a set of symbols, and in the context of his time and place externals had profound symbolic meaning. ... The Hat Law meant an ostentatious break with Islam, which required the faithful to touch his covered head to the ground in his daily prayers. The alphabet change produced its intended effect by cutting off later generations from most of their pre-1928 literary heritage. (p. 229)

Furthermore, Atatürk's Turkey was the only non-Western nation attempting at that time an about-face in its mode of life, seeking to be accepted by the Wes tern world as a Western nation. The West looked less than generously on this aspiration.

It was in 1934, four years before his death, that a new law required Turks to use surnames. Kemal chose the name Atatürk, or "Father Turk." The process of change, with all the struggles change involves, still continues in today's Turkey, many years after the death of Atatürk in 1938 at the age of 57. Before he succumbed to cirrhosis of the liver, related to his habitual drinking, he was already a legend, a virtual deity. The Turks could not bring themselves to inter him, but kept his body preserved for 15 years until a mausoleum to contain it was completed. I believe that grieving over the death of this man as a mortal being has still not taken place in Turkey, and that it is this inability to come to terms with his death that constitutes one of the major psychological forces in the group process at work in Turkey today, affecting popular attitudes toward such issues as whether or not to turn back to the old Islamic reverence for religion.

A formulation

Not only was the young Mustafa linked by name to a dead uncle about whose death his father may have felt guilty, but his mother clearly saw him as a link to his dead siblings, a "living linking object," an immortal.

To her he was a savior, since her memories and representations of the dead were deposited in him. The death of his siblings not only left him with a survivor's guilt, but drove him to long for their return to life so that his mother might cease her grieving, an internal pattern that reinforced his self-concept as an omnipotent savior: if the dead could not actually be returned to life, he could at least "save" his mother from her grieving. Atatürk was one of those who in such a situation was able to actualize the demands of his self-concept by saving the homeland onto which he had displaced his grieving mother's representation. As a national leader he did not find it enough to make political change; he had to create a household of joy to contrast with the household of grief he had known as a child, an idealized motherland in contrast to the actual grieving mother of his early years. He had unconsciously fantasied that if he were able to stop his early mother's grieving and place her in a joyful household, she would in turn stop burdening him with the role of a living link to the family members she had lost to death.

His adherence to the notion that he was chosen to repair or save his mother was clear in the way he conducted his life. He tried to absorb and adapt to his role as an heir of the dead, but also rebelled against it. In 1929 or 1930 he wrote an essay on "Solidarity," a handwritten version of which remains:

> All people are members of a social body and for this reason are linked with each other. Furthermore, such links cover every time and every place since people are *cultural heirs of the dead.* (p. 101; italics added)

However, he also wrote about the burden of being linked to the dead. During his campaign to close the *tekkes* (religious houses), he attacked their practice of exalting the dead and trying to establish contact with them, claiming that this "numbed the mind." He asserted that "to seek help from the dead is a blot on any civilized nation" (Atatürk, 1925).

I have written elsewhere (Volkan, 1980; Volkan, 1981b) about how Atatürk's grandiose self—to borrow a term from Kohut (1971)—developed around his mother's perception of him as a special being—an omnipotent link to the dead. By using him for her own narcissistic ends, and ignoring his need for psychological nurture, she caused the oral frustration that resulted in the development of the grandiose self-concept. This self-concept received ready support from those in the environment because the young Mustafa was in fact constitutionally not only bright but handsome as well.

There is no better description of the grandiose self that was the nucleus of his high-level (Kernberg, 1975) narcissistic personality organization than his own explanation of his psychological makeup in 1927:

> Since my childhood, in my home, I have not liked being together with either my mother or sister, or a friend. *I have always preferred to be alone and independent*, and I have lived this way always. I have the peculiarity of being unable to tolerate being given advice by my mother, my sister, or any close friend according to their mentality and conceptions of the world ....
>
> Because when one is given advice one has either to accept and obey it—or disregard it altogether. Neither response seems right to me. Wouldn't it be a regressive retreat to the past to heed a warning given to me by my mother, who is more than 20 or 25 years older than I? Yet *were I to rebel against it I would break the heart of my mother*, in whose virtue and lofty womanhood I have the firmest belief. (Aydemir, Vol. 3, 1969, p. 484; italics added)

His grandiose self is also apparent in the self-description he wrote while in Karlsbad in 1918 for treatment of an ailment. World War I was still going on, and everything was grim for the Ottomans.

> If I obtain great authority and power I think I will bring about with a coup—suddenly in one moment—the desired revolution in our social life. Because, unlike others, I don't believe that this deed can be achieved by raising the intelligence of others slowly to the level of my own. My soul rebels against such a course. Why, after my years of education, after studying civilization and the socializing processes, after spending my life and my time to gain pleasure from freedom, should I descend to the level of common people? I will make them rise to my level. *Let me not resemble them; they should resemble me!* (Aydemir, Vol. 3, 1969, p. 482; italics added)

Our present psychoanalytic knowledge of the narcissistic personality (Kernberg, 1975; Modell, 1976; Volkan, 1976; Volkan, 1981b) directs us to search in Atatürk's life for evidence of psychological hunger of an oral type, and defenses and adaptations to deal with it. This evidence is readily found in his use of alcohol, his oratorical power, his customary way of describing the fate he desired for his enemies by using the word *boğulmak*, which means to smother by squeezing the neck or stuffing something in the mouth, his habit of putting people he encountered for the first time through "oral examinations" to determine whether or not they were worth his attention. To this evidence, we can add his identification with an idealized father, the fact that he was a loner as a child, and his adoption of the names Kemal and Atatürk as further proof of his grandiose self-concept.

Throughout his adult life he was preoccupied with freedom, and an examination of his utterances on this subject reveals the effects of his childhood dilemma with respect to separation–individuation from a grieving mother. My reconstruction of his early life suggests that he had a fantasy of "repairing" the grieving mother whom he perceived as "bad," and transforming her into a joyful "good" mother from whom it would then be possible to achieve full individuation. Variations on the theme of freedom—appear in many of his writings. For example, he said in 1921, "Freedom and independence are my character" (Aydemir, 1969, Vol. 3, p. 475). Going on to describe how he had been consumed by a love of freedom from childhood on, he declared:

> I put it as a main condition that my country should have the same characteristics. *In order for me to be able to live I should be the child of a free nation.* Thus the national sovereignty is a matter of life for me. (Aydemir, 1969, Vol. 3, p. 475; italics added

Dealing with the mother's grieving

Arnold Hottinger (1977), a distinguished Swiss foreign correspondent, refers, in writing about today's Turkey, to conscious political factors in Atatürk's reform movement, saying that the previous history of Turkish attempts at reform, which began soon after the French Revolution, had always been frustrated by the religious element in the country; he attributes Atatürk's success to the psychological force with which he "persecuted Islam with a personal passion and sought to eliminate it with a zeal that betrayed a deep animus" (p. 78). Careful scrutiny of Atatürk's writings and what is remembered about the living man shows that he was *not* opposed to Islam per se, but was strongly antagonistic to those versions of it that people used to suppress others, as he had perceived his mother to have suppressed him.

He had, I believe, two opposing representations of the early mother; the grief-stricken, religious mother and the "merry widow" mother who was the object of his thinly disguised incestuous strivings. Atatürk wanted to rid himself of the grim image and transform it into a joyous one, as evidenced by certain repeated activities of his adult life, one of which was his adopting as "daughters" a number of young girls, most of whom he took into adoption at puberty, recalling the child bride his mother had been. It can be assumed that in this practice he not only repeated behavior much like incest, reversing it now from mother–son to father–daughter relationships, but that he was also by this behavior repairing the unity with his mother that had been violated during his puberty by her second marriage. The manner in which he had these girls brought up is suggestive. He sought to *create* in them images of womanhood that were the opposite of the religious and grieving "bad mother" image. The girls were to be Westernized and liberated, free from the bonds of the old religion. He told them to smile, and warned them against trusting anyone who did not have a smiling countenance (Gökçen, 1974). They were to be free from the contamination of the grim and grieving mother.

One of these girls decided her fate when, an orphan at puberty, she ran out of the house in which she was staying and welcomed Atatürk, who was visiting next door. He asked her at once if she wanted to become his daughter. When I interviewed her in her later years, she made it evident that she had been seeking a father in him. Later, in her mid-teens, she became aware that he was not only a father but also a mother to her and to the other girls. She explained how she had played Galatea to his Pygmalion: " Atatürk wanted so much to create something with his own hands" (Gökçen, 1974). Following the pattern of idealized Western womanhood that he approved, she became the first female military pilot in Turkey after he gave her a name that means "of the sky." She was free to fly, to glide away from mother earth, and she was ready to attack any religious elements in the country that might revolt against him, as on occasion they did. Another adopted daughter, who functioned like a wife toward the end of his life, was pushed into becoming a professor of history bent on the "purification" of the history of Turkey.

Although he was callous to the needs of women as individuals, except in the case of those who were useful to him in one way or another, he was zealous in the liberation of Turkish women en masse, bringing them out of the confines of the Moslem home. As representatives of his early "bad mother," they should, he felt, be out in the open and thus no longer menacing. As "good mothers" they were to be made into polished Western women. Meanwhile, he kept distant from and devalued his "bad" objects—religious, smothering mother representations. He closed down the *tekkes* or dervish chapels, for example, and during the late 20s and early 30s sought to transform the dusty little city of Ankara, following the "merry widow" mother image, into an ambitious imitation of the glittering gaiety of Paris or Berlin as he saw it. I am indebted to Niederland (1977) for his suggestion that Atatürk was attempting to turn his childhood "house of death" into a great "house of life." He attended one party after another, and he personally taught people to dance, forcing the reluctant to participate. He sometimes had two orchestras perform simultaneously, one playing traditional Turkish music and the other European music. Sitting between the two orchestras with his entourage, he would ask his guests to distinguish the kind of music each orchestra played, and to compare them. In this he kept the "good" and the "bad" apart, although, paradoxically, this helped close the gap between the opposing units, since before long the Turkish musicians began to write some of the traditional Turkish tunes in the European style.

The new Turkey, as the representation of the "good mother," got one face lift after another, as he compulsively carried out his drive to idealize it. Such activity made him a patriot in the true sense, and validates the saying that he spent every day of his public life thinking about Turkey. Perhaps he never consciously recognized his fantasies of resurrecting the dead and rescuing the grieving mother as they were displaced onto his adult fantasies of rescuing a grieving nation; but he might well have been aware of his creative urges. In a speech he made on March 17, 1937 (Melzig, 1974), he spoke of the pleasure of a gardener who cultivates flowers, and compared such a gardener with one who likes to "cultivate men," in an obvious reference to himself. Here he saw himself as "the creator" of men, someone able to bring them to life and even to bloom. In this musing there is perhaps the implication that if he could "raise" men in so omnipotent a way, he could also undo the death of his siblings and thus rescue his mother from her grief. He indicated that the man who cultivates men should act with the mentality of the flower gardener who expects no tangible return for his efforts. But beneath his altruism was the wish to rescue himself from oral aggression, from the burden of being the depository of the images of dead siblings, from being the early mother's linking object, and from the guilt he felt for living while others had died. Only by actualizing his fantasies of being an omnipotent savior could he identify with the idealized father image and become "Father Turk."

CHAPTER 14

A living linking object: The case of the *Night of the Living Dead*

In this chapter I describe the case of a young woman in her mid-twenties who claimed to communicate with "good" and "bad" spirits from another world, and who felt herself to be half-woman, half-man, half-alive and half-dead. A believer in reincarnation, she was convinced of having had a previous existence in some bygone time. At the age of four days, she had been adopted to replace her adoptive mother's brother, a pilot shot down in combat. I will demonstrate how the way in which she was regarded by important others in her early environment—as a living link to the dead man—passed into the little girl's self-concept when her self-image as a child could not be integrated with the concept of the dead man.

The reason why the use of a person as a living linking object sometimes causes psychosis, and sometimes stimulates the production of some masterpiece of art or of bold and successful political leadership (like Atatürk's, described in the previous chapter), points to the presence of numerous variables, and suggests that the constitution of the person in question is a strong determinant. Although we cannot list all the variables that need to be considered generally, we can, through analysis, clearly identify most of them in any individual case. The case described here highlights the concept of the "living linking object," and clarifies further what I have referred to as "generational continuity."

More on "generational continuity"

Psychoanalysis has clearly shown that an affective flow exists between the early mother and the child; in fact, the observations of Mahler (1963, 1968), Mahler and Furer (1960), Spitz (1965), and others concerning the symbiotic phase of child development indicate that the early mother and her child function as though they were one psychological unit. One of the most important clinical contributions of Sullivan (1956, 1962) was his emphasis on the way in which a mother's anxiety is conveyed to her child, and this process is graphically exemplified in the observations of Anna Freud and Dorothy Burlingham (1942) of children in England during World War II. They note that if very young children were not separated from their mothers or mother substitutes, they were not traumatized by repeated exposure to bombing. The mothers or their substitutes provided a protective environment, psychologically speaking, for the youngsters, and shielded them against the dangers of the world. This in a sense offers proof that the mother performs certain executive functions for her child, even when he has outgrown his infancy. Under the hazardous conditions that then prevailed, the young child reflected the anxiety of an anxious mother, but was not himself anxious if the mother remained calm. There are countless clinical vignettes in the literature to show the affective flow between the early mother and her child, and, in a later stage of development, between the patient and his therapist. The latter is beautifully described by Searles (1965, 1979), especially in connection with severely regressed patients.

We are now able to study more clearly another although related type of phenomenon in which something is conveyed to the child from the early mother. Unassimilated object or self-representations that are located, so to speak, within the mother, can be deposited within the child during the early mother–child interaction. If we compare the conveying of anxiety from the early mother to her child with the conveying of an infection by the transmission of germs, we may compare the passage of unassimilated self- and object representations, with their related affect dispositions, from mother to child with the inheritance by the child of the mother's genes. Since these unassimilated self- and object representations, once thrust upon the child, will affect his characterological makeup and adaptive mechanisms, we may in fact talk about a kind of psychological heredity that promotes generational continuity of the sort evident in the case of Linda, cited in Chapter 2. There I used the term *generational continuity* to account for the interaction within a child of his own self-representation with his mother's representation of her own dead father.

Of course, unassimilated representations of others may in time become depersonalized and absorbed by means of identification into the child's developing ego and superego systems. My focus here, however, is on those representations conveyed to the child that remain unintegrated with his dominant self-concept and that continue to have a life of their own, so to speak. Such phenomena contribute to the primitive splitting of the child's self-concept.

The literature notes the existence of what is called "the replacement child syndrome," occasioned by the death of a child whose mother has been guilt-ridden, depressive, phobic, or compulsive. Such a mother may replace her lost child with another who still lives, an assignment likely to cause psychological difficulties for the living child chosen as the surrogate (Cain & Cain, 1964). Following the Cains' formulation, Poznanski (1972) elaborates the potential hazards for the substitute child, offering the case of Susie as an example. Susie was a 15-year-old girl whose family had considered her to be a replacement for a dead sibling. Her life seemed to center around death and dying; she not only had nightmares about death but acquired a boyfriend who actually attempted to kill her. "Replacing a child with another allows the parents partially to deny the first child's death. The replacement child then acts as a barrier to the parental acknowledgement of death, since a real child exists who is a substitute" (Poznanski, 1972, p. 1193). Susie automatically acquired a "past history," and inherited a legend of performance and expectations generated by a child no longer alive. Poznanski felt that the idealization of the dead child was a usual component of the replacement child syndrome.

Green and Solnit (1964) include in their collection of children "vulnerable" in their psychosocial development those who represented for a parent—usually the mother—some figure from the past who died prematurely. The substitute child is also expected to die prematurely.

> ... the child regularly senses the mother's expectation of his vulnerability and accepts his mother's distorted mental images of himself. This is communicated in many subtle ways but mainly through the

> mother's moods and in her way of granting him autonomy and independence with fearful inhibiting reservations. It can also be observed in the mother's way of experiencing separation from the child. (p. 64)

Susie's case and the others briefly described by Green and Solnit were studied either in pediatric inpatient units or in outpatient clinics, and were not subject to searching psychoanalytic scrutiny. No attempt was made to understand metapsychologically the self-concepts of these children as they included—or related to—the representations of the dead individuals whom they replaced; they may have identified with them in toto, or they may have simply taken in such representations in an unassimilated and unintegrated way. The studies cited nonetheless provide graphic illustration of the dilemma involved in being a replacement child.

The psychoanalytic literature includes some further references to the replacement child phenomenon, but these are usually brief. Loewald (1962), for example, writes about a patient who, having become a substitute for his father's beloved brother, was victimized by his father's clinging to him with all the force of this never relinquished attachment. This patient had great difficulty emancipating himself from his father because of the guilt involved in severing this tie. Loewald was quick to add in his review of this case that the patient's neurotic attachment to his father included other aspects as well.

Pollock (1972) provides a new perspective on the case of one of the most famous patients in psychoanalytic history—Anna O (Bertha Pappenheim) (Breuer & Freud, 1893–1895). Pollock writes that Bertha felt herself to be a replacement for a dead sister—and, at a later point in her life, perhaps for another dead sister as well. He adds:

> We know that children who are dead may remain powerfully in the mother's mind and so can become even more important rivals for the surviving sibling, who has no ability or opportunity for reality confrontation and correction of the image of the idealized dead child. The dead sibling usually remains remembered at the age he was at the time of his death, and hence there is some arrest of the image of the sibling in the minds of the survivors. (p. 478)

Agreeing with the Cains (1964) and Rogers (1966), Pollock adds that the unresolved mourning of the parents of a dead child plays a role in their establishment of another child as a replacement.

I hope that my metapsychological understanding of the linking object and linking phenomenon will shed light on the replacement child syndrome. The living child is used by his parents (or important others) as a living linking object and thus as an embodied meeting place for the mother representation and the unassimilated representation of the dead. Not only is the substitute child given a "past history," but he is made to feel to some extent immortal, since the one lost to death is kept alive in him. The aspect of the child that links him to the dead person may or may not be integrated with his more "normal" aspects—those that represent someone who feels himself to be uniquely himself as a child, and who is able to feel that his parents so perceive him. In any case, such a child must make an internal adaptation to what might be considered an unusual "psychological gene" in his makeup. Some children make this adaptation in ways that from a social point of view are seen as creative, but others respond to the situation in ways that from a clinical viewpoint are seen as "crazy." In what follows, I offer an example of a psychotic adaptation. This patient's repetition of childhood perceptions, expectations, and fantasies on the transference–countertransference axis of her psychoanalytic treatment supports my metapsychological understanding of the living linking object. Aspects of her story that have no direct bearing on her being a living linking object will provide a balance in my understanding of her as a total human being.

A young woman in contact with "spirits" from another world

Frances, a woman in her mid-twenties, was referred to me by a caring woman psychiatrist who had treated her on two occasions for acute psychotic excitement; she had been giving her therapeutic support and anti-psychotic drugs for two years, but felt that the patient needed more than the supportive therapy she was able to provide. The patient was tall, slim, and flat-chested, with a clumsy carriage. At our first encounter, she greeted me with a forced smile, and took her place in ghostly silence. She spoke of having become aware four years earlier of presences around her, especially when she was alone in her own room. At first, what she called "the spirits" did not speak, but one night, when a candle in her room lit itself and she felt suffused with warmth at what she interpreted as a signal that her spectral visitors were good spirits, she was told by the spirits that they had come to make her "all good," and cautioned her to eat only what they designated as "good." They then took command of her life, counseling her when to take her vacation, when to smile, when to blow her nose, etc. She wrote down their orders and obeyed them. Some time later, however, she began to feel that her spirits were impostors, and that they were actually messengers of the devil who had come to trick her by entering her body, and thereby conquer the whole world through her. Frightened, she sought help from a religious cult that she had recently joined. A priest of this cult performed an exorcism for her, placing her on the floor surrounded by a circle of his followers, who loudly demanded that the devil leave her body. Although this exorcism was considered successful by those who performed it, she continued to feel the devil's presence within her. She ran through the city streets, half-naked in the rain, and was picked up by the police and put in a hospital.

Her second hospital admission, this time for a suicide attempt, came a year later. While on a bus, she had sat next to a beautiful young woman whom she had never seen before. She had asked her about her favorite colors, and the reply—"black and red"—had led her to think of the girl as a witch who could read her mind. Some months later she had hallucinated seeing this girl as a lesbian, and had masturbated. She had felt that in a previous incarnation the girl had been a sister with whom she had shared some mysterious unfinished business, and that her "sister" still lived in her earlier incarnation and came to drive her to suicide in order that they might be reunited in another world.

She was still under the control of her spirits when I first saw her. I later learned that she had been symptomatic long before the acute illness that seemed to have begun with the visits of her spirits. She had been "very shy" in childhood and had been told by the adults around her that she was slow in her "social" development, although she did well in school. She thought of herself as unlike her peers, and felt isolated. When she went to college she was unable to associate with those she felt were compatible with her own middle-class background, becoming the girlfriend of a drug pusher and taking drugs herself. While she was in high school, she had been in the habit of pilfering trifles from store counters. Her open psychotic break took place during a visit to her parental home.

Her former psychiatrist had made home visits, and on occasion given her patient tea in her own home. Although the patient had responded to her physician's warmth, she told me much later that she had resented being unable to have a therapeutic alliance with her psychiatrist and that she had felt burdened by the obligation to please her. She was on anti-psychotic medication when I first saw her, and seemed able to function adequately in her daily life in spite of her bizarre stories. It seemed likely that she would finish college satisfactorily. She not only dressed rather well, but bore no visible physical mark of her long adherence to the meatless diet of "good" food advised by her spirits.

After the diagnostic interview, I explained how we would work, meeting four times a week, and said that I would give her no drugs. Since she lived at a distance, I expressed concern about her ability to keep this schedule, particularly in bad weather, but she seemed determined to adhere to it; I learned that her psychiatrist had indicated to her that treatment at my hands was her last chance for recovery, making me a kind of special person in her eyes. I was struck by her courageous determination to go through with her treatment, and noted that her ego was functioning in the service of her recognition of her condition as a sickness and her insistence on getting well.

Her family and her psychiatrist helped her to make arrangements to begin treatment in ten months, when my first opening for a new patient would occur. They then helped her find a nearby apartment to share with two other young women, and she enrolled as a part-time student and began looking for a part-time job. Her ability to make these moves indicated some competence in the outside world, but she had no real friends, did not socialize with her roommates, and never dated. Her mind was preoccupied with her "spirits," although she carefully refrained from mentioning them to the people with whom she associated in her daily life. Under these circumstances, our work together began.

The initial phase of treatment

Frances was the kind of patient long considered untreatable by outpatient psychoanalytic therapy. Boyer (1961, 1967, 1971, 1977) writes about office (outpatient) treatment of such patients with minimal use of parameters. I have been able to report similar cases of my own in which like efforts proved successful (Volkan, 1975a, 1976). As our theories about the development of an integrated self-concept and the internalization. of object relations became increasingly refined in this country, psychoanalytic techniques for the treatment of borderline patients—and even of those considered schizophrenic, like the patient described here—have acquired theoretical backing, so that it is now possible to explain technical maneuvers in terms of internalized object relations. I now take into outpatient analytic treatment selected patients who are severely regressed. An account of my first 18 months of treating this young woman will, I think, help us to formulate how she was used as a depository of the representation of a dead person.

As we began work, I told her that she was to feel free to tell me whatever came into her mind during her hours with me and whatever bodily sensations she experienced. I was to speak whenever I felt that my comment might be useful for us both. I explained that silence on my part would mean that I was listening to her. She spent the first two and a half months with me describing in detail aspects of the psychotic breaks she had had, which I have summarized here. During this time, I saw her face to face. I planned to put her on the couch after my summer vacation overseas. Even had I not taken my vacation at this time, however, I might have wanted to work with her face to face before putting her on the couch; I find preliminary face to face work useful with such patients in the establishment of what I have called (Volkan, 1976) a "reality base" for the psychotic. At first, I thought of postponing her treatment until my return from vacation in order to avoid having a significant break occur so early, but I decided against the postponement because I had originally told her that we could begin work within ten months. She had made her arrangements accordingly. I was unwilling to disillusion her by asking her to wait longer to begin our work together. I made minimal intervention during the first two and a half months, although I made sounds to indicate that I was listening to her recitals. What I heard was that her inner life was populated with "good" and "bad" self- and object images, now differentiated, now fused again. They moved about, sometimes being felt "inside" and then "outside." I heard her descriptions of the "spirits" as representing these images or representations, and I heard them coalesce into either "good" or "bad" camps, as is usual in a borderline patient (Kernberg, 1966). However, the fusion of self- and object images and their fragmentation even within each camp suggested to me that my patient was functioning at a lower level than a borderline person would. The images, as she felt them in or outside herself, were involved in a typical introjective–projective relatedness. At times she would regress even further toward a defensive autistic position, and would state that she was unable "to carry" herself with any of these images, and that she felt "empty." She would say, "I have no opinions of my own. I am empty. But I am afraid of taking in the opinions of others." In addition to describing her relationship with spirits from another world, she described two other symptoms: that she was half-female, half-male; and that she was half-alive, half-dead. I had picked up her "half-dead" aspect when she had behaved at our first encounter like a zombie.

I showed my interest in her personal history, which I will summarize here in an organized way although she conveyed the particulars in a very uneven fashion, spending at times a whole hour on a single detail. I learned that she was an adopted and only child. Her adoptive mother had miscarried after a five-month pregnancy, and her physician, aware of her strong desire for a child, had arranged for her to take Frances home from the hospital as a four-day-old infant. The child had been given no information about her biological parents. The adoptive mother had had a hysterectomy after her miscarriage; her health had not been good, and there were indications that she had been depressed for months after miscarrying. It was known that the maternal grandmother had taken over the mothering of the adopted infant during her first months of life; the maternal grandparents had lived near my patient's adoptive parents at the time. When the grandfather died, Frances was eight, and the grandmother began living in the home of her daughter. She was an invalid at the time of the treatment. I learned that my patient's mother had acted as a slave toward her mother, who had suffered from phobias about countless evil possibilities, from thunderstorms to holocausts, and had been hypochondriacal about her digestive system, centering her whole life around her bowel habits.

My patient suspected that her adoptive parents had had no sexual relations after her adoption. As she spoke of this, rather unrepressed oedipal material poured out, and she talked openly of incestuous fantasies. She would say, "I came into my father's life and since then my parents have had no sex." She described at length how her father kissed her on the lips when she returned home for a visit, and so on. Patients like this, who function on a level in which fragmented self- and object images are reactivated and who have a severe deficiency in reality testing, use oedipal material as "upward resistance." I usually pay little attention to such material at this point in treatment except to make note of it as a form of resistance, usually resistance against early conflicts of fantastic internalized object relations. I agree with Boyer (1967, 1977), the Ornsteins (1975), and Rosenfeld (1966) that premature oedipal interpretation—even direct attention to such issues—precludes the development of the preoedipal transferential states, which, as Boyer insists, must be worked through before the patient can reach a classical transference neurosis.

My patient noticed my failure to react to the oedipal material, and expressed some surprise. The therapist she had formerly worked with had spent hours analyzing the behavior patterns of her mother and father. I was impressed once again by her ability to make spontaneous and accurate observations about our relationship in the midst of lower-level general functioning; this persuaded me further that she would be accessible to analysis. Since my initial aim with this kind of patient is to help her to develop a "new" object relationship with the analyst (Loewald, 1960), and to take in the analyst's representation in a fashion tinged with an analytical attitude—what Giovacchini (1972) calls "an analytic introject"—I verbally acknowledged her differentiation of me from the psychiatrist she had previously had. Without either attacking or protecting that therapist, I stated that I seemed to have a different way of dealing with patients. It is assumed that the analytic introject becomes the focal point within the patient as he attempts to increase the integrative capacity of his ego. Such an introject grafts over, as it were, the split or fragmented self- and object representations, and binds them together in a cohesive way (Volkan, 1968, 1976).

Soon my vacation separated us. We had agreed that since this absence came so soon after she began treatment, she was to go to her parents' home if she felt uncomfortable while I was away. Her former psychiatrist was available there. On my return I learned that she had not gone home, and at first she said nothing about my absence. A week later she told me that she had kept a secret from me; after she had seen me again on my return a master spirit had told her to go to a vacation spot 100 miles away. She had gone, but while there, had stayed in her room, living on orange juice and emerging only four times a week—to drive 100 miles for her appointment with me. I suggested that she might have been hurt by my failure to tell her where I was going on my holiday, but I noted with appreciation how she had kept her commitment to our common task by driving so far to keep working during her holiday. She then told me her first fantasy about me. During my vacation she had had an image of me walking in a big city like New York where there were many fragmented ethnic communities. Then she had thought of me in Istanbul, having been told by her former psychiatrist that I am of Turkish origin. It had occurred to her then that Istanbul might be a place in which fragmentations are mended, different religions living there in harmony. My reply to this was that she had wanted me to be someone who could help her put together all of the images she had, including her spirits, and make sense of them all. She wept for a moment, and I felt that she was relieved to have me back and ready to work with her. However, such unguarded moments, in which she would respond to a psychological proposition with appropriate emotion, were short-lived. Distant once again, an emotionless ghost, she commented that we came from different backgrounds, hers being metaphysical and mine psychological. She said that she knew that one day I would tell her that her spirits were simply products of her unconscious, and that they had no real existence, and that she would not believe me. I made no reply to this.

She then brought me a diary in which over the years she had written everything she claimed the master spirit had told her. She confided that, although she was not supposed to share it with anyone, the spirit had told her to "*feel free* to tell Dr. Volkan anything." (I had used the phrase "feel free" in our first encounter to encourage her free association.) It was at this point that I decided, after discussion with her, to have her use the couch.

I kept the diary in my office for some months, at her request, before she took it away. I am always reluctant to take for safekeeping any item belonging to a neurotic patient in analysis, but I felt that this diary had magical, frightening qualities for this patient and that my keeping it might reduce her anxiety as she embarked on the analysis of the meaning of the spirits' orders. I did not analyze the meaning of "the act" of keeping the diary in my office for a few months, and she was told from the beginning that it belonged to her and not to me, and that she could take it back whenever she wanted to. I commented on her wish for me to read it, saying that I preferred that she point out which aspects of it were important to her when the time came, and that although I would look it over, our work would essentially depend on direct communication during her hours. Later, I did look it over, and found it full of descriptions and pseudophilosophical statements about life, as well as the spirits' directions about what to think and what to buy, etc.

Lying for the first time on the couch, she kept one foot on the floor so that she was actually half sitting up. I sensed her anxiety and noted the throbbing of the vein in her neck. In view of her fear, I increased my "hm, hm's" to reassure her that I was there. By the next session she seemed more comfortable and better adjusted to the new situation between us. I continued for a while, however, to make throaty noises to encourage her. Boyer (1967) uses the term "noisy phase" about such patients, saying that they cannot tolerate silence on the part of the analyst, who may provide reassurance by making noncommittal noises as evidence that he has neither deserted nor magically committed murder. Lying on the couch initially increased this patient's "upward resistance." I heard again her fear and desire concerning being raped by her father, whose representation she at times displaced onto me.

Further regression, evidencing her open inclusion of me in her introjective–projective relatedness, appeared within a few days. (I use the term *introjective–projective relatedness* here in a general way to include the concept of fusion. *Introjective–projective* seems semantically correct when the patient is able to differentiate the self-representation from the object representation. Fusion refers to the loss of boundary between the two representations. However, I choose to use *introjective–projective* in a general way because I believe this term shows graphically a dynamic flow into and out of the patient.)

My patient reported becoming what she called "a therapeutic instrument." With the aid of a spirit, she became a "psychoanalyst" herself. Feeling that one of her roommates needed psychiatric help, she spent hours listening to her "problems." However, she soon became "frustrated" and then became the "patient" of her friend, telling her for the first time that she herself was troubled. Soon she reported holding inner conversations with me after leaving my office. I noticed this first reference to my having become an introject, an introject subject at this point to being tinged by her expectations and contaminated by her "spirits."

Now, sitting behind her, I observed my own regression, that type of regression which Olinick (1969) sees as being "in the service of the other," and I began to make more sense out of my emotional–ideational responses to her verbal and nonverbal productions. I felt that she had a purpose in her long monologues with their belaboring of unimportant details even while she described the feverish particulars of psychotic excitement. This purpose was twofold, I felt: (1) to offer entertainment, as though it were expected of her, and (2) to mock me, as though she were very slyly making a fool of me. I remembered her many statements that, when during her visits home her grandmother demanded her time, she felt obliged to entertain her, as she had always done ever since she was a child. It occurred to me that her mockery might be hiding rage, and one day I asked her if she felt that she was lying on the couch for my entertainment, whether she assumed that my superior age made it necessary to entertain me as she did her grandmother. She told me that when she was five she amused herself by making a stage with wooden blocks and having toy singers perform on it. "Of course, the blocks belonged to *him*," she explained. "Him?" I asked. "He" turned out to be her mother's younger and only brother, a pilot shot down in Europe during World War II. When she told me his name, I realized that she had been given its feminine version; we might call him her Uncle Francis.

The death of a pilot

Francis had been "God's gift to the world," according to her grandmother. "God took him away and then He gave us you." The old lady even referred to my patient as "a reincarnation of Francis." I responded to this story by saying, "No wonder you sometimes ask 'Who am I?' " My patient felt that spirits lived on an astral plane, on the highest level of which lived Francis. I began to sense that her preoccupation with spirits, astral planes, and reincarnation had something to do with her having been chosen as a living "linking object" by her parents, and especially by her grandmother. Although my patient had initially been chosen to replace a dead fetus, I learned now that she was the replacement for a dead pilot who would have been replaced by the child lost in miscarriage. Since, as I would learn later, talk about the dead pilot was never-ending in my patient's home, whereas there was no mention of the aborted infant, in her fantasies my patient associated the immortal representation of the dead chiefly with her perception of the dead pilot. I did not share my initial thinking about this with her, but proof of the psychological impact of her being a living linking object quickly became evident.

It was soon after the shocking death of the pilot Francis that my patient's adoptive mother married her husband, also a pilot. No living children came of this marriage. Interestingly, my patient herself became a pilot, learning to fly when she was 16. After the grandfather's death and the grandmother's move into her daughter's house, the house became a monument to the dead pilot, whose picture hung on almost every wall. It even appeared on the wall of one bathroom—perhaps the most important room in the house in view of the grandmother's preoccupation with her bowel habits. The kind of woman who cannot let anyone die, the grandmother brought her dead husband's bed with her, and slept in a room in which it stood unoccupied except when my patient was on occasion allowed to sleep on it. It is possible that the adopted child who replaced a dead fetus and a dead man came later to some extent to replace the grandfather as well.

I certainly do not ascribe my patient's emotional illness solely to the presence of her grandmother in the home, but I noticed at this point in Frances's analysis that a relationship like symbiosis, existing between the grandmother and her daughter, as well as the depression of my patient's mother after her miscarriage, may have contributed to the psychologically inadequate mothering given the little girl adopted into the family. She had been "chosen" by both her mother and her grandmother to replace Francis, and their perception of this substitute as half-alive and half-dead, half-girl and half-boy, passed into the child's self-concept as it developed through interaction with the mothering persons, making impossible the integration of a total self-concept and the corresponding internalized object representations.

There was further evidence of this. Soon after I learned about the dead Francis, my patient told me that spirits made her unable to see the whiteheads on her face. I learned then about a longstanding symptom of spending inordinate periods of time gazing at her face in the mirror. During the few days just past she had not been able to see and remove her whiteheads, and she feared that her face would "look terrible." She would pick "bad" things from her face besides the whiteheads—dried bits from inside her nose which she would eat, for example. (What was graphically externalized had to be internalized.) Convinced that her face was hideous, she felt that it would disturb me to look at her, and she tried to protect me by covering her face as she passed by me on her way to the couch. Once she stretched out on the couch, she stopped trying to hide her face; it may be that since she could not see me from where she lay, she thought that I would magically be unable to see her. She spoke of frantic masturbation when as a girl she heard that sexual activity keeps the face from breaking out, but reported that her face had been disfigured in spite of her efforts.

She was fascinated with Edgar Allen Poe, that death-obsessed poet known to have faced early childhood loss with the death of his mother. She recalled his tale *The Masque of the Red Death*, which tells of a prince and his followers hiding away in a castle to escape a pestilence that overtook them in spite of their precautions and that made blood spring from the pores of their faces. Such a story might suggest in a neurotic woman a perception of the ugliness of menstruation displaced to the face. When I inquired if she were having her menses on the day she told the story, she answered in the negative. Even if the story did hold such a meaning for her, it was insignificant compared to the following contribution the notion of the Red Death made to her self-concept. She reported a dream about the Poe story that she had had a few years earlier. In it she was in a castle, afflicted by the Red Death but with its characteristic disfigurement in only *half* of her face. She was wearing a sheet-like dress that reminded her of a hospital gown or a shroud. At this point in her narration, I asked about Francis's plane crash and learned that his face had been badly burned and that all of the plane's three occupants had been burned beyond recognition. When the bodies had been sent home, it had been impossible to identify which was the body of Francis, but at the funeral of the three men, the grandmother, "feeling the hand of God on her shoulder," had been able to see the ascent of her son's image from one of the coffins. She had stopped crying, struck by the recognition of her son's ghostly body and the realization that he was both dead and alive. This story was repeated over and over in the family during the childhood of my patient; it had become the family myth.

As soon as she lay down on the couch on the day after telling about all this she cried out, "My heart is beating!" I confirmed, "You are alive!" I tried to see how much connection she made between her symptoms (talking to spirits; being half in this world and half on an astral plane; being half-boy, half-girl; half-deformed, half-not-deformed) and her initial partial self-concept as a linking object. Although I made the attempt cautiously, it was premature. She let me know that she was not ready to hear about such things. "If I don't believe in spirits there is something wrong with my chemistry," she said. "And if something is wrong with my chemistry that is unchangeable."

I became a devil in her eyes, and she accused me of having her on the couch to get her money. By the next day she had written a poem, each line of which began with "I am"—"I am a leaf, I am the rain," etc. Although this was an attempt to integrate the concept of self, it was unsuccessful, since she spent the rest of the hour giving a lecture that reflected primitively split internalized object relations, a monologue on "the principle of polarity," in which she spoke of "good" and "bad," "the master of light" and "the master of darkness," etc.

Transference manifestations of the patient's wish to protect others from the pain of mourning

The linking object a mourner creates functions to save him from the pain of mourning and of letting the dead die. If the linking object is a child, the child will be conscious of a mission, a charge from the mourner, to keep the mourner from pain and to keep externalized his struggle to retain but simultaneously destroy the lost object.

In her seventh month of treatment my patient's sense of having been chosen to "save" her grandmother by becoming in part the reincarnation of the dead pilot began to appear in her transference. She had become my "therapist" (Searles, 1975). She reported fantasies about my having been the victim of famine and earthquake in Turkey as a child, a needy person whom she feverishly tried to save. I was the grieving grandmother, sometimes fused with the adopted child who also needed to be saved. By now, although Frances continued to attend school so as to qualify as an elementary school teacher, she had found a new part-time job with a health food newsletter, a job compatible with her preoccupation with nutrition.

A female associate who spoke accented English as I do became an extension of me; my patient felt obliged to entertain her. This activity was consistent with her new feeling of being "the psychoanalyst." Her "here and now" version of wanting to save me, and the fusion and alternation of savior and saved was followed by an attempt to differentiate her self-concept as a woman from the deformed image of Francis's face. When she looked into the mirror, she saw one face superimposed on the other. She wanted surgery on her chin, and discussion of this acquainted me with how her first acute psychotic episode had followed plastic surgery of the nose. The failure of the attempted external solution to an internal problem had triggered the psychotic break.

After a visit home she poured out memories and descriptions of events that had taken place there. She thought, probably accurately, that her father was chronically unhappy as a result of her mother's being virtually housebound by the care of her mother. She felt, moreover, that her parents had stayed together because of her; she had once overheard them discuss divorce. She spoke of her grandmother's having talked about Francis during her visit, and I suspect that she had led the old lady, now in her eighties, to the subject. I felt that she had wanted to investigate where she ended and he began. She openly expressed anger for the first time about being obliged to send twice-weekly cards to her grandmother. During her visit her mother had warned her that her grandmother was dying—although her hypochondriacal fears had been bringing her to death's door for as long as my patient could remember. "Humor her," her mother had said. "She has been good to you!" After reporting this the patient went to a movie, treating herself to pleasure for the first time since we started working together. She soon felt guilty about this, however.

Christmas break, in the eighth month of her analysis, pushed her into contact with the astral bodies. She lay on a couch at home and talked aloud to herself. When I suggested that she might have missed me, she agreed. Soon she reported a dream in which she saw herself as a man in a military uniform in an office where the Nazis spied on her (him). She ran through ballrooms like those in Poe's story, and found herself again in the office, but this time as a woman. She found a Russian spy there and began talking with an accent to avoid being recognized as American. Before I could ask, she said that the man in the uniform was not Francis but someone resembling a well-known conservative Republican associated with America, apple pie, Patton, and Eisenhower. I felt that although he did not represent the real Francis, he did represent Francis as he had been idealized during her childhood. The Russian woman was a condensation of "bad" and "good" analyst; my patient had a female dentist who resembled the dream figure and who was both "healer" and "torturer" to her.

A dream indicating a wish to mend opposing representations

In the next night's dream the patient saw me undisguised. Her primitive splitting was evident in her seeing me as having a twin brother. I was going to teach her to swim. A cousin named Francis was at the side of the pool, and someone brought a jar and poured the contents into the water. I wanted her to practice her backstroke but she thought that I had tricked her into doing the dead man's float. She had no control over her thoughts. She then felt that I was also under the control of astral creatures, and was an impostor. She awakened with anxiety.

After relating this dream she announced that although they continued to pester her, her spirits were not entering into her any longer. Associating to her dream of my twin, she spoke of a childhood fantasy of having a twin herself; she had once been told of a girl who resembled her. One twin could be "good," the other "evil." Since I could not watch over her all 24 hours of the day, I should have a twin brother who was also an analyst.

Her father had succeeded in teaching her to water ski after many humiliating failures. I sensed from this association to the dream that she was hopeful about our work together even while she was being humiliated by "bad" me. The jar in the dream contained oyster juice, and before the dream ended she heard chanting—"OKAHARA-OKAHARA." *Oka* reminded her of okra, the favorite food of her father's stepmother, who had also liked oyster juice. She said *Oka* represented death since this woman had died at the time such strange happenings as the self-lighting candle had occurred. *Hara* sounded, she thought, like what Hare Krishna groups chant, extolling peace. Her associations emphasized that she was joining what was dreaded with what was comfortable, the "natural" with the "artificial," the living with the dead, just as the oyster juice was poured into the pool in her dream. At this point she recalled the chanting at her exorcism, and b.er body began to shake.

I have come to know from my experiences in the analytic treatment of severely regressed patients that attempts at mending may result in "emotional flooding" (Volkan, 1976), and certainly Frances was now flooded. Her libidinally invested self- and object representations were primitively split from those laden with aggression, and I now think that the part of her split self-concept that was a living girl and the part that was a dead man were condensed in or associated with her "good" and "bad" self- and object representations respectively. The defensive benefit of primitive splitting is protection from the diffuse anxiety that the patient would experience were he to try to put together opposing representations contaminated with opposing affect dispositions. Nevertheless, developmental needs force him to turn toward mending, and as his analytic therapy progresses this inclination is activated and the patient, wanting to coalesce opposing constellations, may actively attempt to do so. Such an advance requires the patient to surrender the "good" units that the pleasure principle encourages him to keep, so that the unprepared individual, faced with the possibility of such a loss, is overwhelmed by anxiety.

With the report of her dream and her associations to her push toward mending, Frances felt anxious and greatly afraid of an evil spirit. I made soothing sounds, and recalled to her how greatly her father had humiliated her by forcing her to water ski, by shaping her into a success. I denied having any predetermined idea as to what she was to accomplish in my hands, and indicated that she would have a choice for herself as we worked together. I asked her if she were too frightened to continue, but she said bravely that she wanted to go on. She now associated me more openly with the evil spirit; in her dream I had told her what strokes I would teach her, and then taught her the dead man's float instead!

Consolation via hands and mouth

Throughout this month and the one that followed Frances began her hours by reporting dreams. Since her associations to them recalled much of her childhood and her perceptions about herself and her early environment, I learned a great deal about her. I observed, however, that she was becoming a "dream addict." I sometimes wondered during those months if she were using the dream reports as a means of resistance—transference resistance against frighteningly open introjective–projective relatedness between us. She appeared now as though she were a typical neurotic, and I decided to go with her pace and style for a while. I felt especially that her beginning to feel appropriate emotions about her experiences as a child and a teenager was highly desirable. Her life was being put into an organized perspective. This attempt at organization began with a dream about her being married in a funeral parlor, in a ceremony about which she had had nothing to say since it had been organized by others. Was it a wedding or a funeral? In associating to this, she said that she had had no choice about her reincarnation into this life, and I told her that she had had no choice about her adoption. This dream ended with the sight of a terrarium under a light, which had burned some of the leaves. On my couch, which is green, the patient lies beneath a ceiling light that is not kept burning during therapy sessions. The burned leaves in her dream recalled her poem "I am a leaf," and I suggested that they might represent the burned Francis whose image others saw in her at the beginning of her life. After this interpretation she felt heavy and said that she felt "consolidated into her hands and mouth," recalling Hoffer's (1949) paper, "Mouth, Hand, and Ego-Integration." By way of confirming my interpretation about burned leaves, she spoke of having as a child been afraid of volcanoes, of being burned and buried. My name—Volkan—I thought might be connected with these fears now. She said, "It must have sunk into me as a child that Francis died a terrible death. The story that he was unrecognizable—I always supposed his face was messed up—and that he could not be distinguished from the other two dead men made a horrible impression on me. My destiny was controlled by others! I want to choose!" This was a moving hour. In those that followed, her dream associations led her to direct expressions of anger toward her grandmother and mother.

Many of her dreams dealt with garbage and cleaning. She also dreamed about people with protruding body parts that resembled penises. The meaning of the protruding body parts was later revealed.

Her "dream addiction" ended when she declared one day that she wanted to talk about the diary still in my office. She spoke of the diary published by the woman founder of the cult she had joined during her first psychotic excitement. This woman had been engaged to a pilot who had died. After his death, she had seen him in a dream, still clad in his uniform, and, deciding that he was still alive in another world, had started a religious movement based on a belief in an astral plane. My patient now realized how greatly this book had affected her, and how closely it had resembled the story she had heard in her own home. She told me that after the death of Francis her grandmother had become depressed; she had consulted a psychiatrist, who, with the help of the appropriate governmental agency, had facilitated the return of the three dead airmen for burial in their homeland. My patient recalled being seven when she had asked a girl on the school bus, "Do you ever think about committing suicide?" With further discussion, we reconstructed the possibility that her grandmother had been suicidal and had been saved from destroying herself only by her son's "reincarnation" in my patient, whose burden of obligation was thereafter severe, to say the least.

This hour was followed by a report of childhood memories of picking her face. She had had fantasies about having leprosy. Her face-picking was in the service not only of reassuring herself that she was alive, but also of attempting to separate her image from the image of Francis with which she had identified. As a teenager she had worn layers of makeup like a mask, superimposing one face on another. She had consulted a dermatologist and had gotten him to put a mask of paste on her face that would peel off the top layer of skin. I was delighted to see how insightful she had become and that she was able to see humor in her behavior. She laughed and said, "I got the dermatologist involved in my psychological processes."

The fantasy of eating (introjecting) the flesh of the dead

Our working alliance bloomed, and she told me how much she appreciated my helping her make sense out of the bizarre and disorganized material she had brought to analysis. I noticed a warmth and aliveness in her. Fortified by our alliance, she talked about a movie, *Night of the Living Dead*, which had fascinated, but not frightened her as a teenager. It was like a Frankenstein or Dracula entertainment, in which the dead ate the living in order to live themselves. I told her that Francis ate her to stay alive, and she ate him in turn to identify with him. She said. that when she felt a spirit enter her for the first time it felt as though cancer were eating her inside. I have already noted her early incorporative fantasies.

The next day she missed an hour for the first time. Two days later she came to tell me how badly she felt over failing to appear, but explained that she had had "a sore throat." I interpreted her incorporative anxieties, cannibalistic fantasies, and her defensive refusal to eat meat. During this hour she felt extreme anxiety, and as the hour concluded, she let herself express identification with the dead by feeling her body turn cold. Once the experience was over she burst out sobbing. She had passed the test—had done something under the gaze of the observing ego that formerly she had done unconsciously, with accompanying pathological defenses and adaptations. We were now in the tenth month of her analysis. A few days later she took back her diary.

Early trauma and sexual aggressive fantasies in childhood

Beginning with her associations to *Night of the Living Dead*, Frances visited her early pathogenic fantasies of orally taking in the dead pilot's representation, which had remained inside her like a cancer, invading but not totally overwhelming her. The collision of the dead pilot's representation with her own self-representation had laid the scene for the expression of her object relations conflict. Now, she seemed to be more confident in herself, as though one round in her struggle toward health had been won; during the following months she showed a marked improvement in her ability to deal with everyday issues.

Analysis now uncovered information about her very first year of life. It seemed that her mother, while pregnant with the child she had lost, had perceived her fetus in a peculiarly split way. Her pregnancy had been likely undertaken with the hope of having a male child to replace her brother and thereby end her mother's grief, although apparently, like Frances, she had never established the sex of the aborted fetus. Frances had been impulsively adopted after the miscarriage to replace the (putatively male) fetus, and thus the dead pilot. Although the mother wanted Frances, she may have resented her for being an infant of the wrong sex; she may have felt her to be "bad" and perceived her lost (presumably male) fetus as "good." The mother was unable to help her baby become an integrated child.

Mahler, Pine, and Bergman (1975) hold that the infant must have a satisfactory symbiotic relationship with the mothering person before it can advance to the next step of separation–individuation. It seems that in the absence of satisfactory "mutual cueing" (Pao, 1974) between mother and child one can expect "experiential core disturbance," which, I think, can be understood best in terms of an internalized object relations conflict between different opposing representational units. One evidence of what I describe here was the phobia Frances's mother had had about having her daughter touch her breast. This phobia had endured, and when the adult Frances had once "accidentally" touched the breast of her fully clothed mother she had seen her mother's automatic response of disgust and anxiety. Frances felt that she had not been "touched" in any motherly warm way by her mother when she was small; she had been taken care of by her grandmother, whose "touch always felt rough."

So far I have given a rather detailed account of the first ten months of Frances's analysis, during which the material that emerged clearly demonstrated, I believe, that she was a living linking object. I now propose to show how the conflicts stemming from her childhood traumas and her sexual–aggressive fantasies (and the defenses against them) were superimposed on her object relations conflict. A summary of the next year's analysis will make for a more balanced presentation of this case, since it will show that circumstances other than her replacing a dead person had contributed to her illness. Such circumstances and their appearance on the transference–countertransference axis will not be discussed in detail, however, since they do not directly involve the subject under discussion.

Frances idealized me, and her dream of romantic love between us led her to masturbate. She ceased to idealize me when she had fantasies of my giving her enemas for sexual stimulation. Then she disclosed some repeated childhood traumas. Even before she was eight years old (before her grandmother joined her parents' household) she had seen her mother giving her grandmother enemas. The older women had thought the child was asleep. She would watch the process and hear her grandmother cry out, "Stop, stop! You are hurting me!" even as she had urged her daughter to keep on. The fascination with protruding parts that Frances had revealed in earlier associations returned; it was evident that enema tubes had been condensed with female phalluses. Frances's delusion of being half-woman and half-man, previously understood as her being half her real self and half the dead pilot, could now be re-examined in terms of a superimposed phenomenon, i.e., a fantasy of women with penises.

Frances's sadistic–masochistic sexual fantasies as a teenager had included early perceptions of the sexual interaction between two women. When she was 16 she inserted a finger in her vagina, and because penetration was possible, thought that someone must have had intercourse with her when she was a child; she had fantasies of being molested by her mother. She recalled having had "air bubbles" in her vagina, and her mother pushing her hand at her genitals to release them. This performance was often repeated during her childhood.

The memory of her mother's giving her an enema when she was four years old, while her adoptive grandfather looked on, evoked embarrassment and rage; in the transference, I became a monster who gave enemas. On occasion, this transference constellation was on the psychotic level; she actually believed that I would attack her sexually and with enema tubes. Then, feminizing me, she would fantasize my having a hairless chest. In other fantasies I would be monk clad in a robe that looked like a dress; a woman with a phallus.

Different images of others that had been externalized onto me were now reactivated, along with corresponding images from her childhood; these were sometimes felt to exist inside her, and sometimes outside. For example, where once I was a "torturer, a Hitler," there would now be an "inner Hitler" to combat the one outside, etc. I helped her to appreciate the splitting and fragmentation of these images, and helped her to understand her powerlessness before the frightening images of her mother, and how they were condensed with her horrible perceptions of the dead pilot.

In a few months she thanked me for helping her to re-examine her old perceptions. One day, while on the couch, she gave an imitation of her grandmother grumbling about her bowels as she sat on the toilet. On the following day she was amazed at having done this, and began a feverish attempt to differentiate herself from others in her childhood environment. She pointed out that, since she had been adopted, she would not genetically inherit anything bad from her adoptive family.

The next day she insisted that I share with her my first impression of her. This insistence was understood and interpreted to her as arising from fear that I would be just like her adoptive parent, and from longing that I would be different. Her childhood fears that if she weren't good she would be sent to an orphanage poured out. At work she practiced being aggressive as she toyed with the danger of being discharged from her job. She reported that her analysis had put her in touch with her emotions and acquainted her with what she was made of. After remarking on this, she said that she wanted to tell me the details of her second acute psychotic break, the memory of which still frightened her. She spent the next five hours going into the details of this experience, a summary of which I gave at the beginning of my report of her case. Her recall of this acutely psychotic event with considerable accompanying emotion was again full of references to her being a living link to the dead pilot.

During this phase of her analysis she received a telephone call from her mother telling her that an elderly relative had died. She thought, "Now I must cry. I must feel sorry," and she began crying, only to stop herself with the realization that she had never known the dead relative at all well, and that she was simply automatically assuming her grandmother's attitude toward death. She attended the funeral, and her grandmother, who was too frail to go herself, questioned her eagerly about all who attended the services, wanting to know who had wept, who had seemed unmoved, etc.

I could now better understand her unmended early self- and object images and their attendant affect dispositions. She had given these images names; her aggressively tinged self-image was called the Incredible Hulk. Since television's Incredible Hulk is also a gentle doctor, the term referred also to her split perception of me, which would from time to time fuse with her self-perception. On a higher level, the Incredible Hulk represented the phallus of a woman.

A little more than a year after beginning treatment, Frances left her part-time job and began work in her chosen profession, having by then finished the necessary program in school. From time to time her delusion would reappear, reminding me of Freud's (1923) observation that in the course of an illness delusions are decathected and recathected, and his later statement (Freud, 1939) that they remain as "A State Within a State:

an inaccessible party," in spite of my feeling that Frances would be able to modify them, given treatment. Discussing her case, Pao (1978) stated that

> Influenced earlier by the maternal preoccupation and reinforced now by the grandmother's tutelage, Frances chose the basic theme of her fantasy-delusion by assigning herself as the link between the living and the dead and as a person neither of the male nor female sex.

The fantasy-delusion referred to by Pao had been described earlier by Lichtenberg and Pao (1974), who indicated that fantasy is formulated in accordance with the pleasure–unpleasure principle whereas fantasy-delusion, like delusion, is created from the necessity of keeping anxiety at a minimum and of maintaining a minimal degree of what Sandler (1960) calls a "sense of well-being." I agree with Pao that Frances turned to her cognitive ability, which was in the ascendance of its development, to formulate a fantasy-delusion or what Freud (1922) called a preformed delusion, in order to ward off profound regression.

At this point in her treatment I felt that when Frances's wish to individuate, to be a "normal" girl, to date, to have "normal" sexual activity appeared, and was reflected in the transference, she became anxious, and regressive defenses against such wishes appeared. Moreover, she faced the realization that if she were to continue in her chosen profession she must leave the area. Her anxiety increased further.

A plane crash followed by a car crash

One day, after a particularly stressful and embarrassing day at her new job, Frances came to her hour with loose associations, and with the delusion that something was wrong with her car and that when she took it to a garage she would meet her future husband. At the end of this hour she seemed to have recovered somewhat, but the next day her father called to tell me that she had had a car accident on the way to visit them, and that she was in a hospital. She was not physically injured, but appeared to be acutely psychotic.

As I thought about these events I suddenly realized that on the day before her last hour in my office there had been a widely publicized plane crash that had tragically resulted in many deaths, many of the passengers having been burned beyond recognition. On the day of Frances's accident there had been hourly accounts of the crash on the radio, and the story had led all others on television. I wondered if the plane crash, coming as it had at a time when Frances was anxiously trying to be a "total" woman, had functioned as a "releaser" for her behavior, as though she were having an anniversary reaction.

I talked about her situation on the phone with the physician caring for her. He spoke of her bewilderment, and her account of how she had lost control of her car under the influence of spirits; she had been trying to kill a big spider in the car. The doctor, who had not seen her before her admission, was impressed by her description of herself as two people. When I received a copy of his notes on her admission, I found that he had taken her statements verbatim. Frances felt that she had been controlled by beings from space. She had told him, "I am two people—half and half. I experience a transfusion of my two souls, one black and one white, and I was forced to look at my black soul through my white soul."

Her acute psychosis lasted only five days, and she returned to my couch. When in due time I asked her about the plane crash, she denied having heard about it, although, since she was in the habit of watching news reports on television, she must have known of it. In any case, she described her car crash as an act to kill Francis once and for all so that she could be free as a woman. It also involved resistance to analysis in the sense that at that time in her analysis she was trying in piecemeal fashion to be a "total woman," and feeling some anxiety about this. It was as though her dangerous act expressed a wish to be over with this task once and for all. She did not seem to be especially disturbed after her brief stay in the hospital, but I noticed hypomanic behavior, elation, an air of celebration as though she had now become a woman. She had a new coiffure, a new style of makeup, etc. I helped her to "slow down" by making remarks about our needing to gradually gain an understanding of what had happened. If we went slowly, we would more easily assimilate things, and assimilate them better, etc. She responded favorably to this, but once again returned to an intense examination of her being a living linking object. Her brief psychosis seemed to have been a turning point for a new integration. During the next few months she threw her diary away, and discarded other material such as her religious magazines as "junk." The symptom of refraining from eating meat disappeared totally, having begun to disappear after the *Night of the Living Dead* interpretation. She referred to the pictures of the dead pilot displayed in the family home as "those stupid pictures." One day she told me that she disliked the painting on my office wall, and wanted me to change it for something "livelier." She changed the pictures on the walls of her apartment for more "lively" ones. She dreamed of giving children a lecture on death and funerals, and reported that her delusions and hallucinations were "dying" as if "a door is closing in my head." She reported more death-related memories; it turned out that her grandmother had lost a younger brother a year before her son's death, and that she had also been talking about him over the years. Frances pondered once again how extensively her grandmother's life was peopled with the dead. Commenting on her grandmother's diabetes, she said, "At least one good thing about being adopted—I missed that disease!"

Elements of father transference now appeared in her treatment. She realized how lonely her father had been, pushed aside by the symbiotic-like union of his wife with her mother; over the last years his wife had, of course, very seldom left the house, devoting herself to her mother, who had become an invalid. She slept near her mother, watched over her bowel habits, etc. Frances saw herself as a fell ow traveler with her father in the family constellation. The sexualization of her relations with the father/analyst caused anxiety and subsequent regression to fantasies of having sexual relations with a captain from the space ship Battle Star Galactica (the dead pilot).

Frances's treatment continues. She has told me that she is entering "an area of trust," of becoming a woman and relating to me "on a personal basis." This is, of course, a difficult task for her, but she has proven to me that she is a courageous person, and I look forward to more work with her; we will have a long way to go before completing our mutual task. Nevertheless, I believe that the report of her story up to this point offers a good example of the complications—however condensed they may be with other conflicts—that occur when representations of a dead person, conveyed to a child in his interaction with important others, are not assimilated in the developing self-concept, resulting in continuing identity confusion and object relations conflict.

Part IV

Coda

CHAPTER 15

Magical inanimate objects

I have reserved this final section for a comparison of linking objects and phenomena with transitional objects, fetishes, and other magical inanimate objects (and phenomena). My discussion of linking objects and phenomena has so far "linked" the topics introduced throughout this volume. I have described their "discovery"—their appearance in the clinical setting—and given examples. I have outlined their role in keeping the mourning process in a "frozen" state, while at the same time keeping the patient "protected" from full-blown depression and/or suicide. I have indicated their usefulness in the special treatment called re-grief therapy, designed for persons who have met with complications in their mourning. I have explained how living beings can be used as the linking object of a parent, replacing a child who has died.

This book deals, of course, with death-related losses. But I suspect that linking objects and linking phenomena appear in other kinds of separations such as divorce. Since my clinical research has dealt only with those conditions arising from loss by death, I have deliberately refrained from applying my formulation to other situations.

Throughout this book, especially in the detailed case reports, it is clear that linking objects and phenomena contain references and responses to castration and separation anxiety, and to the defenses against them.

I have suggested that linking objects serve some of the same purposes as do fetishes or transitional objects. One might be led to question whether a new designation is required for the inanimate objects and parallel phenomena discussed in this book. The following discussion addresses itself to this question.

A comparison of transitional objects, fetishes, and other magical inanimate objects (and phenomena) with linking objects (and phenomena)

Greenacre (1969, 1970) uses the term fetish in its limited sense to refer to a means of adult perversion. I will use her views—as well as those of some others—to summarize what is known about the fetish and the transitional object, and I will compare them with what I mean by the linking object. I will also make reference to fetishism in children as described by M. Sperling (1963), and to the "instant mothers" used by psychotic children studied by Speers and Lansing (1965), who applied Mahler's (1963, 1968) concepts. Although all these kinds of uniquely significant objects overlap in function and description, they are recognizably different from one another. They should also be differentiated from the common keepsake or talisman, and from the inanimate objects psychotics endow with magic powers.

Keepsakes and talismans

A talisman, amulet, or charm is invested with magical powers and is used to defend against separation and castration anxieties, but usually in a way sanctioned by cultural or religious belief (or stereotyped symbolization of the same) so that its use cannot be considered evidence of psychopathology. It contains some aspects of the fetish, transitional object, or linking object, but not on a clinical-diagnostic level. The belief in the Evil Eye, for example, is characteristic of people living in the Near East. A symposium on the Evil Eye, held at the 1972 Annual Meeting of the American Anthropological Association (Maloney, 1976), made references to the openly displayed devices used to protect against it; for example, miniature Korans or Bibles are carried by people who believe themselves the target of the Evil Eye. It is not my purpose here to review critically the papers offered at this symposium. (It is noteworthy, however, that those which dealt with the psychological aspects of the phenomenon appeared to place little emphasis on its sexual significance.) I simply cite the symposium here as evidence that millions of people share this belief system. I myself saw protective devices against the influence of the Evil Eye when I was a child in Cyprus; people afraid that the jealousy of others would call down upon them the baleful force of the Evil Eye wore about their necks bits of paper called *muska* upon which prayers were written before they were folded into triangles. And in the United States it is not necessarily considered symptomatic to carry about a rabbit's foot, or to insist on wearing some supposedly lucky garment when going into a competitive sport.

A talisman may reflect the psychological influence of an overwhelming event, and retain a significance specifically related to the inner conflicts that event brought about. Group trauma may bring about the adoption by many of the same sort of talisman, which, although best understood in relation to the historic event in question, contains some defenses against basic separation and castration anxiety.

In 1975 I had the opportunity to observe the development of a kind of talisman shared by the inhabitants of Cyprus after the 1974 war. The Turkish army had intervened in the dangerous situation existing between the two ethnic groups on the island, the Turks and Greeks. When I went into the northern section of the island less than six months after the war's end—and on several later occasions—I studied the kind of mourning and adaptation that had followed it (Volkan, 1977, 1979a). In the post-war culture, the shell cases that had so recently meant death had suddenly become collectors' items, displayed in the home in new guise as umbrella stands or vases, and were so greatly valued that people who had not acquired them as a matter of salvage had actually bought them in order to be in style. For a year or two after the war, people postponed having the evidences of shot and shell repaired in their homes; when children came for visits they were given something sharp with which to probe the holes for bullets, as though they were discovering Easter eggs hidden out of sight for their amusement. A host would take pride in pointing out the bullet holes in his furniture, as though he had gained distinction from having survived an attack so immediate and so savage. It seemed that being close to the evidence of fire made fire appear to be less dangerous.

Found bullets were used for necklaces. The necklaces made from bent bullets were particularly prized, since such bullets had been fired and thus represented a defused explosive, a disarmed attack.

Many meanings were condensed in those shared talismans of the survivors of war. They kept bullets near their bodies as though to identify with their countrymen who had been killed. But the talismans were counterphobic as well, since they were a continual reminder of an escape from death.

The transitional objects (and the transitional phenomenon)

The transitional object is something chosen by the small child himself, usually during the first year of his life and from among those things that he can see, touch, and smell—perhaps a teddy bear, blanket, or something similar. Winnicott (1953) pointed out the importance of such an object to the child, who may regard it as more necessary to him than his own mother. He stated:

> I have introduced the terms 'transitional object' and 'transitional phenomena' for designation of the intermediate area of experience, between the thumb and the teddy bear, between the oral erotism and true object-relationship, between primary creative activity and projection of what has already been introjected, between primary unawareness of indebtedness and the acknowledgment of indebtedness ('say: ta!').
>
> By this definition an infant's babbling or the way an older child goes over a repertory of songs and tunes while preparing for sleep come within the intermediate area as transitional phenomena, along with the use made of objects that are not part of the infant's body yet are not fully recognized as belonging to external reality. (p. 89)

The main function of this inanimate object (or phenomenon) is to allow the infant to develop, in response to the ministrations of the "good enough" mother, "the *illusion* that there is an external reality that corresponds to [his] own capacity to create" (Winnicott, 1953, p. 95). A first "not-me" possession is created. In certain situations the mother herself can be used by the infant as a transitional object. The transitional object is in any case "almost ubiquitous," states Greenacre (1969, p. 315), "a temporary construction to aid the infant in the early stages of developing a sense of reality and establishing his own individual identity. It is of positive value in monitoring growth and expansion" (p. 334), and "does not generally forecast abnormal development" (p. 315).

In her review of the transitional object, Greenacre agrees that it is first "not-me" but never totally "not-me," since it links "not-me" with "mother-me." She describes its odor as a fusion of "me-odor" with "mother-odor," and its softness as being associated not only with the softness of the mother's breast but with the softness of pillows and blankets that comfort the child when the mother is absent. It is usually something soft, fragrant with body odors, and portable. It provides a "cushion" against frustration while reality testing is still insecure, and it is particularly useful in helping the child drop off to sleep, since it bridges the experience of cuddling close to the mother's body and having to get along separated from her. The child whose transitional object is mislaid or lost is usually single-minded in his distress over its absence until he can find or, perhaps, replace it. He will never attack it in anger, but he does require that it absorb neglect as well as provide loving closeness.

It has been observed that the child's resort to his transitional object becomes less and less frequent as he grows older until at last he ignores it altogether. Winnicott (1953) suggests that active repression of its memory is not the process involved in its surrender, however, a view with which Greenacre agrees. Influenced by Kohut's (1971) concept of "transmuting internalizations," Tolpin (1972) states that certain aspects of the transitional object, i.e., the soothing functions, "go inside" as mental structure. Other writers (Coppolillo, 1967; Kahne, 1967; Kafka, 1969; Fintzy, 1971; Volkan, 1976; Volkan & Kavanaugh, 1978) observe that in some persons the transitional object or its memory can persist into adult life, sometimes covertly, but sometimes reactivated. Modell (1963, 1968) has suggested that borderline patients are arrested at the stage of transitional object *relatedness*, emphasizing that the transitional object has regressive and progressive sides that are directly correlated with the relative rejection or acceptance of the external object. Kavanaugh and I (Volkan, 1976; Volkan & Kavanaugh, 1978) followed Modell when we demonstrated how borderline patients use reactivated transitional objects—altered in function—to defend against conflicts of object relations.

The childhood fetish

M. Sperling (1963), differing from Winnicott, states that the transitional objects Winnicott describes as universally found in healthy, normal development are in fact pathological manifestations of a specific disturbance in object relationships. Dickes (1963) speculates as to whether the transitional object was indeed the child's creation as held by Winnicott, or something presented pathologically to the child by his mother. Sperling sees Winnicott's concepts as "not only fallacious but dangerous," and prefers to refer to those inanimate objects to which the small child becomes extravagantly attached as "childhood fetishes." They are always real and concrete; in cases where they are a part of the child's own body, they are replaceable parts such as fingernails. The child resentful at being weaned replaces the mother's breast with his fetish, the symbolic function of which is to deal with separation anxiety at weaning; the child at the height of the anal phase (clinging to or releasing feces—the mother equivalent), or the child in the oedipal phase during which the mother is being renounced as the sexually gratifying object may turn to such fetishes. In summary, the childhood fetish represents a pathological defense against separation from mother prior to the resolution of the oedipal conflict, and it may or may not lead to adult fetishism.

In their observations of psychotic children, Speers and Lansing (1965) noticed something that resembled Sperling's childhood fetishism in its psychodynamic meaning; the children created "instant mothers" through the use of portable inanimate objects. Mahler (1968) gives clinical examples of the "psychotic preoccupations" of children with an inanimate object (the "psychotic fetish") such as a fan, a record player, a jar—or even a thread wound around a finger—describing these as a form of transitional object, although great differences among such objects in form, texture, odor, etc., are clearly evident.

In previous articles (Volkan, 1976; Volkan & Kavanaugh, 1978), I wrote that I did not agree with Sperling that the transitional object was a pathological manifestation. I see it, along with the childhood fetish that originates with it, as located on a spectrum that ranges from normality to pathology: when the child's development is normal, the transitional object helps him to separate from his mother, but when the mother–child relationship is disturbed, the transitional object may change in function to become something used defensively to repair the illusion of body defect that stems from incomplete individuation from the mother. The idea of such a spectrum also appears in Dickes's (1978) recent paper on the topic, although he differs from me in restricting the use of transitional objects and phenomena to children who do not value this prized possession above their caretakers, classifying the object valued more than the mother herself as a childhood fetish.

The adult fetish

In the classical sense, the adult fetish represents the illusory penis of the mother at perhaps the last moment in which she could have been regarded as truly phallic (Freud, 1927). It is utilized as a special solution to the threat of castration by an adult, usually a male adult, so as to ensure his ability to perform genital sexual intercourse. The roles of pregenital sexual experiences, of aggression, and of other aspects of fetishism have been extensively studied since Freud. Bak (1953), summarizing factors contributing to the development of fetishism, includes: weakness of the ego structure; fixation in pregenital phases; the representation of breasts, skin, buttocks, feces, nipples, and the female phallus, separately or in combination, in the fetish. He emphasizes the importance of identification with the penis-less mother, in which the wish to give up the penis creates marked intrastructural conflict, and, psychodynamically speaking, puts the adult's fetish on the same line as that of the child. He writes:

> Historically, the pregenital identification with the phallic mother cannot be given up in the phallic phase in spite of the new reality (penislessness) because separation from the mother is experienced as an equal, if not greater, danger than the loss of the penis. Both phases of danger, i.e., of separation and castration, are defended by the fetishistic compromise (biphasic). (p. 286)

In a series of papers, Greenacre (1953, 1969, 1970) shows how fetishism develops against varying backgrounds, in certain cases resulting from a disturbance during the first two years of life, perhaps an illness or inconsistent mothering. She points to the important role of vision in the two types of experience that lead to severe castration anxiety and that contribute specifically to the development of a fetish.

> *First*, there is the exposure of the infant during the first two or three years, frequently or even consistently, to awareness of the genitals of the opposite sex, whether of the parent or of a sibling. *Second*, there is the acute experience of witnessing an injury (usually bloody) to the self or even more importantly to another, more often the mother, another child, or a pet. (1969, p. 331)

The palpable concreteness of the adult fetish leaves no doubt as to its reality. It usually contains, in addition to male characteristics, some association with the female body, thus offering a combination of male and female attributes. It is usually an article of clothing—a part of the mother's costume of which the child in latency or in the prepubertal phase caught a glimpse when peeking beneath his mother's skirt (Freud, 1927). A shoe is a common fetish—usually a shoe that combines hard and soft textures. The color black, which represents pubic hair, is important, as are odor and visibility (Greenacre, 1969).

Inanimate objects prized by adults psychotics and borderline patients

Searles (1960), noting that many schizophrenics utilize certain inanimate objects—as well as nonhuman animate ones—in a magical way, studies the impact of nonhuman aspects of the environment on the child and the psychotic. His initial thesis is that what is nonhuman in the environment has an influence on the child above and beyond that of persons, but he later (1963) revises this view, proposing that the nonhuman realm represents by displacement some increment of the child's essentially mother-directed feelings of love, dependency, etc. Even later, Searles (1965), still addressing himself to this issue, states that the mother "humanizes" the whole of both the inner and outer reality of the infant and young child, and differentiates for him the nonhuman from the human. At a considerably later date (1976), he writes about the transitional aspects of nonhuman objects such as the couch, the analyst's notes, the tape recorder, the psychotropic drug. Such items he sees as functioning as transitional objects for *both* analyst and patient. He further suggests that the patient's symptoms, as well as his transference image of the analyst, must become transitional objects (phenomena) for both the patient and his analyst if any effective transference analysis is to occur in the case of that patient, whether neurotic, borderline, or psychotic.

Luttrell and I (1971) describe an 18-year-old "mechanical boy" (so named after a patient designated as such by Bettelheim in 1959; both patients at times regarded themselves as machines). Our patient used a tape recorder with many auxiliary gadgets to relate to other people, recording their heartbeats and then playing them back to help him get to sleep. He had absolute control over this tape recorder, and it gave him something Janus-like to place between himself and other people so that he had control over contact with them. Its use as a reactivated transitional object is thus clear.

Burnham (1969) observes the schizophrenic's" use of either an inanimate object or some phenomenon such as a religious idea. Like Fenichel (1945), he calls these "substitutes for objects" or, more briefly, "substitute objects." He notes that these objects were somewhat similar to transitional objects, and I add to this concept my finding that

> Closer examination of the "substitute objects" used by schizophrenic and borderline patients may reveal elements of "mother-me" and "not-me" as well as a link between the two, a link under the patient's illusory global control. (1976, p. 213)

In other words, the normal developmental relatedness with the transitional object characteristic of early childhood continues in the adult borderline individual, in the schizophrenic patient, and in the neurotic patient in regression, but the object undergoes a change in function so that it is defensively used mainly against a conflict of object relationships—a conflict between opposing self- and object representations with their accompanying affective ties. However, in therapeutic regression, the normal developmental properties of the object can be captured once again. The borderline or psychotic individual feels primitive anxiety whenever he tries to mend, as it were, his primitively split or fragmented self- and object representations. I see such attempts as inevitable because I believe that each of us has an urge to travel up the developmental ladder. The reason such mending is so difficult is that some self- and object units are excessively laden with aggressive drive derivatives so that mending is perceived as necessitating the annihilation of the "all good" representational units that the patient wants to keep in accordance with the pleasure principle. A psychotic (or borderline) maneuver in this direction may involve the use of a (reactivated) transitional object as a buffer between "all good" and "all bad" self- and object units. Since the individual has absolute control over his transitional objects, he can sustain the illusion of absolute control over the contact between his opposing representational units—the illusion that he can bring them together or keep them apart. There are thus clear similarities between the transitional object of infancy (a bridge between "not-me" and "mother-me") and the reactivated transitional object (substitute object) of the borderline and psychotic, for whom the object is a defensive buffer between what can be admitted and what must be kept outside.

Linking objects

I now turn to a different link or bridge, related to those described in the foregoing, but important for the clinician to identify as unique.

The bridge provided by the transitional object enables the healthy child to travel from "mother-me" to "not-me," and to become acquainted with the world of reality. If he is impeded in traveling this developmental course, or faced by difficulties in the real world, he can use it as a buffer between different "mother-me's" and different "not-me's," and, later, even between internalized and externalized "me's" and internally located and externally located object representations. The original transitional object, then, can be seen as being reactivated in difficult childhood and, later, in severely regressed adulthood with a change of function. In the adult fetish the bridge is seen as being more highly focalized, with a more durable symbolic meaning. As Greenacre (1969) notes:

> Whereas the transitional object is derived from mother-me association and is somewhat focused on the mouth-nose and breast, the fetishist's mother-me combination is distinctly concerned with genitals (p. 321)

The bridge here is in effect the place at which the rejection and acceptance of the existence of human beings without a penis come together. Since this bridge (the fetish) is under the individual's absolute control, it enables him, as Glover (1933) showed some time ago, to patch "over flaws in the development of reality-sense" (p. 499). The more the pregenital aspects, i.e., anxieties pertaining to separation from the breast or feces, are included in the adult fetish, the more compulsively the individual will find the fetish necessary to the maintenance of his reality sense. But the classic fetish of the adult male, in spite of the condensation of pregenital issues in it, represents the mother's penis; this is its primary significance.

A look at the linking object suggests that it also involves elements that respond both to separation and castration anxieties. Jerry's handkerchief (see Chapter 6) was used as a scrotal bag for the reception of his father's bequest, a testicle, and was probably useful to him in dealing with castration anxiety. In this sense it was fetishistic, but Jerry did not need the handkerchief at hand in order to have intercourse. The linking object appears at a time of loss (death) of an important other, and, paraphrasing Freud, I have suggested that it is a "token of triumph" over the loss. Although the childhood fetish or the fetish of the psychotic adult deals chiefly with the loss on the preoedipal level of the part-representations of the mother (object), as well as the part-representations of the self, a loss by death may represent to the mourner separation from representations of a greater diversity of important objects from every level of psychosexual development, including the oedipal, with a more focalized symbolization as a link between the mourner's representation and that of the deceased. Its main function is to provide an illusion of being able to keep or "kill" someone now dead with whom the ego perceives the mourner has unfinished business. In the example that follows, the dead father, who had died one minute after midnight and was accordingly associated with Father Time, was needed by his mourner to help him resolve his oedipal conflict and to complete the integration of his superego. This patient wanted to avoid separation on the oedipal level so that he could, in turn, have help in avoiding some unpleasant aspects of his preoedipal phase.

The patient, Andrew, was a 38-year-old man who had undergone an operation for a hiatus hernia two years before he was seen as a psychiatric patient. The surgery had been considered successful. A year after it took place, the patient's 79-year-old father died, and soon after this death Andrew became impotent and felt pain in his surgical scar. These symptoms were brought to a psychiatrist's attention on the first anniversary of the father's death. Andrew was preoccupied with the fantasy that physical activity would open the scar on his chest, and his association to the scar tissue made it clear that, surrounded by hair, it represented a vagina to him. He had regressed to dependency, and needed constant care from his wife and his mother, toward both of whom he felt unexpressed rage.

As a child he had perceived that his mother had preferred his younger brother to him, and had "reached up" to his father in an attempt to pair with him. Luttrell and I (1971) described this kind of "reaching up" in connection with another case, seeing it as a defensive maneuver designed to solve earlier problems, one not only futile but also symptomatic because compulsive. Andrew's sense of having been rejected by his mother, and his intense sibling rivalry, had interfered with the development of normal oedipal conflicts, renunciations, and identifications. Accordingly, motivated by an unconscious attempt to avoid the unpleasant aspects of the pregenital phase by reaching up the ladder of psychosexual development, he had become his father's constant and obsessive companion and competitor, and had cut a manly figure in athletic activities. These efforts had not, however, led to any real solution of the oedipal conflict, nor to the establishment of an adaptively useful identification with the father. The original oedipal father of the external world survived in the actual father of later years, and although Andrew married in the course of time, and worked in his own profession, he remained geographically near his father.

The operation for hiatus hernia was a symbolic castration and, on a lower level, an obstruction to the satisfaction of his oral needs in that it involved his stomach. The death of his father within a year of the surgery had caused him to connect the mutilation of the operation with his wish for the death of his oedipal father; he thus felt feminized, and experienced pain in his chest, as the retaliation of his oedipal father. When Andrew reported that "Father Time caught up with me," Father Time was his real father, who, like Time's symbolic representation, wore a beard, lived a long time, and died at one minute after midnight. Andrew's associations showed a clear condensation of Father Time, his real father, with the surgeon who had put a "vagina" on his chest.

With the oedipal ambivalence thus unresolved, Andrew could not "kill" his father, and went into established pathological mourning for him. What interests us here is his use of his father's old car as a linking object. Although Andrew was poor, he spent as much as a thousand dollars a year to keep this car and its motor in good condition, although he never took it out on the road. It had no value as an antique. It had simply become magical, and a link between Andrew and the representation of the dead man as oedipal father. The car, as his phallic father, stayed within his reach and, now that it belonged to him, became a meeting ground for the representation of both men, a meeting ground over which he had the illusion of absolute control.

Jerry's case (Chapter 6) tells us more about the main function of the linking object. Once his treatment had helped him recall some of his early memories, I learned that his stained handkerchief was condensed with the stained bed linen of the dead black child. The first memory we uncovered thus had a definite reference to separation anxiety from his early childhood, and so, it seemed clear that both castration and separation anxieties were condensed in his linking object. But the linking object was mainly a bridge between the representation of the mourner and the dead. This is so because, while transitional objects link primitive representations, linking objects link formed representations or parts of such representations, as in the case of Jerry.

The typical transitional object, as noted, is soft and impregnated with the odor of the mother and of the child himself, whereas the fetish can be cold and bizarre, perhaps reflecting the chill of a difficult child–mother relationship. The substitute objects of borderline and psychotic individuals may be unusual items, or they may reflect the original softness of the typical transitional object, now turned to defensive purposes. I describe elsewhere (Volkan, 1976) a borderline patient who came to her hours with "fuzz balls" with which she would toy while on the couch. They were made of lint taken from cushions, and she ensured their magic by putting them into her panties so that they would smell of her body. The typical adult fetish, often a shoe, reflects genital body aspects both male and female, and the greater the involvement of pregenital issues in the adult fetish, as it maintains its main function of dealing with castration anxiety, the more unusual the fetish may be.

The symbolism with which the linking object is invested is more ideational. The notion that an object can provide a meeting place for a reunion of the mourner with the one he mourns may be enough for its establishment, as may be the idea that the object was the last thing seen by the mourner just before he learned about the death. Thus, in striking contrast to the original transitional object or the adult fetish, in both of which the inclusion of aspects of body image are necessary, the texture, odor,[3] portability, and visibility of the linking object are not important. The linking object is in a sense a higher-level symbol, its relation to body parts more ideational. The sexual symbolism is more hidden in these than it is in the adult fetish. For example, a dead father's eye-glasses may reflect his visual aspect adequately enough to serve as a linking object, particularly if they are broken and thus eloquent of the father's decline in health. Their symbolic reference to genitals is not obvious, at least on the surface.

The transitional object seems more heavily invested with libido than the other objects considered, however much they may also absorb the child's aggression. I agree with Greenacre that the fetish contains congealed anger born of castration panic. The linking object also contains anger and is similarly an instrument for controlling the expression of anger, especially anger that arises from narcissistic hurt relating to separation panic. I would further suggest that the linking object is more significantly invested with the aggressive drive (to "kill") than is the fetish (to "castrate"). Because of this intense contamination with aggression, one characteristic of the linking object distinguishes it clearly from the typical adult fetish: patients usually "distance" themselves from it, sometimes even locking theirs away. Although it is important to know where it is, the mourner avoids embracing it, as it were. Jerry had to lock up his handkerchief in order to sleep, and never used it in the daytime, although it was always on his person. Some linking objects produce eerie feelings in their owner when he looks at them. In contrast, the child holds, smells, and sees his transitional object all the time, and the adult pervert must have at least a glimpse of his fetish in order to feel sexually potent. The need to "distance" is characteristic of

[3] I once had a patient who became enraged when her mother sent to the cleaners a flag that had been her link with a father whose coffin it had covered. Cleaning did away with its characteristic musty odor, and my patient said that it was no longer the same to her. Her behavior was, in fact, very much like that of the small child who laments that the blanket he has used as a transitional object is no longer the same now that it is full of laundry smells. However, this was the only case in which the odor of a linking object was important; I noticed nothing like this among my other cases.

the ownership of linking objects (it may also be present in connection with the inanimate objects treasured by some psychotics).

Linking objects also have another distinguishing characteristic. They absorb, as it were, some of the conflicts pertaining to the work of mourning. In other words, aspects of the work of mourning are externalized onto the linking object, and the pain or other sensory perception involved in the usual work of mourning is not felt. Mourning is not resolved, and, as we have seen, unresolved mourning may be as productive of creative activity as it is of troublesome symptom formation. Jerry included the wiping away of his tears in his linking object, for example, and I have described how Mike's tears were also externalized onto the water that dripped onto his father's photograph.

Conclusion

In comparing the different inanimate objects for which different kinds of use require different labels in the psychoanalytic literature, I think it accurate to say that we can classify them all as variations on the theme of the transitional object. This classification is acceptable as long as we understand that the reactivation of the transitional object (and phenomenon) in adult life is associated with changes in function from its original use, as a means toward healthy growth, to defensive use that is almost always pathological.

These magical inanimate objects can, however, be distinguished from one another on a phenomenological level and according to the psychodynamic processes that are involved in each, in spite of the overlapping of some of their functions. I have yet to see a mourner use a linking object that directly reflects a transitional object he may have had in early childhood. In talking about the reactivation of a transitional object (or phenomenon), I thus refer to the reactivation of a form of psychological relatedness. The reactivated magical inanimate object will show influences from different levels of psychosexual development, and will be used to patch the flaws of reality and to control aspects of object relations. What was originally a powerful tool for healthy growth has thus become a defense against pathology.

References

Abraham, K. (1911a), Notes on the psycho-analytical investigation and treatment of manic-depressive insanity and allied conditions. In: *Selected Papers*, ed. D. Bryan & A. Strachey. New York: Basic Books, 1960, pp. 137–156.

Abraham, K. (1911b), Giovanni Segantini: A psychoanalytical study. In: *Clinical Papers and Essays*. New York: Basic Books, 1955, pp. 210–261.

Abraham, K. (1916), The first pregenital stage of the libido. In: *Selected Papers*, ed. D. Bryan & A. Strachey. New York: Basic Books, 1960, pp. 248–279.

Abraham, K. (1924), A short study of the development of the libido, viewed in the light of mental disorders. In: *Selected Papers*, ed. D. Bryan & A. Strachey. London: Hogarth Press, 1927, pp. 418–501.

Abse, D. W., & Jessner, L. (1961), The psychodynamic aspects of leadership. *Daedalus*, 90: 673–710.

Abse, D. W., & Ulman, R. B. (1977), Charismatic political leadership and collective regression. In: *Psychopathology and Political Leadership*, ed. R. S. Robins. New Orleans: Tulane University, pp. 35–52.

Atatürk, M. K. (1925), *Atatürk'ün Söylev ve Demeçleri* (The Speeches and Statements of Atatürk), 3 vols., ed. E. Z. Karal. Ankara: Türk Tarih Kurumu, 1952–1959.

Atatürk, M. K. (1929-30), Bağlılık (Solidarity). In: *M. Kemal Atatürk'ten Yazdıklarım*, ed. A. Afetinan. Istanbul: Milli Eğitim Basımevi, 1971, pp. 101–104.

Atatürk, M. K. (1930), Hürriyet (Freedom). In: *M. Kemal Atatürk'ten Yazdıklarım*, ed. A. Afetinan. Istanbul: Milli Eğitim Basımevi, 1971, pp. 77–97.

Aydemir, S. S. (1969), *Tek Adam* (The First Man), 3 vols. Istanbul: Remzi Kitabevi.

Bak, R. C. (1953), Fetishism. *Journal of the American Psychoanalytic Association*, 1: 285–298.

Beres, D. (1959), The contributions of psycho-analysis to the biography of the artist: A commentary on methodology. *The International Journal of Psycho-Analysis.*, 40: 26–37.

Berg, M. D. (1977), The externalizing transference. *The International Journal of Psycho-Analysis*, 58: 235–244.

Bergmann, M. S. (1973), Limitations of method in psychoanalytic biography: A historical inquiry. *Journal of the American Psychoanalytic Association*, 21: 833–850.

Berman, L. E. A. (1978), Sibling loss as an organizer of unconscious guilt: A case study. *The Psychoanalytic Quarterly*, 47: 568–587.

Bettelheim, B. (1959), Joey, a mechanical boy. *Scientific American*, 200: 116–127.

Bibring, E. (1953), The mechanism of depression. In: *Affective Disorders*, ed. P. Greenacre. New York: International Universities Press, pp. 13–48.

Bibring, E. (1954), Psychoanalysis and the dynamic psychotherapies. *Journal of the American Psychoanalytic Association*, 2: 745–770.

Blos, P. (1979), *The Adolescent Passage*. New York: International Universities Press.

Bonaparte, M. (1933), *The Life and Works of Edgar Allen Poe: A Psychoanalytic Interpretation*. London: Imago, 1949.

Bowlby, J. (1960), Grief and mourning in infancy and early childhood. *The Psychoanalytic Study of the Child*, 15: 9–52. New York: International Universities Press.

Bowlby, J. (1961), Process of mourning. *The International Journal of Psycho-Analysis.*, 42: 317–340.

Bowlby, J. (1963), Pathological mourning and childhood mourning. *Journal of the American Psychoanalytic Association*, 11: 500–541.

Bowlby, J. (1969), *Attachment and Loss. Vol. 1: Attachment*. New York: Basic Books.

Bowlby, J., & Parkes, C. M. (1970), Separation and loss within the family. In: *The Child in His Family*, Vol. 1, ed. E. J. Anthony & C. Koupernik. New York: Wiley Interscience, pp. 197–216.

Boyer, L. B. (1961), Provisional evaluation of psycho-analysis with few parameters employed in the treatment of schizophrenia. *The International Journal of Psycho-Analysis.*, 42: 389–403.

Boyer, L. B. (1967), Office treatment of schizophrenic patients: The use of psychoanalytic therapy with few parameters. In: *Psychoanalytic Treatment of Characterological and Schizophrenic Disorders*, ed. L. B. Boyer & P. L. Giovacchini. New York: Science House, pp. 143–188.

Boyer, L. B. (1971), Psychoanalytic technique in the treatment of certain characterological and schizophrenic disorders. *The International Journal of Psycho-Analysis*, 52: 67–85.

Boyer, L. B. (1977), Working with a borderline patient. *The Psychoanalytic Quarterly*, 44: 386–424.

Boyer, L. B., & Boyer, R. M. (1972), Effects of acculturation on the vicissitudes of the aggressive drive among the Apaches of the Mescalero Indian Reservation. *The Psychoanalytic Study of Society*, 5: 40–82. New York: International Universities Press.

Boyer, L. B., & Boyer, R. M. (1977), Understanding the individual through folklore. *Contemporary Psychoanalysis*, 13: 30–51.

Boyer, L. B., & Giovacchini, P. L. (1967), *Psychoanalytic Treatment of Characterological and Schizophrenic Disorders*. New York: Science House.

Breuer, J., & Freud, S. (1893–1895), *Studies on Hysteria. Standard Edition*, 2. London: Hogarth Press, 1955.

Brown, F., & Epps, P. (1966), Childhood bereavement and subsequent crime. *British Journal of Psychiatry*, 112: 1043–1048.

Buckman, J., & Greyson, C. B. (1977), Attempted suicide and bereavement: Symbiosis, ambivalence, and magical reunion. In: *Suicide and Bereavement*, ed. B. L. Danto & A. H. Kutscher. New York: Foundation of Thanatology/ MSS Information Corp., pp. 90–104.

Burnham, D. L. (1969), Schizophrenia and object relation. In: *Schizophrenia and the Need-Fear Dilemma*, by D. L. Burnham, A. I. Gladstone, & R. W. Gibson. New York: International Universities Press, pp. 15–41.

Cain, A. C., & Cain, B. S. (1964), On replacing a child. *Journal of the American Academy of Child & Adolescent Psychiatry*, 3: 443–456.

Cobb, S., Bauer, W., & Whiting, I. (1939), Environmental factors in rheumatoid arthritis. *JAMA*, 113: 668–670.

Coppolillo, H. P. (1967), Maturational aspects of the transitional phenomenon. *The International Journal of Psycho-Analysis*, 48: 237–246.

Crisp, A. H., & Priest, R. G. (1972), Psychoneurotic status during the year following bereavement. *Journal of Psychosomatic Research*, 16: 351–355.

Deutsch, H. (1937), Absence of grief. *The Psychoanalytic Quarterly*, 6: 12–23.

Dickes, R. (1963), Fetishistic behavior: A contribution to its complex development and significance. *Journal of the American Psychoanalytic Association*, 11: 303–330.

Dickes, R. (1978), Parents, transitional objects, and childhood fetishes. In: *Between Reality and Fantasy: Transitional Objects and Phenomena*, ed. S. A. Grolnick, L. Barkin, & W. Muensterberger. New York: Jason Aronson, pp. 307–319.

Dorpat, T. L. (1976), Structural conflict and object relations conflict. *Journal of the American Psychoanalytic Association*, 24: 855–874.

Emin, A. (1922), Interview with Mustafa Kemal. Reported in the newspaper *Vakit*, January 10.

Engel, G. L. (1961), Is grief a disease? A challenge for medical research. *Psychosomatic Medicine*, 23: 18–22.

Engel, G. L. (1971), Attachment behavior, object relations and the dynamic-economic points of view: Critical review of Bowlby's *Attachment and Loss. The International Journal of Psycho-Analysis*, 52: 183–196.

Engel, G. L. (1975), The death of a twin: Mourning and anniversary reactions: Fragments of 10 years of self-analysis. *The International Journal of Psycho-Analysis*, 56: 23–40.

Erikson, E. (1958), *Young Man Luther*. New York: Norton.

Erikson, E. (1969), *Gandhi's Truth*. New York: Norton.

Evans, P., & Liggett, J. (1971), Loss and bereavement as factors in agoraphobia: Implications for therapy. *British Journal of Medical Psychology*, 44: 149–154.

Fenichel, O. (1945), *The Psychoanalytic Theory of Neurosis*. New York: Norton.

Fintzy, R. T. (1971), Vicissitudes of the transitional object in a borderline child. *The International Journal of Psycho-Analysis*, 52: 107–114.

Fleming, J. (1972), Early object deprivation and transference phenomena: The working alliance. *The Psychoanalytic Quarterly*, 41: 23–49.

Fleming, J., & Altschul, S. (1963), Activation of mourning and growth by psycho-analysis. *The International Journal of Psycho-Analysis*, 44: 419–431.

Freud, A. (1936), *The Ego and the Mechanisms of Defense. The Writings of Anna Freud*, Vol. 2. New York: International Universities Press, 1966

Freud, A. (1960), Discussion of Dr. John Bowlby's paper. *The Psychoanalytic Study of the Child*, 15: 53–62. New York: International Universities Press.

Freud, A. (1965), *Normality and Pathology in Childhood. The Writings of Anna Freud*, Vol. 6. New York: International Universities Press.

Freud, A. (1967), About losing and being lost. *The Psychoanalytic Study of the Child*, 22: 9–19. New York: International Universities Press.

Freud, A., & Burlingham, D. (1942), *War and Children*. New York: International Universities Press.

Freud, S. (1887–1902), *The Origins of Psycho-Analysis: Letters to Wilhelm Fliess, Drafts and Notes: 1887–1902*, ed. M. Bonaparte, A. Freud, & E. Kris. New York: Basic Books, 1954.

Freud, S. (1895), Project for a scientific psychology. In: *The Origins of Psycho-Analysis: Letters to Wilhelm Fliess, Drafts and Notes: 1887–1902*. New York: Basic Books, 1954, pp. 347–445.

Freud, S. (1900), *The Interpretation of Dreams. Standard Edition*, 4 & 5. London: Hogarth Press, 1953.

Freud, S. (1907), Delusions and dreams in Jensen's Gradiva. *Standard Edition*, 9: 3–95. London: Hogarth Press, 1959.

Freud, S. (1908), Creative writers and day-dreaming. *Standard Edition*, 9: 141–153. London: Hogarth Press, 1959.

Freud, S. (1912), Types of onset of neurosis. *Standard Edition*, 12: 227–238. London: Hogarth Press, 1958.

Freud, S. (1914a), Remembering, repeating and working-through (Further recommendations on the technique of psycho-analysis II). *Standard Edition*, 12: 145–156. London: Hogarth Press, 1958.

Freud, S. (1914b), On narcissism. *Standard Edition*, 14: 67–102. London: Hogarth Press, 1957.

Freud, S. (1915), Thoughts for the times on war and death. *Standard Edition*, 14: 273–301. London: Hogarth Press, 1957.

Freud, S. (1916), On transience. *Standard Edition*, 14: 303–307. London: Hogarth Press, 1957.

Freud, S. (1917a), Mourning and melancholia. *Standard Edition*, 14: 237–258. London: Hogarth Press, 1957.

Freud, S. (1917b), A childhood recollection from *Dichtung* und *Wahrheit*. *Standard Edition*, 17: 145–156. London: Hogarth Press, 1955.

Freud, S. (1920), Beyond the pleasure principle. *Standard Edition*, 18: 1–64. London: Hogarth Press, 1961.

Freud, S. (1921), Group psychology and the analysis of the ego. *Standard Edition*, 18: 65–143. London: Hogarth Press, 1961.

Freud, S. (1922), Some neurotic mechanisms in jealousy, paranoia, and homosexuality. *Standard Edition*, 18: 223–232. London: Hogarth Press, 1955.

Freud, S. (1923), The ego and the id. *Standard Edition*, 19: 3–59. London: Hogarth Press, 1955.

Freud, S. (1926), Inhibitions, symptoms and anxiety. *Standard Edition*, 20: 77–175. London: Hogarth Press, 1959.

Freud, S. (1927), Fetishism. *Standard Edition*, 21: 149–157. London: Hogarth Press, 1964.

Freud, S. (1939), Moses and monotheism. *Standard Edition*, 23: 7–137. London: Hogarth Press, 1964.

Freud, S. (1940), Splitting of the ego in the process of defence. *Standard Edition*, 23: 271–278. London: Hogarth Press, 1964.

Friedlander, K. (1940), On the longing to die. *The International Journal of Psycho-Analysis.*, 21: 416–421.

Fuchs, S. H. (1937), On introjection. *The International Journal of Psycho-Analysis*, 18: 269–293.

Furman, R. (1964), Death and the young child: Some preliminary considerations. *The Psychoanalytic Study of the Child*, 19: 321–333. New York: International Universities Press.

Furst, S. S. (Ed.) (1967), *Psychic Trauma*. New York: Basic Books.

Gedo, J. E., & Goldberg, A. (1973), *Models of the Mind*. Chicago: University of Chicago Press.

Gill, M. M. (1954), Psychoanalysis and exploratory psychotherapy. *Journal of the American Psychoanalytic Association*, 2: 771–797.

Giovacchini, P. L. (1967), The frozen introject. *The International Journal of Psycho-Analysis*, 48: 61–67.

Giovacchini, P. L. (1972), The symbiotic phase. In: *Tactics and Techniques in Psychoanalytic Therapy*, ed. P. L. Giovacchini. New York: Science House, pp. 137–169.

Glover, E. (1933), The relation of perversion-formation to the development of reality-sense. *The International Journal of Psycho-Analysis*, 14: 486–504.

Gökçen, S. (1974), Interview with the author on December 2 in Ankara.

Gray, S. M. (1978), Brief psychotherapy: A developmental approach. *Journal of the American Psychoanalytic Association*, 5: 29–40.

Green, N., & Solnit, A. J. (1964), Reactions to the threatened loss of a child: A vulnerable child syndrome. *Pediatrics*, 34: 58–66.

Greenacre, P. (1953), Certain relationships between fetishism and the faulty development of the body image. In: *Emotional Growth*, Vol. 1. New York: International Universities Press, 1971, pp. 9–30.

Greenacre, P. (1955), *Swift and Carroll: A Psychoanalytic Study of Two Lives.* New York: International Universities Press.

Greenacre, P. (1969), The fetish and the transitional object. In: *Emotional Growth*, Vol. 1. New York: International Universities Press, 1971, pp. 315–334.

Greenacre, P. (1970), The transitional object and the fetish: With special reference to the role of illusion. *The International Journal of Psycho-Analysis*, 51: 447–456.

Greene, W. A. (1965), Disease response to life stress. *The Journal of the American Medical Association*, 20: 135–140.

Greene, W. A., & Miller, G. (1958), Psychological factors and reticuloendothelial disease. *Psychosomatic Medicine*, 20: 124–144.

Greenson, R. R. (1954), The struggle against identification. *Journal of the American Psychoanalytic Association*, 2: 200–217.

Greenspan, S. I. (1977), The oedipal–pre-oedipal dilemma: A reformulation according to object relations theory. *The International Review of Psycho-Analysis*, 4: 381–391.

Hamilton, J. W. (1969), Object loss, dreaming and creativity: The poetry of John Keats. *The Psychoanalytic Study of the Child*, 24: 488–531. New York: International Universities Press.

Hamilton, J. W. (1975), The significance of depersonalization in the life and writings of Joseph Conrad. *The Psychoanalytic Quarterly*, 44: 612–630.

Hamilton, J. W. (1976), Some comments about Freud's conceptualization of the death instinct. *The International Review of Psychoanalysis*, 3: 151–164.

Hamilton, J. W. (1979a), Joseph Conrad: His development as an artist, 1889–1910. *The Psychoanalytic Study of the Child*, 8: 277–329. New York: International Universities Press.

Hamilton, J. W. (1979b), The Doppelgänger effect in the relationship between Joseph Conrad and Bertrand Russell. *The International Review of Psychoanalysis*, 2: 175–181.

Hartmann, H. (1939), *Ego Psychology and the Problem of Adaptation*. New York: International Universities Press, 1958.

Hartmann, H. Kris, E., & Loewenstein, R. (1946), Comments on the formation of psychic structure. *The Psychoanalytic Study of the Child*, 2: 11–38. New York: International Universities Press.

Hartmann, H., & Loewenstein, R. M. (1962), Notes on the superego. *The Psychoanalytic Study of the Child*, 17: 42–81. New York: International Universities Press.

Hill, O. W. (1972), Child bereavement and adult psychiatric disturbance. *Journal of Psychosomatic Research*, 16: 357–360.

Hoffer, W. (1949), Mouth, hand, and ego-integration. *The Psychoanalytic Study of the Child*, 3/4: 49–56. New York: International Universities Press.

Hottinger, A. (1977), Turkey's search for identity: Kemal Atatürk's heritage. *Encounter*, 48: 75–81.

Itzkowitz, N. (1974), Mustafa Kemal Atatürk's relationship with women: A psycho-historical inquiry. Paper presented at Princeton University before the Princeton Near Eastern Studies Group and the Task Force on Psychiatry and Foreign Affairs of the American Psychiatric Association, March 8, Princeton, New Jersey.

Jacobson, E. (1964), *The Self and the Object World*. New York: International Universities Press.

Jacobson, E. (1971), *Depression*. New York: International Universities Press.

Jaffe, D. S. (1968), The mechanism of projection: Its dual role in object relations. *The International Journal of Psycho-Analysis*, 49: 662–677.

Jones, B. (1967), *Design for Death*. New York: Bobbs-Merrill.

Kafka, J. S. (1969), The body as transitional object: A psychoanalytic study of a self-mutilating patient. *British Journal of Medical Psychology*, 43: 207–212.

Kahne, N. (1967), On the persistence of transitional phenomena into adult life. *The International Journal of Psycho-Analysis*, 48: 247–258.

Kernberg, O. F. (1966), Structural derivatives of object relationships. *The International Journal of Psycho-Analysis*, 47: 236–253.

Kernberg, O. F. (1967), Borderline personality organization. *Journal of the American Psychoanalytic Association*, 15: 641–685.

Kernberg, O. F. (1975), *Borderline Conditions and Pathological Narcissism*. New York: Jason Aronson.

Kernberg, O. F. (1976), *Object Relations Theory and Clinical Psychoanalysis*. New York: Jason Aronson.

Kernberg, O. F. (1978), Contrasting approaches to the psychotherapy of borderline conditions. In: *New Perspectives on Psychotherapy of the Borderline Adult*, ed. J. F. Masterson. New York: Brunner/Mazel, pp. 76–104.

Kinross, L. (1965), *Atatürk: A Biography of Mustafa Kemal: Father of Modern Turkey*. New York: William Morrow.
Klein, M. (1940), Mourning and its relation to manic-depressive states. *The International Journal of Psycho-Analysis*, 21: 125–153.
Klein, M. (1946), Notes on some schizoid mechanisms. *The International Journal of Psycho-Analysis*, 27: 99–110.
Klein, M. (1955), On identification. In: *Our Adult World and Other Essays*. New York: Basic Books, pp. 55–98.
Knight, R. (1940), Introjection, projection, and identification. *The Psychoanalytic Quarterly*, 9: 334–341.
Koff, R. H. (1961), A definition of identification: A review of the literature. *The International Journal of Psycho-Analysis*, 42: 362–370.
Kohut, H. (1960), Beyond the bounds of the basic rule. In: *The Search for the Self*, ed. P. H. Ornstein. New York: International Universities Press, 1978, pp. 275–303.
Kohut, H. (1971), *The Analysis of the Self: A Systematic Approach to the Psychoanalytic Treatment of Narcissistic Disorders*. New York: International Universities Press.
Kohut, H. (1977), The Restoration of the Self. New York: International Universities Press.
Kramer, P. (1955), On discovering one's identity. *The Psychoanalytic Study of the Child*, 10: 47–74. New York: International Universities Press.
Kubie, L. S. (1964), Multiple determinants of suicidal efforts. *The Journal of Nervous and Mental Disease*, 138: 3–8.
Lehrman, S. R. (1956), Reactions to untimely death. *Psychiatric Quarterly*, 30: 565–579.
Lewis, R. (1971), *Everyday Life in Ottoman Turkey*. London: B. T. Batsford.
Lichtenberg, J. C., & Pao, P. (1974), Delusion, fantasy and desire. *The International Journal of Psycho-Analysis*, 55: 273–281.
Lichtenberg, J. C., & Slap, J. W. (1973), Notes on the concept of splitting and the defense mechanism of the splitting representation. *Journal of the American Psychoanalytic Association*, 21: 772–787.
Lidz, I. (1949), Emotional factors in the etiology of hyperthyroidism. *Psychosomatic Medicine*, 11: 2–9.
Lindemann, E. (1944), Symptomatology and management of acute grief. *The American Journal of Psychiatry*, 101: 141–148.
Lipson, C. T. (1963), Denial and mourning. *The International Journal of Psycho-Analysis*, 44: 104–107.
Loewald, H. (1960), On the therapeutic action of psycho-analysis. *The International Journal of Psycho-Analysis*, 41: 16–33.
Loewald, H. (1962), Internalization, separation, mourning, and the superego. *The Psychoanalytic Quarterly*, 31: 483–504.
Loewald, H. (1973), On internalization. *The International Journal of Psycho-Analysis*, 54: 9–17.

Loewenstein, R. (1957), A contribution to the psychoanalytic theory of masochism. *Journal of the American Psychoanalytic Association*, 5: 197–231.

Mack, J. E. (1971), Psychoanalysis and historical biography. *Journal of the American Psychoanalytic Association*, 19: 143–179.

Mahler, M. S. (1963), Thoughts about development and individuation. *The Psychoanalytic Study of the Child*, 18: 307–324. New York: International Universities Press.

Mahler, M. S. (1968), *On Human Symbiosis and the Vicissitudes of Individuation: Infantile Psychosis*. New York: International Universities Press.

Mahler, M. S., & Furer, M. (1960), Observations on research regarding the "symbiotic syndrome" of infantile psychosis. *The Psychoanalytic Quarterly*, 29: 317–327.

Mahler, M. S., Pine, F., & Bergman, A. (1975), *The Psychological Birth of the Human Infant: Symbiosis and Individuation*. New York: Basic Books.

Malan, D. H. (1979), *The Frontier of Brief Psychotherapy*. New York: Plenum.

Maloney, C. (1976), *The Evil Eye*. New York: Columbia University Press.

Marris, P. (1958), *Widows and Their Families*. London: Routledge & Kegan Paul.

Matchett, W. F. (1972), Repeated hallucinatory experiences as a part of the mourning process among Hopi Indian women. *Psychiatry*, 35: 185–194

McDermott, N. T., & Cobb, S. (1939), A psychiatric survey of fifty cases of bronchial asthma. *Psychosomatic Medicine*, 1: 203–245.

Melzig, H. (1944), *Inönü Diyorki* (Inönü Speaking). Istanbul: Ülkü Basımevi.

Miller, A. A., Pollock, G. S., Bernstein, H. E., & Robbins, F. P. (1968), An approach to the concept of identification. *Bulletin of the Menninger Clinic*, 32: 239–252.

Mintz, I. (1971), The anniversary reaction: A response to the unconscious sense of time. *Journal of the American Psychoanalytic Association*, 19: 720–735.

Modell, A. H. (1963), Primitive object relationships and the predisposition to schizophrenia. *The International Journal of Psycho-Analysis*, 44: 282–292.

Modell, A. H. (1968), *Object Love and Reality: An Introduction to a Psychoanalytic Theory of Object Relations*. New York: International Universities Press.

Modell, A. H. (1976), The "holding environment" and the therapeutic action of psychoanalysis. *Journal of the American Psychoanalytic Association*, 24: 285–307.

Moellenhoff, F. (1939), Ideas of children about death: A preliminary study. *Bulletin of the Menninger Clinic*, 3: 148–156.

Moore, B., & Fine, B., Eds. (1967), *A Glossary of Psychoanalytic Terms and Concepts*. New York: American Psychoanalytic Association.

Nagera, H. (1970), Children's reactions to the death of important objects: A developmental approach. *The Psychoanalytic Study of the Child*, 24: 360–400. New York: International Universities Press.

Niederland, W. G. (1956), Clinical observations on the "Little Man" phenomenon. *The Psychoanalytic Study of the Child*, 11: 381–396. New York: International Universities Press.

Niederland, W. G. (1965), An analytic inquiry into the life and work of Heinrich Schliemann. In: *Drives, Affects, Behavior*, Vol. 2, ed. M. Schur. New York: International Universities Press, pp. 369–396.

Niederland, W. G. (1977), Personal communication.

Noble, D. (1951), Hysterical manifestations in schizophrenic illness. *Psychiatry*, 14: 153–160.

Novey, S. (1968), *The Second Look: The Reconstruction of Personal History in Psychiatry and Psychoanalysis*. Baltimore: Johns Hopkins University Press.

Novick, J., & Kelly, K. (1970), Projection and externalization. *The Psychoanalytic Study of the Child*, 25: 69–95. New York: International Universities Press.

Olinick, S. L. (1969), On empathy and regression in the service of the other. *British Journal of Medical Psychology*, 42: 41–49.

Ornstein, A., & Ornstein, P. H. (1975), On the interpretive process in schizophrenia. *International Journal of Psychoanalytic Psychotherapy*, 4: 219–271.

Pao, P. (1974), The relationship of the infantile period to the etiology of schizophrenia. Read at the Winter Meeting of the American Psychoanalytic Association.

Pao, P. (1978), Discussion of Dr. Vamık Volkan's paper, "Night of the Living Dead." Read at the Winter Meeting of the American Psychoanalytic Association.

Parkes, C. M. (1964a), The effects of bereavement on physical and mental health: A study of the case records of widows. *British Medical Journal*, 2: 274–279.

Parkes, C. M. (1964b), Recent bereavement as a cause of mental illness. *British Journal of Psychiatry*, 110: 198–204.

Parkes, C. M. (1970), The first year of bereavement: A longitudinal study of the reaction of London widows to the death of their husbands. *Psychiatry*, 33: 444–467.

Parkes, C. M. (1972), *Bereavement: Studies of Grief in Adult Life*. New York: International Universities Press.

Parkes, C. M., & Brown, R. J. (1972), Health after bereavement: A controlled study of young Boston widows and widowers. *Psychosomatic Medicine*, 34: 449–461.

Peck, M. W. (1939), Notes on identification in a case of depressive reaction to the death of a love object. *The Psychoanalytic Quarterly*, 8: 1–18.

Plank, E. M., & Plank, R. (1978), Children and death: As seen through art and autobiographies. *The Psychoanalytic Study of the Child*, 33: 593–620. New Haven: Yale University Press.

Pollock, G. H. (1961), Mourning and adaptation. *The International Journal of Psycho-Analysis*, 42: 341–361.

Pollock, G. H. (1970), Anniversary reactions, trauma and mourning. *The Psychoanalytic Quarterly*, 39: 347–371.

Pollock, G. H. (1971), Temporal anniversary manifestations: Hour, day, holiday. *The Psychoanalytic Quarterly*, 40: 123–131.

Pollock, G. H. (1972), Bertha Pappenheim's pathological mourning: Possible effects of childhood sibling loss. *Journal of the American Psychoanalytic Association*, 20: 476–493.

Pollock, G. H. (1975a), On anniversary suicide and mourning. In: *Depression and Human Existence*, ed. E. J. Anthony & T. Benedek. Boston: Little, Brown, pp. 369–393.

Pollock, G. H. (1975b), On mourning, immortality, and Utopia. *Journal of the American Psychoanalytic Association*, 23: 334–362.

Pollock, G. H. (1977), The mourning process and creative organizational change. *Journal of the American Psychoanalytic Association*, 25: 3–34.

Poznanski, E. O. (1972), The "replacement child": A saga of unresolved parental grief. *Journal of Developmental and Behavioral Pediatrics*, 81: 1190–1193.

Rado, S. (1956), Adaptational development of psychoanalytic therapy. In: *Changing Concepts of Psychoanalytic Medicine*, ed. S. Rado & G. E. Daniels. New York: Grune & Stratton, pp. 89–100.

Rangell, L. (1959), The nature of conversion. *Journal of the American Psychoanalytic Association*, 7: 632–663.

Rapaport, D. (1952), Projective techniques and the theory of thinking. In: *The Collected Papers of David Rapaport*, ed. M. M. Gill. New York: Basic Books, pp. 461–472.

Ritvo, S., & Solnit, A. (1958), Influences of early mother–child interaction on the identification process. *The Psychoanalytic Study of the Child*, 13: 64–85. New York: International Universities Press.

Rochlin, G. (1965), *Griefs and Discontents: The Forces of Change*. Boston: Little, Brown.

Rogers, R. (1966), Children's reactions to sibling death. *Psychosomatic Medicine* Proceedings of the First International Congress of the Academy of Psychosomatic Medicine, Spain, Excerpta Medica International Congress Series, No. 134.

Rosenfeld, H. A. (1966), Discussion of "Office Treatment of Schizophrenic Patients by Psychoanalysis," by L. H. Boyer. *The Psychoanalytic Forum*, 1: 351–353.

Rossner, J. (1975), *Looking for Mr. Goodbar*. New York: Simon & Schuster.

Rustow, D. A. (1970), Atatürk as founder of a state. In: *Philosophers and Kings: Studies in Leadership*, ed. D. A. Rustow. New York: George Braziller.

Sandler, J. (1960), The background of safety. *The International Journal of Psycho-Analysis*, 41: 350–356.

Schafer, R. (1968), *Aspects of Internalization*. New York: International Universities Press.

Schafer, R. (1972), Internalization: Process or fantasy? *The Psychoanalytic Study of the Child*, 27: 411–436. New York: Quadrangle.

Schmale, A. H. (1958), Relationship of separation and depression to disease. I. A report on a hospitalized medical population. *Psychosomatic Medicine*, 20: 259–277.

Schofield, W. (1966), The structured personality inventory in measurement of effects of psychotherapy. In: *Methods of Research in Psychotherapy*, ed. L.A. Gottschalk & A. H. Auerback. New York: Appleton-Century-Crofts, pp. 536–550.

Schur, M. (1960), Discussion of Dr. John Bowlby's paper. *The Psychoanalytic Study of the Child*, 15: 63–84. New York: International Universities Press.

Schuster, D. B. (1969), A note on grief. *Bulletin of the Philadelphia Association for Psychoanalytic Studies*, 19: 87–90.

Searles, H. F. (1960), *The Nonhuman Environment in Normal Development and Schizophrenia*. New York: International Universities Press.

Searles, H. F. (1963), The place of neutral therapist-responses in psychotherapy with the schizophrenic patient. *The International Journal of Psycho-Analysis*, 44: 42–56.

Searles, H. F. (1965), *Collected Papers on Schizophrenia and Related Subjects*. New York: International Universities Press.

Searles, H. F. (1975), The patient as therapist to his analyst. In: *Tactics and Techniques in Psychoanalytic Therapy: Countertransference*, Vol. 2, ed. P. L. Giovacchini, A. Flarsheim, & L. B. Boyer. New York: Jason Aronson, pp. 95–151.

Searles, H. F. (1976), Transitional phenomena and therapeutic symbiosis. *International Journal of Psychoanalytic Psychotherapy*, 5: 146–203.

Searles, H. F. (1979), *Countertransference and Related Subjects*. New York: International Universities Press.

Sifneos, P. E. (1972), *Short-Term Psychotherapy and Emotional Crisis*. Cambridge, Mass.: Harvard University Press.

Smith, J. H. (1971), Identificatory styles in depression and grief. *The International Journal of Psycho-Analysis*, 52: 259–266.

Smith, J. H. (1973), If you think you might be dying and the doctors (and your friends) aren't telling you – worry. Foundation of Thanatology Symposium on Bereavement, Columbia-Presbyterian Medical Center, New York, November 2 and 3.

Smith, J. H. (1975), On the work of mourning. In: *Bereavement: Its Psychological Aspects*, ed. B. Schoenberg, I. Gerber, A. Wiener, A.H. Kutscher, D. Peretz, & A. C. Carr. New York: Columbia University Press, pp. 18–25.

Speers, R. W., & Lansing, C. (1965), *Group Therapy in Childhood Psychosis*. Chapel Hill, N. C.: University of North Carolina Press.

Sperling, M. (1963), Fetishism in children. *The Psychoanalytic Quarterly*, 32: 374–392.

Spitz, R. A. (1960), Discussion of Dr. John Bowlby's paper. *The Psychoanalytic Study of the Child*, 15: 85–94. New York: International Universities Press.

Spitz, R. A. (1965), *The First Year of Life*. New York: International Universities Press.

Sterba, R. (1948), On Hallowe'en. *American Imago*, 5: 213–224.

Stierlin, H. (1973), Interpersonal aspects of internalizations. *The International Journal of Psycho-Analysis*, 54: 203–213.

Strachey, J. (1934), The nature of the therapeutic action of psycho-analysis. *The International Journal of Psycho-Analysis*, 15: 127–159.

Sullivan, H. S. (1956), *Clinical Studies in Psychiatry*. New York: Norton.

Sullivan, H. S. (1962), *Schizophrenia as a Human Process*. New York: Norton.

Tessman, L. H. (1978), *Children of Parting Parents*. New York: Jason Aronson.

Tolpin, M. (1972), On the beginning of a cohesive self: An application of the concept of transmuting internalization to the study of the transitional object and separation anxiety. *The Psychoanalytic Study of the Child*, 26: 316–353. New York: Quadrangle.

Tucker, R. C. (1970), The. theory of charismatic leadership. In: *Philosophers and Kings*, ed. D. A. Rustow. New York: George Braziller, pp. 69–94.

Volkan, V. D. (1965), The observation of the "Little Man" phenomenon in a case of anorexia nervosa. *British Journal of Medical Psychology*, 38: 299–311.

Volkan, V. D. (1966), Normal and pathological grief reactions—A guide for the family physician. *Virginia Med. Monthly*, 93: 651–656.

Volkan, V. D. (1968), The introjection of and identification with the therapist as an ego-building aspect in the treatment of schizophrenia. *British Journal of Medical Psychology*, 41: 369–380.

Volkan, V. D. (1970), Typical findings in pathological grief. *Psychiatric Quarterly*, 44: 231–250.

Volkan, V. D. (1971), A study of a patient's re-grief work through dreams, psychological tests, and psychoanalysis. *Psychiatric Quarterly*, 45: 255–273.

Volkan, V. D. (1972), The linking objects of pathological mourners. *Archives of General Psychiatry*, 27: 215–221.

Volkan, V. D. (1975a), Cosmic laughter: A study of primitive splitting. In: *Tactics and Techniques in Psychoanalytic Psychotherapy*, Vol. 2, ed. P. L. Giovacchini, A. Flarsheim, & L. B. Boyer. New York: Jason Aronson, pp. 425–440.

Volkan, V. D. (1975b), Tekrar yaslandırma tedavisi. *Tıp Dünyası*, 48: 85–91.

Volkan, V. D. (1976), *Primitive Internalized Object Relations: A Clinical Study of Schizophrenic, Borderline, and Narcissistic Patients*. New York: International Universities Press.

Volkan, V. D. (1977), Mourning and adaptation after a war. *American Journal of Psychotherapy*, 31: 561–569.

Volkan, V. D. (1979a), *Cyprus: War and Adaptation: A Psychoanalytic History of Two Ethnic Groups in Conflict*. Charlottesville, VA.: University Press of Virginia.

Volkan, V. D. (1979b), The "glass bubble" of a narcissistic patient. In: *Advances in Psychotherapy of the Borderline Patient*, ed. J. LeBoit & A. Capponi. New York: Jason Aronson, pp. 405–431.

Volkan, V. D. (1980), Narcissistic personality organization and "reparative" leadership. *International Journal of Group Psychotherapy*, 30: 131–152.

Volkan, V. D. (1981a), Transference–countertransference: An examination from the point of view of internalized object relations. In: *Object and Self: A Developmental Approach*, ed. S. Tuttman, C. Kaye, & M. Zimmerman. New York: International Universities Press, pp. 429–451.

Volkan, V. D. (1981b), Immortal Atatürk: Narcissism and creativity in a revolutionary leader. In: *Psychoanalytic Study of Society*, Vol. 9. New York: Psychohistory Press, pp. 221–255.

Volkan, V. D., & Akhtar, S. (1979), The symptoms of schizophrenia: Contributions of the structural theory and object relations theory. In: *Integrating Ego Psychology and Object Relations*, ed. L. Saretsky, G. D. Goldman, & D. S. Milman. Dubuque, Iowa: Kendall/Hunt, pp. 270–285.

Volkan, V. D. Cilluffo, A. F., & Sarvay, T. L. (1975), Re-grief therapy and the function of the linking object as a key to stimulate emotionality. In: *Emotional Flooding*, ed. P. T. Olsen. New York: Human Sciences Press, pp. 179–224.

Volkan, V. D., & Josephthal, D. (1980), The treatment of established pathological mourners. In: *Specialized Techniques and Psychotherapy*, ed. T. B. Karasu & L. Bellak. New York: Brunner/Mazel, pp. 118–142.

Volkan, V. D., & Kavanaugh, J. G. (1978), The cat people. In: *Between Reality Fantasy: Transitional Objects and Phenomena*, ed. S. Grolnick, L. Barkin, & W. Muensterberger. New York: Jason Aronson, pp. 291–303.

Volkan, V. D., & Luttrell, A. S. (1971), Aspects of the object relationship and developing skills of a "mechanical boy." *British Journal of Medical Psychology*, 44: 101–116.

Volkan, V. D., & Showalter, C. R. (1968), Known object loss, disturbance in reality testing, and "re-grief work" as a method of brief psychotherapy. *Psychiatric Quarterly*, 42: 358–374.

Wahl, C. W. (1957), Suicide as a magical act. *Bulletin of the Menninger Clinic*, 21: 91–98.

Wahl, C. W. (1958), The fear of death. *Bulletin of the Menninger Clinic*, 22: 213–214.

Wahl, C. W. (1970), The differential diagnosis of normal and neurotic grief following bereavement. *Psychosomatics*, 11: 104–106.

Winnicott, D. W. (1953), Transitional objects and transitional phenomena. *The International Journal of Psycho-Analysis*, 34: 89–97.

Wolfenstein, M. (1966), How is mourning possible? *The Psychoanalytic Study of the Child*, 21: 93–123. New York: International Universities Press.

Wolfenstein, M. (1969), Loss, rage, and repetition. *The Psychoanalytic Study of the Child*, 24: 432–460. New York: International Universities Press.

Wolfenstein, M. (1973), The image of the lost parent. *The Psychoanalytic Study of the Child*, 28: 433–456. New Haven: Yale University Press.

Wolpe, J. (1958), *Psychotherapy by Reciprocal Inhibition*. Palo Alto, CA: Stanford University Press.

Zinner, J., & Shapiro, R. (1972), Projective identification as a mode of perception and behavior in families of adolescents. *The International Journal of Psycho-Analysis*, 53: 521–530.

Name index

Abraham, K., 2, 238
Abse, D. W., 242
Akhtar, S., xiii, 5, 86, 146, 147, 154, 156–158, 161–162
Altschul, S., 9
Anna O, 258
Atatürk, Mustafa Kemal, xx, 237, 239–240, 241, 242–250
Aydemir, S. S., 242–243, 250–251

Bak, R. C., 291
Bauer, W., 55
Beres, D., 241
Berg, M. D., 94
Bergman, A., 277
Bergmann, M. S., 241
Berman, L. E. A., 230
Bernstein, H. E., 56
Bettelheim, B., 293
Bibring, E., 11, 65, 128–129, 164, 168
Blos, P., 54, 107
Bonaparte, M., 238
Bowlby, J., 14–15, 35, 37, 40, 54, 71, 228–229
Boyer, L. B., xvi, 72, 78, 86, 261, 264
Boyer, R. M., 72, 78, 261, 264
Breuer, J., 10, 258
Brown, F., 55, 191, 215
Buckman, J., 67
Burlingham, D., 256
Burnham, D. L., 293
Buxton, R., xiv, 51

Cain, A. C., 257
Cain, B. S., 257, 259
Cilluffo, A. F., xiii, 79, 184, 195, 197, 198
Cobb, S., 55
Conrad, Joseph, 240
Coppolillo, H. P., 289
Crisp, A. H., 55

Deutsch, H., 11, 47
Dickes, R., 290–291
Dorpat, T. L., 85–86

Eliot, T. S., 208
Emin, A., 244–245
Engel, G. L., 15, 29, 32, 34, 39–40
Epps, P., 55
Erikson, E., xv, 241
Evans, P., 55

Fenichel, O., 42, 44, 64–65, 66, 293
Fine, B., 5, 13, 195
Fintzy, R. T., 289
Fleming, J., 9
Fletcher, W. B., xiv, 195, 197–198
Freud, A., xv–xvi, 2–3, 7, 10–11, 15, 28, 34–35, 37, 42, 55–57, 63–64, 76, 82, 84, 87–88, 98, 109, 121, 181, 228–229, 238, 256, 258, 279–280, 291–292, 295
Freud, S., xv–xvi, 2–3, 7, 10, 11, 15, 28, 34–35, 37, 42, 55–57, 63–64, 76, 82, 84, 87–88, 98, 109, 121, 181, 228–229, 238, 256, 258, 279–280, 291–292, 295
Friedlander, K., 98
Fuchs, S. H., 55–56
Furer, M., 256
Furman, R., 229
Furst, S. S., 42

Gedo, J. E., 86
Gill, M. M., 129–130
Giovacchini, P. L., 56–57, 76, 86, 264
Glover, E., 294
Goethe, J. W. von, 238
Gökçen, S., 252
Goldberg, A., 86
Gray, S. M., 61, 75, 165, 201, 211
Green, N., 75, 257, 258, 274
Greenacre, P., 241, 286, 288–289, 291–292, 294, 298
Greene, W. A., 37, 55
Greenson, R. R., 56
Greenspan, S. I., 86
Greyson, C. B., 96–97

Hamilton, J. W., 238, 240–241,
Hartmann, H., 13, 15, 55–56, 63
Hastings, B., xiii, 131, 133, 135, 138
Hill, O. W., 55
Hoffer, W., 274
Hottinger, A., 251

Itzkowitz, N., 241, 247

Jacobson, E., 12–13, 64–65, 66, 79
Jaffe, D. S., 58
Jessner, L., 242
Johnson, Lyndon Baines, 50
Jones, B., 81
Josephthal, D., xiv, 9, 172, 189, 205

Kafka, J. S., 289
Kahne, N., 289
Kavanaugh, J. G., 289, 290
Keats, John, 240
Kelly, K., 57–58, 94
Kennedy, John F., 113
Kennedy, Robert, 178
Kernberg, O. F., xvii, 12–14, 15, 79, 86, 87, 130, 250, 262
King, R., 230, 231, 234
Kinross, L., 242
Klein, M., 7, 35, 40, 58
Knight, R., 55
Koff, R. H., 56
Kohut, H., 57, 80, 86, 241, 249, 289
Kramer, P., 3
Kris, E., 63, 272
Kubie, L. S., 95

Lansing, C., 286, 290
Lehrman, S. R., 55
Lenin, V. I., 239
Lewis, R., 247
Lichtenberg, J. C., 87, 280
Lidz, I., 55
Liggett, J., 55
Lindemann, E., 33, 34, 37, 40, 42–43

Lipson, C. T., 34
Loewald, H., 63, 258, 264
Loewenstein, R. M., 56, 63, 95, 98
Luttrell, A. S., 293, 296

McDermott, N. T., 55
Mack, J. E., 241
Mahler, M. S., xvi, 12–13, 65, 228, 256, 277, 286, 290
Malan, D. H., 165
Maloney, C., 286
Marris, P., 37
Matchett, W. F., 77–78
Melzig, H., 254
Miller, A. A., 56
Miller, G., 55
Mintz, I., 29
Modell, A. H., 86, 250
Moellenhoff, F., 34
Moore, B., 13

Nagera, H., 230
Niederland, W. G., 3, 239, 241, 253
Noble, D., 85
Novey, S., 29, 161
Novick, J., 57–58, 94

Olinick, S. L., 267
Ornstein, A., 264
Ornstein, P. H., 264

Pao, P., 277, 280
Pappenheim, Bertha (see Anna O)., 258
Parkes, C. M., 15, 35, 37, 54–55, 70–71, 75, 77
Peck, M. W., 55
Phillips, N., xiv, 183
Pine, F., 277
Plank, E. M., 239
Plank, R., 239
Poe, Edgar Allan, 239, 269
Pollock, G. H., 12, 29, 32, 34–36, 37, 40, 56, 74–75, 81, 95, 98, 238–240, 258–259
Poznanski, E. O., 232, 257
Priest, R. J., 46, 55, 170, 260

Rado, S., 171
Rangell, L., 85
Rapaport, D., 57
Ritvo, S., 63
Robbins, F. P., 56
Rochlin, G., 12, 40
Rogers, R., 259
Rosenfeld, H. A., 264
Rossner, J., 146
Russell, Bertrand, 240
Rustow, D. A., 247–248

Sandler, J., 280
Sarvay, T. L., xiv, 79, 184, 189, 195, 198–200, 201–203
Schafer, R., 28, 56, 79, 89, 92–93
Schliemann, Heinrich, 239
Schmale, A. H., 55
Schofield, E., 195
Schur, M., 15, 229
Schuster, S. B., 34, 36, 76
Searles, H. F., xxiii, 256, 270, 292
Segantini, Giovanni, 238
Shakespeare, William, 104
Shapiro, R., 58, 94
Showalter, C. E., xxi, 7–9, 167
Sifneos, P. E., 165
Slap, J. W., 87, 134
Smith, B., xiv, 32, 42, 61, 62–63, 183, 195, 197–198
Smith, J. H., xiv, 32, 42, 61, 62–63, 183, 195, 197–198
Solnit, A. J., 63, 257–258
Speers, R. W., 286, 290
Sperling, M., 286, 290
Spitz, R. A., 15, 229, 256
Sterba, R., 34
Stierlin, H., 63
Strachey, J., 129, 301
Sullivan, H. S., 256

Tessman, L. H., 82
Thomson, J. A., xiii, 5, 146, 147, 149, 150–151
Tolpin, M., 289
Tucker, R. C., 242

Ulman, R. B., 242

Volkan, V. D., xi, xv–xvi, xvii–xxiii, 2–4, 7–9, 10, 12, 14, 16, 30, 32, 40, 41, 44–45, 49, 55, 56–57, 63, 71, 79, 81–82, 86, 87, 90, 93, 94, 123, 172, 175, 184, 195, 198, 205, 229, 241, 244. 246, 249–250, 261–262, 264–265, 273, 274, 287, 289, 290, 297

Wahl, C. W., 11, 34, 50, 98
Whiting, I., 55
Winnicott, D. W., 16, 82, 288–289, 290
Wolfenstein, M., 54, 229, 239
Wolpe, J., 6, 9

Zinner, J., 58, 94

Subject index

Abreaction, 46, 128, 130, 168–169
Absence of grief reaction, xviii, 6, 11, 40, 81, 175, 228
Ambivalence, 13, 16, 57, 59, 62, 64, 67, 70, 71, 74, 76, 77, 78, 90, 108–109, 114–116, 142, 168, 171, 175, 190, 197, 201, 209, 216, 240, 296
  clarification of, 55, 128, 129, 130, 166, 168, 169, 170
  in dreams, 42
  overcome in analysis, 62
  See also "Unfinished business"
Anger, 9, 25–26, 32, 36, 37, 38, 46, 48, 49–50, 60, 92, 100, 107, 110, 116–117, 135–136, 142, 151, 153–154, 160, 168, 170, 192, 193–194, 200, 204, 209, 215, 216, 219, 232, 271, 274, 289, 298
Anniversary reaction, 28, 29, 99, 101, 281
Anticipatory grief, 42, 43
Attachment behavior, 14, 15, 16, 71

Body image, 239, 298
Borderline personality, 14, 85, 86, 87
Burial, 25, 74, 99, 112, 118, 135, 169, 178–179, 194, 215, 220, 275

Case examples (in order of appearance)
  Anorectic Alice, 2–4
  The "Daughters of Goodbar," 146, 161
  Mary, who attempted suicide with her mother's suicide weapon, 7–8
  Linda, her father's "second wife," 21–28
  Millie's wedding date, 98
  Fred, who denied his brother's death, 43, 46
  Will, delayed anniversary somatization, 47–48
  Carl, a potential sniper, 48–50
  Gregory's continuing dreams, 51
  The woman who found her husband hanged, 51
  Tina, "the brain," 59–62
  Phyllis, a dead horse, and a stone, 68–70
  Bernard and the movable coffin, 73

Mike, son of the snorkeling surgeon, 172–174
Clyde and the "poisoned" coffee, 214–215
Joe and his dead brother's clothing, 81
Helen and the appointment card, 83
Martin, the suddenly wayward physician, 91–92
Jerry and Othello's handkerchief, 104
Carol's uneasy femininity and a dead brother, 132
Roberta, a widowed lawyer, 166, 205–211
Julie's red robe, 191
Chip and the bloodstone ring, 198, 202, 204
Barbara's search for a father, 229
Polly, the physician with a dull "inner tapestry," 231–236
Susie, a replacement child, 257–258
Frances, a schizophrenic replacement child, 259–261
The "mechanical boy," 293
Andrew and Father Time, 295–299
Charlottesville Psychoanalytic Psychotherapy Study Group, 8
Chicago Institute for Psychoanalysis, 9
Coconut Grove disaster, 33
Constitutional determinants, 119, 230, 237, 250

Delayed reactions, 47–48
Demarcation exercises, 167
Denial of death, xix, 38, 123, 214
Depression *see* Reactive depression
Displacement of personal issues to a "motherland," 245, 246, 249
manifestation of ambivalence, 109
repeating, 47, 51, 74–75, 89, 99, 115, 119, 170, 194, 216
theories of, 261
types in established pathological mourning, 67
Dream examples and types (in order of appearance)
of the decaying body of the dead, 10, 32
of the body still "living" in the coffin, 76
of trying to save (or "kill") the dead, 99–100, 216
of a life-and-death struggle, 74, 76, 113
of flowers being squeezed, 114, 115
of the dead preparing to vanish, 116
of a falling coffin, 118
masturbation dreams, 134
of an auto crash, 159
of being pregnant, 137, 138
of "bodies, blood, and babies," 139
of tornadoes, 151
of sex and the therapist, 274
of bliss, 159
of the dead and an operation, 64, 166, 176, 177, 182, 186, 295, 296
of the gift of a dismantled telephone, 177–178
the "Safeway dream," 180
examination dream, 181
of the grave, 73, 179, 181, 220
of shoes, 60, 61, 62, 194, 218
of five pterodactyls, 208
"termination dream" of portrait, 166, 209
of a neighborly call, 219
a review dream, 222
of the white stone swan, 235
of the Red Death, 269
of Russian spies, 271
of oyster juice in a swimming pool, 272
of a wedding in a funeral parlor, 274

Established pathological mourning, defined, 32, 67, 85, 90
Externalization, xviii, 23, 55, 57–58, 80, 89, 94, 95, 152, 169

Fetish, 16, 84, 286, 290, 291, 292, 294, 295, 297, 298
Fixation, xix, xxi, 41, 42, 46, 48, 55, 67, 74, 75–76, 168, 171, 214, 291

Generational continuity, 28, 30, 255, 256–257
Grief as a disease, 39
Guilt, 9, 26, 32, 33, 35, 42–43, 50, 60, 62, 64–65, 68–69, 77, 91, 94, 96, 106, 109, 117, 123, 134, 136, 148, 153, 154, 156, 159, 161, 162, 167, 169, 170, 184, 187, 190, 193, 198, 200, 203, 216, 218, 229, 230–231, 233, 234, 235, 236, 246, 249, 254, 257–258

Hallucinations, xviii, 68, 77–78, 191–192, 282

Identification with the dead, 2, 61, 112, 200, 231, 276
Imitation of the deceased, 55, 156, 242, 253, 278
Incestuous strivings, 106, 252
Incorporative fantasies, 276
Internalization, 55, 56–58, 63, 80, 89, 92, 95–96, 262, 289
Internalized object relations, 11, 12, 14, 15–16, 42, 86, 164, 262, 264, 270, 277
Introject, 7, 31, 35, 56–57, 79–80, 90, 91, 96, 218, 235–236
  the "analytic" introject, 264
  cannibalistic fantasies related to, 276
  composite, 13, 184, 231
  defined in context, 55, 80, 87, 115, 165, 248
  personified, 80, 91
Introjection, xviii, 53, 54–55, 56, 62, 64, 79, 89

Linking objects
  defined, 58, 248
  diagnostic significance, 166, 200
  and introjection, xviii, 53, 54, 55, 56, 62, 64, 79, 89
  "last minute" objects, 83
  as protection against suicide, 84
  See also Living linking objects
Linking phenomena, ix, xviii, 16, 40, 58, 80, 82, 84, 97, 285
"Little man" phenomenon, 57
Living linking objects, 248, 255, 259, 268, 270, 277
  See also placement children
Loss in childhood, 228
  influence of object constancy, 85, 227, 228
  positive outcomes of, 238, 239
Loss as a feature of growth, 33, 75, 216

Maternal grief, 236, 238, 242, 248–249, 252, 253–254, 263
  See also Replacement children; Savior role
Merging, 92, 93, 95, 97–98, 100–101, 135, 174, 176, 178, 265

Narcissistic personality, 12, 250

Oedipal issues, 150, 157
Oral orientation, 65, 234, 240, 249, 251, 254, 288, 296

Projection, xviii, 53, 54–55, 57–58, 94, 233–234, 288
Psychoanalytic techniques, 262
Psychological testing of patients in re-grief therapy, xiii, 184
Psychopathology, coexistent or antecedent with complications following death, 5, 6, 119, 222, 278, 281
  See also Schizophrenia

Reactive depression, xviii, 11, 40, 53, 54–55, 59, 62, 63–65, 66, 68, 89, 94, 95–96, 143, 145, 158, 163–164, 213, 227, 229
loss of self-esteem in, 63, 65, 70, 91, 106, 110, 154, 190
suicide in, 53, 65, 66, 68, 93, 95, 96, 260
Re-grief therapy, ix, xiii, xiv, xx, 7–8, 10, 17, 127, 163, 164–166, 167, 170, 171, 172, 174, 181–182, 184, 186, 189, 195, 197, 198, 205, 213, 216–217, 220, 222, 285
Reincarnation, 72, 207, 237, 255, 267, 270, 274–275
Religious and cultural influences, 72, 84, 96–97, 114, 275
Apache beliefs, 72, 78
cults, 260
Hopi hallucinations, 77
magical objects, 16, 27, 67, 83, 95, 97, 103, 104, 119–120, 122, 169–170, 175–177, 180, 189, 191, 203, 230, 265–266, 269, 285, 286, 292, 297, 299
Replacement children, 16, 46, 160, 209, 232, 257, 258, 259, 267
Reunion, wish for, 98, 100, 101, 208

Savior role, 25
Schizophrenia
need to differentiate from established pathological mourning, xix, 85, 214
"substitute objects" in, 293, 297
treatment in, 118, 159, 184, 191, 261
Somatization, 55, 184
Splitting, 13, 14, 31, 34, 38, 46, 49, 58, 86–87, 88–89, 94, 169, 178, 183, 202, 213, 257, 272–273, 278
appearance in initial stage of grief, 41, 44, 45–48, 50–51, 169, 179
in complicated mourning, ix, xiii, 7, 17, 29, 166, 214, 228
high-level, 85, 86, 87–88, 169, 250
primitive, 13, 14, 42, 55, 86, 87–88, 230, 243, 257, 272, 273, 293, 297
Stages of mourning, 21, 64, 76
Suicide, xiv, xxiii, 7, 8, 21, 30, 43, 50–51, 53, 61, 65, 66, 68, 72, 78, 93, 95, 96, 97–98,101, 110, 236, 260, 275, 285
fended off by linking object, 95
fended off by introject, 95–96
parental, 23, 107, 135, 137, 242, 257, 260
See also Reunion, wish for

Termination of mourning process, 37, 54
Tombstone, xx, 49, 74, 170, 193, 194
Transference, 4, 6, 116, 150, 158, 171–172, 186, 232, 278, 292–293
interpretations and clarifications of, 130
place in re-grief therapy, 164
Transitional objects, 82, 84, 285–286, 288–289, 290–291, 292, 293–294, 297

"Unfinished business," 23, 209, 260, 295

Violent death, effects of, 43, 69, 72